Happiness Is...

Happiness Is...

How to become a Happy Entrepreneur

KT EUZEN

Archway Publishing books may be ordered through booksellers or by contacting:

Archway Publishing
1663 Liberty Drive
Bloomington, IN 47403
www.archwaypublishing.com
844-669-3957

ISBN: 978-1-6657-5756-0 (sc)
ISBN: 978-1-6657-5758-4 (hc)
ISBN: 978-1-6657-5757-7 (e)

Library of Congress Control Number: 2024904146

Print information available on the last page.

Archway Publishing rev. date: 03/06/2024

Contents

Preface

It is a profound thought to think that our place in the vast cosmos, which is intricate, is unique. We as human beings often feel limited by time and space, perceiving ourselves as entities distinct from the whole. Yet, this perception might be just a narrow glimpse of a broader reality, a reminder that our perspective is but a single thread in the rich tapestry of existence.

Happiness Is … is my modest attempt to step out of that delusion and to capture, however fleetingly, the boundless and multifaceted nature of happiness.

It all started with some very simple encounters, with my fingers dancing on the keys, delving deep into the recesses of my memories, emotions, and experiences. The more I ventured, the more I realized how vast the terrain was. I began to see happiness as both immeasurable and infinite.

In the grand theatre of life, it is often the simplest things that bring us the greatest joy. A burst of laughter from a baby, the aroma of a home-cooked meal, the delicate touch of a loved one's hand, the comforting hug of a friend—these moments, though seemingly trivial, hold within them the essence of the universe. But it is not just the moments of spontaneous elation that define happiness. Happiness is also found in our struggles, in the resilience with which we face life's myriad challenges, and in the silent, sometimes painful understanding that everything is fleeting.

To my children, the stars in my universe: every anecdote, every tear, and every joyful moment in this memoir owes itself to you. Your very existence has been my compass, leading me through the labyrinth of emotions to the very heart of happiness.

Families are the lighthouses in the human journey. They stand tall, guiding us through our darkest nights. My family, with its idiosyncrasies, warmth, and never-ending support, is the bedrock upon which this memoir stands.

The tapestry of my life is interwoven with the threads of friendships that have stood the test of time, friends who have laughed with me, cried with me, and held my hand as we navigated the undulating terrain of existence. To them, I owe the colours that make this tapestry vibrant.

Writing *Happiness Is …* has been an exercise in introspection. It has been a journey, not of miles and landscapes, but of memories and emotions. Every word, every line, has been a step closer to understanding the enigma that is happiness.

It's fascinating, isn't it, how memories of the past, once thought to be buried deep within, come rushing back with a mere nudge. The act of reminiscing, of delving into the archives of our minds, is a testament to the eternal nature of happiness. The universe, in all its grandeur, is but a reflection of the emotions we house within ourselves. And happiness, that elusive emotion, is perhaps the most luminous of all the stars in our internal galaxy.

There is no definitive manual for happiness, no guidebook with rules and steps. Happiness is as varied as the individuals who seek it. What brings joy to one might bring sorrow to another. But in its essence, happiness is universal.

The journey of writing has been transformative for me. The process has been a pilgrimage, not to distant lands, but to the deepest corners of my soul. And what I've found is that happiness, in all its myriad forms, resides there.

Throughout these pages, you'll find fragments of my soul, scattered like stars in the night sky. Some shine brightly, while others are faint. But each holds a story, a memory, a piece of the puzzle that is happiness.

While we may be bound by our perceptions, it is our endeavour, our eternal quest, to break free from them and to embrace the universe in its entirety, letting its beauty seep into our very beings. In this quest, we find happiness, not just in the milestones and grand celebrations, but also in the mundane, the routine, the everyday.

Happiness Is … is not an endpoint, but a milestone on the continuous journey of understanding, of introspection, of discovery—a journey that I invite you, dear reader, to embark upon with me.

"Happiness is … " is not just a phrase. It is a question, an exploration, a challenge, and an answer. It is the culmination of experiences, of moments that have left an indelible mark on my soul.

While penning down these memories, I was reminded of the interconnectedness of it all, how every individual we meet, every experience we have, contributes to our understanding of happiness.

In this memoir, I've bared my soul, opened up my heart, and shared snippets of my life, not to serve as a guide or issue a directive, but to be a companion, a fellow traveller on the road to understanding happiness.

The encounters that birthed this memoir were spontaneous, often raw, and always genuine. They were conversations with myself, with the universe, and with the emotion of happiness itself.

In the end, this is not just my story. It is the story of every individual who has ever pondered upon the nature of happiness. It is a tapestry of human emotions intricately woven with threads of joy, sorrow, love, and hope.

As you delve into these pages, I hope you find a piece of yourself—a memory, an emotion, a moment that resonates with your soul. For in the end, *Happiness Is …* is a reflection, a mirror held up to the soul, capturing the myriad hues of human emotion.

To all who have been a part of my journey, my story, my universe: thank you. In you, I've found pieces of myself. In your joys, your sorrows, your struggles, and your victories, I've found fragments of my own happiness.

Here's to the journey, to the exploration, to the eternal quest for happiness. May we never cease to seek, to understand, or to cherish.

With gratitude and love, my story begins …

Chapter 1

RENEWAL IN FRANCE

1.1 Le Voyage

In the wake of heartbreak and mourning, I stood at a precipice. The winds of change swirled around me, cutting as sharply as the divorce papers I'd just signed and the deaths of my beloved father and maternal grandmother. These were three separate blows, all equally brutal, each one a testament to the transience of life and love.

As I stood on the literal and metaphorical edge of my old life in Malaysia, I clutched the grief in my fists, my heart pulsating with the rawness of the loss. Yet amidst the grief, there was a spark, a glimmering ember of hope and anticipation, the prospect of a journey that beckoned me.

Embracing the comforting solitude of my study, I ran my fingers over the document that represented a new life, a PhD offer letter from a Franco-American university. I had always been a seeker, curious and passionate, and the ivory tower of academia seemed to me a refuge, a lighthouse in the storm. It promised the balm of intellectual pursuit, an opportunity to immerse myself in my passions, and more importantly, a place to heal.

Thus, the decision to leave my children, my home in California, my familiar life, and to journey to the heart of France was not just a choice but a lifeline. It was a chance to rebuild, to redirect the energy of my loss into something potent and transformative.

With one last lingering glance at my old life, I boarded the plane, the hum of its engines a lullaby to my grief. As the aircraft ascended, I saw the vibrant tapestry of California fading into the distance. A new journey was beginning, bringing with it an opportunity to craft my narrative anew in a foreign land and to find friendship, purpose, and myself again.

As the French countryside unfurled beneath the aeroplane, I felt a tingling sense of anticipation. The silver thread of the Seine, the patchwork of vineyards, the terracotta rooftops of quaint villages, all whispered tales of romance and resilience, matching the rhythm of my heart.

This was my voyage—a journey of discovery, of reinvention, and most importantly, of healing. I had lost parts of myself, and now I would find them in my new life amidst the scholarly halls of academia, in the cobblestone streets of France, and deep within my resilient heart. This was my leap of faith, my embrace of the unknown, my grand adventure. And so the tale begins …

1.2 A Parisian Awakening

My journey continued as the plane landed on the tarmac of Charles de Gaulle Airport, the city of Paris laid out before me like an open invitation. The city was both a tapestry of centuries-old structures and bustling modern life and a symphony of cultures, and was replete with the thrill of new beginnings. It was alluring, yet I carried in my heart a weight, a maternal guilt that threatened to overshadow the city's charms.

I had left my young children in the safety of their home in the USA, promising them countless bedtime story sessions over video calls, a promise that was as much for them as it was for me. As I manoeuvred through the City of Lights, I held onto the belief that my academic journey was not just for me, but for them too. I longed to present them with a living example of the power of resilience, the importance of aspirations, and the beauty of a passionate pursuit.

Navigating through the 7th arrondissement of Paris, I stepped into the heart of my academic journey. In my solitude, the hallowed halls of the university welcomed me like an old friend, appearing much like a sanctuary where I could immerse myself in the pursuit of knowledge.

However, Paris had more to offer than just academic enlightenment, as I would soon find out. Between lectures and studies, I found myself swept up in the city's rhythm, a tempo as flavourful and rich as the French cuisine. I spent evenings in brasseries, learning the subtle differences between Bordeaux and Burgundy wine, and enjoying the creamy texture of camembert and the sweetness of a perfectly baked tarte Tatin or *pain au chocolat.*

It was here I forged new friendships, a mosaic of like-minded individuals who, like me, were in pursuit of knowledge, self-discovery, and the quintessential joie de vivre. Their conversations were as rich as the food they savoured, flavoured with tales of their journeys, their sharing of their dreams, and laughter, which seemed to heal my wounded heart a little more each day.

The Parisian outlook on life and love intrigued me, and the French philosophy of living life fully was refreshing and liberating. The Parisians' open, unabated approach to sensuality and sex made the Asian girl in me blush at first, then gradually, it helped me view my own desires and identity through a new lens, one that was free of judgement and full of self-acceptance.

This was my Parisian awakening. I was a mother, a student, a friend, a woman, and a professional, not defined by any one role, but beautifully complex in my plurality. And though my children were miles away, I felt them close to my heart, memories of their laughter and smiles a constant reminder of why I was here: to grow, to learn, to heal, and to become a beacon of courage and resilience for them. I was crafting a legacy of love, strength, and passion, which I hoped one day my children would not just understand, but also be proud of.

1.3 Un Nouveau Commencement

France welcomed me with a painter's palette of breathtaking landscapes, each a masterpiece in its own right. My journey through the country was akin to walking through a vividly painted canvas, the colours and textures shifting with every region I visited.

In Paris, the charming arrondissements captivated me. I often lost myself in the labyrinth of cobblestone streets, each turn revealing quaint boutiques, bustling cafes, and historic landmarks. The River Seine wove through the city like a shimmering ribbon, the Cathedral of Notre Dame casting dramatic reflections onto the tranquil water. At night, the Eiffel Tower glittered like a thousand stars against the dark velvet of the Parisian sky.

I awoke each morning in my Parisian apartment, greeted by the fresh scent of a new day wafting from the bakeries below. I would wrap myself in a blanket, cradle a cup of café au lait, and gaze at the serene River Seine from my balcony. Every day was an opportunity, a chance to dive deeper into French culture and move farther away from the confines of my past.

I found an almost addictive sense of liberation in riding a scooter through the cobblestone streets, the wind kissing my cheeks and whispering tales of French freedom into my ears. This was a departure from the more rigid and traditional culture I had grown up back in Malaysia, a culture that had stifled my spirit for too long. The freedom of France was like oxygen to my soul, allowing me to breathe deeply and fully, to live each moment in its entirety.

Bordeaux

I began to branch out from Paris, journeying to Bordeaux, the wine capital of the world, where I revelled in the intricacies of the vineyards and the silent poetry of the rolling hills cloaked in vines. Here, I immersed myself in the world of wine tasting, learning to appreciate the subtle notes of oak, fruit, and terroir and the stories each bottle of Bordeaux held within its depths. The narrow road to the Bordeaux countryside led me through a tapestry of vineyards, the emerald-green vines heavy with clusters of purple grapes. The rolling hills were an orchestration of lines and curves converging to form a harmonious natural melody. Majestic châteaux dotted the landscape, their stone façades bearing testament to centuries of winemaking heritage.

Lacanau

In Lacanau, an hour west of Bordeaux, I was greeted by an entirely different palette. The Atlantic Ocean stretched out into the horizon, its surface a shifting kaleidoscope of blues. The sandy beaches were dotted with surfboards, their bright colours stark against the pale sand. I would sit on the shore, watching the sun dip into the ocean, setting the sky aflame with hues of pink, orange, and gold. I challenged myself with the ebb and flow of the Atlantic waves. The freedom of surfing mirrored my new life; each wave was an opportunity; each fall, a lesson; and each successful ride, a celebration of my resilience.

Nice and Côte d'Azur

Farther south, in Nice and Côte d'Azur, the French Riviera unfurled in all its glamour. The pebbly beaches sparkled under the sun, the turquoise waters of the Mediterranean lapping gently against the shore. The palm-lined promenades were alive with the bustle of beachgoers, the air scented with the salty sweetness of the sea. The colours here were vibrant and lively, echoing the spirit of the Riviera. Feeling the warmth of the sun and the cool Mediterranean Sea on my skin, here, I learned to slow down and appreciate the simple pleasures of life such as sunbathing on the pebbled beaches and savouring a bowl of bouillabaisse.

Loire Valley

Back in the countryside in the Loire Valley, I explored the grand châteaux, each boasting sprawling gardens adorned with geometrically arranged flowers. Statuesque trees created leafy canopies under which I would sit, drinking in the peacefulness offered by the French countryside. The grand châteaux, the historic structures, are a testament to France's rich history and culture. Each château represents a chapter in the narrative of France, and I found within their walls inspiration for my own evolving story.

From the iconic landmarks of Paris to the verdant vineyards of Bordeaux, from the rhythmic waves of Lacanau to the glamour of the French Riviera, and with the serene beauty of the countryside, France offered me a myriad of landscapes. Each was a unique tableau, a vivid stretch of scenery that enriched my journey and made my time in France an unforgettable sojourn.

1.4 Les Amis du Voyage

In this new chapter of my life, I began to feel a profound connection to France and its people. I found freedom in the culture, which profoundly differed from the way in which I was brought up. I tasted this freedom in the wines of Bordeaux, felt it in the waves of Lacanau, savoured it on the beaches of Nice, and breathed it in the halls of the grand châteaux. *Un nouveau commencement*, indeed—a new beginning, a blossoming of my spirit, and the unravelling of a life that promised to be as rich and beautiful as France itself.

My journey through France was marked, not only by the places I visited, but also by the bonds I forged. These relationships were as varied and colourful as the French landscape, each one bringing with it lessons, laughter, and shared memories.

The Attorney

At an art-filled soiree in the heart of Paris, I spotted the French attorney, a brooding figure hiding away in a corner. Intrigued, I mustered the courage to introduce myself. The attorney, looking somewhat surprised, merely gave me a polite nod. Undeterred, I began to fill the silence with chatter about the art, the city, and my research, but he remained nonresponsive.

I would later learn that he was a man of few words, reserved in his demeanour and cautious in his interactions. He was not ignoring me but merely observing, assessing, and possibly appreciating my efforts to make conversation.

Then, much to my surprise, he began to speak. His English was fluent with a charming French accent, contrary to his humble assertion that it was "broken". I found his humility endearing and his accent delightful. We decided to meet more often, intending to improve his English—a subtle pretext for what was to become a series of fascinating interactions.

Our rendezvous were typically at quaint Parisian cafes, where amidst laughter, intellectual discussions, and endless cups of café au lait, we formed a bond. I cherished these moments—his warm smiles, his astute observations, and even his occasional bashfulness.

"Sometimes I wonder if I've made the right choices," I shared with the French attorney one evening. "Leaving my children to pursue this path ... it feels like a heavy trade-off."

"But you're doing it for them, aren't you?" he replied, his gaze soft but serious. "We all make sacrifices for the people we love. It's not easy, but it's part of life."

One day, in an attempt to delve deeper into French culture, we embarked on an art-laden journey through various museums. Our tour involved more than mere appreciation of art: it was a profound exploration of perspectives, a silent understanding of shared interests, and a testament to our growing bond.

"Work isn't just about money or power," my attorney friend confessed. "It's about passion. If you don't love what you do, you'll find yourself merely surviving, not living."

"But what if your passion doesn't align with your responsibilities?" I questioned.

"Then you must seek a balance. Life, after all, is about harmonizing our desires with our duties," he answered, his gaze reflecting the wisdom of his words.

France, with its rich culture and diverse perspectives, offered unique insights into subjects often viewed as delicate. Conversations about love, marriage, sex, and even extramarital affairs were tackled with a refreshing openness, a testament to the liberated mindset of the French people.

One evening, the attorney shared his perspective on marriage. "Marriage isn't about ownership," he declared, "it's about partnership. It's about two people, each with their individuality, building something beautiful together."

"And what if this 'partnership' starts to crumble?" I asked.

"Then"—he paused, appearing to choose his words carefully—"it's either time to rebuild or time to part ways. But one must always remember to part with respect and kindness."

Then things took an unexpected turn when he invited me to his apartment. The presence of his girlfriend, coupled with his nonchalant revelation, left me baffled. Yet, he seemed assured of his relationship's dynamics, claiming his girlfriend was OK with our friendship.

In his apartment, under the dim, soft glow of antique lamplight, there was an immediate shift in energy. A velvet seduction seemed to unfold, diffused with the intoxicating scent of rich French wine and the tantalizing aromas of dinner simmering on the stove. The attorney's girlfriend, undeniably beautiful and self-assured, possessed an uncanny grace as she moved around us. She regarded me with eyes that held a curious warmth laced with a hint of a challenge. The couple's home was an exquisite painting of love and companionship, but one that seemed ready to expand its canvas to accommodate another. The ambiance radiated an intriguing blend of warmth and intimacy with an unspoken invitation to engage in their unique companionship paradigm.

This complexity added a new layer to our interactions, opening up uncharted territories that I was yet to navigate. It was a delicate dance, one that promised to reveal more about French attitudes towards relationships and perhaps even my own feelings towards friendship with committed couples.

The Professor

In my academic journey, I encountered an elderly thrice-divorced professor, a man of wisdom and charm, accompanied always by his loyal dog Maxwell. They were an inseparable pair—a testament to unconditional love transcending species lines.

This professor, with his wizened eyes and dark silver hair, shared tales of his numerous heartbreaks and victories, his stories as engaging as the French novels I loved. It was a friendship that held a mirror to my own resilience, showing me that life, with all its trials, was always worth living.

In a corner cafe, over cups of dark, aromatic coffee, he would share his insights.

"Old age," he began one day, "is often regarded with fear and disdain. But I see it as a badge of honour, a testament to a life well lived, to battles fought and lessons learned."

"Isn't it also a reminder of our mortality?" I asked.

"Indeed," he agreed, a contemplative look in his eyes. "But death is not an end, it's a transition. It's the one certainty we all share, and there's a certain comfort in that universality."

As he spoke of death, the professor's thoughts would often drift towards his mother, residing in an aged-care home in New York City. He held a tender love for her, marred by the sadness of seeing her vitality fading.

"My spirit remains strong," he'd often remark, his voice tinged with a mix of pride and sorrow. "It's a reminder of how our spirits can outlive our bodies."

"But how do you cope with the idea of her passing?" I asked on one occasion, my own memories of losing loved ones resonating.

"It's not easy," he admitted, his gaze softening. "But I find solace in knowing that she has lived her life fully, that she's loved and been loved, and that she has touched many lives. I believe that's what truly matters."

His words painted a poignant picture of life, ageing, and death, infusing me with a deeper understanding of these inevitable cycles. The professor, with his thrice-divorced status and his dog Maxwell, embodied the bittersweet symphony of life, filled with love, loss, companionship, and the relentless march of time.

One day, while walking Maxwell in a park, the wise professor shared his view on relationships: "Three divorces taught me a thing or two. Love isn't just about companionship; it's also about growth, respect, and cherishing each other's individuality."

"And what if one gets lost in the process?" I asked.

"Then, my dear, it's time to pause and rediscover oneself," he replied, a knowing smile on his face. "Infidelity is also not a black and white issue. It's a complex interplay of emotions, desires, and circumstances. It's often a symptom of deeper issues within a relationship."

"But isn't it a betrayal?" I questioned.

"Undeniably so," he agreed, "but it's crucial to understand its roots to address it effectively. In many cases, healing is possible, and in others, separation might be the healthier path."

1.5 La Philosophie Française

During my journey, I found myself immersed in rich, enlightening conversations with my French friends. These interactions were a tapestry of laughter, shared experiences, and insightful discussions that greatly shaped my perspective on life.

Conversation 1: The Tunisian Dean

Amongst the academic circles, I found an ally in a Tunisian dean, a stern yet kind-hearted man who held a deep respect for academia. Despite his seriousness, the dean bore a tender heart and was always ready to lend an ear or offer advice. His guidance and friendship was like a lighthouse to me, navigating me through the often choppy waters of academia.

In a discussion about my PhD struggles, the Tunisian dean offered his advice. "Remember, a PhD is a marathon, not a sprint. You need patience and persistence. It's not about the destination, but the journey."

"But what if the journey seems too vast?" I voiced my concerns.

Then narrow your focus. A journey begins with a single step. Find that step in your research."

Conversation 2: At a Parisian Soiree

At a soiree, amidst the clinking of wineglasses, I confessed to a group of friends, "I'm not used to this, the parties, the wine … I am a single mother and a professional with little time for pleasure. It's a lot to take in."

A friend replied, laughing, "But this is life à la française! It's a symphony of experiences. You just need to find your rhythm."

Conversation 3: With a French Artist

During a chance encounter with a French artist, I discovered a different outlook on happiness. "Happiness is not a destination," the artist mused, "it's a way of life. It's in every stroke of my brush, every shade on my palette, every canvas I create."

"So, it's about finding joy in what we do every day?" I asked, my curiosity piqued.

"*Exactement!*" the artist replied, a content smile on his face. "Life is a canvas, and we're the artists. We find happiness when we paint it with colours that bring us joy."

Conversation 4: With an Elderly Frenchwoman

In a quiet French village, I met an elderly woman whose take on life was both simple and profound. "Life, *ma chère*, is like a fine wine. It has its seasons of growth and its moments of sunshine and rain. But with time, it matures, revealing flavours that were hidden."

I looked at her, intrigued. "So, we should be patient with life?"

"Oui." The woman nodded. "Every phase of life has something to offer. We must learn to savour it, just like a good wine."

Conversation 5: With a French Businessman

At a Parisian soiree, I found myself in conversation with a businessman who spoke of success in terms that contradicted conventional definitions. "Success isn't just about the numbers," he explained. "It's about impact. It's about creating value that benefits not just you, but others as well."

"But doesn't that make the pursuit of success even more challenging?" I asked.

"Perhaps," he conceded. "But it also makes success even more meaningful."

These conversations with liberated French men and women opened up new perspectives for me. They revealed the nuances of life, work, and happiness, teaching me to appreciate the subtleties of each and enabling me to adopt a more philosophical approach towards my own journey.

1.6 L'Amour à la Française

Conversation 1: With a Liberated French Woman

An open conversation about sex with a liberated French woman offered me a new perspective. "Sex is not about shame," the woman stated boldly. "It's about pleasure, about connection, about expressing love. It's about embracing your desires without guilt or fear."

"But doesn't that freedom also come with risks?" I asked, intrigued.

"Indeed, it does. But being conscious of our choices, responsible in our actions, and respectful of our partners can guide us through those risks."

Conversation 2: With a French Businesswoman

A conversation with a successful businesswoman illuminated the balance between work, marriage, and personal desires. "My work, my marriage, my desires—they're parts of who I am," she explained. "I strive to honour each without encroaching on the others. It's a delicate dance, but not an impossible one."

"So, it's about harmony," I concluded.

"Exactly." The businesswoman smiled. "It's about finding your personal equilibrium."

These conversations allowed me to openly and honestly explore subjects that in other places I'd lived were often cloaked in taboo. They revealed the complexities of human relationships and emotions, showcasing a frankness that was both liberating and enlightening.

1.7 Les Responsabilités

My journey through France not only broadened my perspectives on personal matters but also gave me a deeper understanding of social responsibility, including our duty to protect the environment, contribute to society, practise ethics, and use sound economics.

Conversation 1: With an Environmental Activist

"Nature is not our possession, it's our home," a passionate environmental activist said to me one afternoon in a Parisian park. "We must protect and cherish it, not exploit it."

"But how can we balance progress and preservation?" I asked.

"By making sustainable choices. Small changes in our everyday lives can lead to significant impacts," he explained.

Conversation 2: With a Social Worker

During my time in Bordeaux, I met a dedicated social worker. "Society isn't something external to us. We are part of it, and we have a responsibility to contribute positively to it," she remarked.

"And how can we best do that?" I questioned.

"By being empathetic, by volunteering our time or resources, by standing up against injustice, and by fostering a sense of community."

Conversation 3: With a Philosophy Professor

In an enlightening conversation, a philosophy professor discussed the importance of ethics. "Ethics are the backbone of any functioning society," he mused. "They guide us in distinguishing right from wrong and ensure fair treatment for all."

"But isn't right and wrong subjective?" I asked, intrigued.

"True, there can be grey areas," he agreed, "but the principle of respecting others' rights and dignity provides a reliable compass."

Conversation 4: With an Economist

A discussion with an economist in Nice revealed to me the dynamics of economics. "Economic prosperity is essential, but it shouldn't come at the expense of societal or environmental welfare," he emphasized.

"So, we need to rethink our definitions of success?" I asked.

"Yes. We need to aim for balanced growth, growth that considers the triple bottom line of people, planet, and profit."

Each of these conversations painted a fuller picture of our collective responsibility. I came to understand that to achieve harmony, it's essential to strike a balance between personal aspirations and social responsibilities, between progress and preservation, and between the individual good and the collective good.

1.8 La Fête à Lacanau

Life in France was not all studying and seriousness; there were parties, soirees that were quintessentially French, filled with the thrill of dance, music, and endless flutes of Champagne. I found myself amidst this swirl of joy, my heart beating in sync with the vibrant music. Though a light drinker, I tried to match the pace of these gatherings, which occasionally led to moments of tipsiness and once to an unforgettable incident of my throwing up at a party. But even these moments were responded to with laughter and camaraderie, another shared tale in my French diary.

These bonds, each unique in its essence, enriched my journey. They became my anchors in a foreign land, turning my voyage into a tapestry of shared stories, laughter, and lessons and providing me with an overwhelming sense of belonging. Through each of these friendships, I experienced the true spirit of France: its warmth, its vibrancy, and its undying zest for life. They were the *amis du voyage*—the friends of my journey, the companions of my heart, the family I found on French soil.

In Lacanau, the day had been filled with excitement. I had ridden my first wave and experienced the thrill and fear of the mighty Atlantic.

My heart was still beating with the intoxication of a new challenge mastered—surfing. Wet, sandy, and exultant, I joined my friends as they made their way back to their holiday home.

The house was a charming seaside bungalow, bathed in the warmth of the setting sun, its white walls reflecting the vibrant hues of the evening. It sat amidst sprawling dunes, facing the restless ocean, a picture of serenity, yet humming with life.

As the last ray of the sun sank beneath the horizon, the party began. A mix of French and American music wafted in the air, a perfect blend of cultures just like the group itself. The scent of barbecue hung heavy, mingling with the fresh sea air and the chlorine of the pool. The clinking of glasses and peals of laughter punctuated the rhythmic beats, creating a symphony of sounds that encapsulated the joy of the moment.

I watched the scene unfold from the edge of the pool, my feet dipped in the warm water, the soft strains of "La vie en rose" filling the air. I saw my friends dancing, their moves unabated, their spirits high. The French attorney, normally composed, was belting out an off-tune rendition of a classic rock song. The professor was engaged in a passionate discussion with a group of young surfers, with Maxwell napping contentedly at his feet. A few adventurous ones had taken a spontaneous dip in the pool, their clothes drenched, their laughter echoing.

In that moment, as I looked at my friends—the relationships I had cultivated, the bonds I had formed—a sense of profound happiness wafted over me. The music, the laughter, the dancing, the camaraderie—it was all so invigorating, so full of life. I had never felt more alive, more connected.

A soft tune began to play, an old American favourite. I felt a hand on my shoulder, and I turned to see the French attorney, his eyes sparkling with mirth. "May I have this dance?" he asked, extending a hand.

With a wide smile, I took his hand, allowing myself to be pulled into the dance, the music, and the laughter. That night, under the starlit French sky, I danced like I never had before: with abandon, with joy, and most importantly, with happiness

1.9 Danse Délicate à Paris

In the coming days, I would wander through the charming streets of Montmartre, marvel at the grandeur of the Louvre, and immerse myself in the bohemian spirit of the Latin Quarter. Paris, with its iconic landmarks and hidden treasures, held endless possibilities for exploration and inspiration.

With an open heart and eager spirit, I ventured forth into the enchanting streets of Paris, ready to embrace the beauty and magic that awaited me. The adventure continued, and I was determined to make the most of every moment, cherishing the experiences that would shape my life forever.

In Paris, I found myself ensconced in the sanctuary of Adrian Leeds Saint-Tropez, a petite slice of heaven, hidden away like a pearl in the oyster of rue Charlot, nestled in the 3rd arrondissement of Le Marais, my most cherished quarter of Paris. Its quaint and tranquil lanes beckoned the wanderer in me, subtly contrasting with the effervescent vitality of the bustling cafes that dotted their intersections.

Café Charlot, poised gracefully at the crossroads of rue Charlot and rue de Bretagne, was my chosen retreat, a haven of conversation and camaraderie, perfumed by the rich aromas of coffee and freshly baked bread. This was more than a cafe; it was my rendezvous with the soul of Paris. A PhD colleague first brought me into its welcoming embrace years ago, and ever since, it has played host to countless memories spun together with a diverse tapestry of friends.

As I sat on the balcony sipping my café au lait, the world below transformed into a beautiful stage where the theatre of life unfolded. It was there, in that enchanting corner of Paris, that I was graced with a sanctuary to marvel at the world, a place where I could live, breathe, and pen my tales. It was a perfect, snug little corner of the universe, a place where I belonged, a place I could call home.

In the City of Lights, Paris, where cobblestone lanes whisper tales of love and life, I found myself enmeshed in a lively ballet of work and camaraderie with this PhD colleague. Our work dynamic was as enthralling as the city itself, though it was not without its subtle undercurrents of apprehension, like two dancers wary of stepping on each other's toes. We were watchful, protective of the sacred territories of our hearts, never crossing those invisible lines of personal space.

I could sense the flickers of discomfort emanating from his girlfriend and see a wariness shadowing her gaze as we worked together, an unease as palpable as the crisp Parisian air. The questions, though, hung unasked between us in a silent agreement not to pry into each other's personal realm. His girlfriend, an enigma in his present, was one of the untouched territories of our conversations.

And yet there was this PhD friend, endearingly referring to his girlfriend as "my honey", a refrain that echoed as frequently as the bells of Notre Dame. The term of endearment seemed less about genuine warmth and more like a constant reminder to both of us, a proclamation of his commitment. It felt very reminiscent of my ex-husband—the need to highlight the lines that should not be crossed, the walls that should not be breached, as a reminder for himself.

In Paris, the attorney and I danced this delicate dance of friendship and professional collaboration, surrounded by the city's timeless charm, forever mindful of the lines we had drawn. Our words and actions formed the rhythm of our interaction, a composition as intricate and beautiful as the Parisian skyline under the watchful gaze of the Eiffel Tower.

One day, stepping out from a local French university in the bustling 3rd arrondissement, I found my afternoon illuminated by an encounter with Mr Encyclopaedia, an enigma of Greek origins, who shone as brightly as the Aegean sun. Over a languid lunch, our conversation wove a tapestry of shared interests and spontaneous laughter that led seamlessly into twilight drinks. Mr Encyclopaedia, in his characteristic exuberance, greeted me as if I were a long-lost friend. "OMG! The one and only KT!" His words echoed with a sense of wonder and delight, painting a smile on my face. "I envisioned an older woman donning Coca-Cola glasses and swathed in an ankle-length skirt," he confessed, his chuckle melodious in the Parisian air.

An inkling stirred within me, a subtle intuition that his interest may have surpassed the bounds of casual camaraderie. Under the stars of the Parisian sky, our conversation meandering through the labyrinths of our lives, I decided to unveil parts of my story. I gently sketched the silhouette of my past: a marriage that once was, and now was only a memory, and the two precious souls that had come from it—my children. I saw Mr Encyclopaedia's eyes absorb my narrative, the light of the streetlamps reflecting the understanding in his gaze.

The evening unfurled in a panorama of tastes and experiences. There was the blissful indulgence of ice cream from Bartholomea, every spoonful a symphony of flavours that melted into sweet sighs on our tongues. We wandered to Bastille, the evening air seasoned with an intoxicating blend of Parisian spirit and camaraderie, and discovered another watering hole, this one curiously bearing the same name as our previous stop.

Through it all, Paris stood as our silent witness, its lamplit streets a testament to this fleeting connection, woven together over shared ice cream, quiet confessions, and the effervescent laughter of a Greek genius named Mr Encyclopaedia.

As the embers of Saturday gave way to the night, Mr Encyclopaedia gave me a fresh invitation, beckoning me to join him. Mr Encyclopaedia, truly a veritable walking encyclopaedia, has a magical knack for etching even the most mundane topics with hues of enchantment. Time, in his company, had the curious habit of hastening, as if eager to reach the crescendo of our shared laughter and playful debates.

The path back to my abode in the 3rd arrondissement from the French university was strewn with windows into my past. Storefronts, standing like silent sentinels, held within their glass panes a reflection of my time in Paris with my PhD friend. The memories tumbled forth, unbidden yet insistent, brushing past my consciousness like wistful ghosts yearning for acknowledgement.

A tidal wave of emotion swelled within me, causing my heart to echo in longing for times now lost. Behind the closed doors of my apartment, the vibrant tapestry of my Parisian adventures became the backdrop to a solitary dance of tears that night. The city of love and light had witnessed the joy and camaraderie of my past and now bore witness to the delicate unravelling of memories, knitting themselves into the very fabric of my Parisian journey.

A sunny ten o'clock rendezvous with Adrian Leeds involved a shared breakfast table, over which we wove dreams of owning Parisian real estate between taking bites of pain au chocolat. Possibilities twinkled in the Parisian morning light, as ripe as the fruits on our plates.

My day continued with a meeting with John from Adrian Leeds, a man who seemed to have a map of French real estate intricately woven into the very fabric of his being. Over a cup of strong, aromatic Parisian coffee, he introduced me to the labyrinthine world of property purchasing in France, specifically, Paris.

His words painted a picture of tangled webs and hidden complexities, of unexpected turns and elusive rewards. I had experience owning properties in Australia and the USA, but this was an entirely different ballgame. It was not for the faint of heart, he cautioned, and I could see the subtle, yet profound truth in his words. Paris was not just a city; it was a living, breathing entity, its real estate landscape reflecting its unique heartbeat.

1.10 Les Premières Étapes

As I moved deeper into my academic journey, the excitement of a new environment began to mingle with the strain I felt in pursuing my PhD. The subject of my thesis was as vast and complex as the nation it centred upon, namely, China, the burgeoning economic powerhouse. The more I delved into the subject, the more I realized the enormity of my task.

China was a puzzle with countless pieces, each representing a unique aspect of the nation's economic might. Struggling to focus on a single piece of this intricate puzzle, I found myself floundering at times, swept up in the vastness of my research.

Alongside my academic struggles were the pangs of motherhood. I found solace in the daily ritual of calling my children, their voices a balm to my weary soul. I missed them, their laughter, their innocence, their endless questions. Promising them I would return in two weeks, I masked my uncertainty, the sacrifices of my journey hidden behind the gentle cadence of my voice.

The Parisian soirees that I had once found charming began to feel overwhelming. The music was too loud, the conversations were too frivolous, and the wine was too intoxicating. I found myself longing for the quiet serenity of my home in California, the vast expanse of the Pacific, the golden sunsets, and the scent of blooming bougainvillea.

My Parisian apartment that I had once found quaint and charming began to feel cramped and suffocating. I missed the sprawling Californian landscapes, the expanses of beaches, the endless blue skies. Winter in Paris was beautiful but harsh, the biting cold a stark contrast to the mild California winters.

Even as I found freedom and liberation in the heart of France, grief began to cast its long shadow. The absence of my father and grandmother, the rawness of my divorce, the miles between me and my children, all culminated in a wave of sadness. The joy of the French countryside, the charm of Paris, and the liberation of my new life were momentarily eclipsed by a sense of loss.

Yet, I understood that this was part of *les premières étapes*, the initial steps. There was a certain beauty in this struggle, a raw authenticity that made my journey even more meaningful. I embraced the struggles, the triumphs, the joy, and the grief, weaving them into the grand tapestry of my life, holding onto the belief that each step, no matter how challenging, was a step towards growth, understanding, and ultimately, happiness.

1.11 L'Entretien

L'École X. It is not just a name, but an institution in itself. One of the finest and most distinguished engineering schools in France, it stands as an edifice to intellectual prowess and academic excellence. Steeped in history and grandeur, it is a place where the cogs of industry and innovation intermesh seamlessly, churning out visionaries and leaders of tomorrow. I felt a palpable thrill, a mix of trepidation and anticipation, as I prepared to cross its threshold for my interview.

I can still clearly picture that moment, which took place a couple of months ago. I was nestled in the corner of a bustling Starbucks in California, surrounded by a spirited group of women volunteers. Our mission: to orchestrate an online auction for my children's elementary school. Amidst the chatter and clatter, the unmistakable ring of my phone broke through the lively hum. The screen displayed an unfamiliar French number as the incoming call. A spark of curiosity ignited in me, and with a swift *excusez-moi* to the group, I navigated through the crowd to a quieter corner, then answered the call.

A familiar voice met my ear—my old friend from my PhD group, his words brimming with an excitement that was contagious even across continents. He got straight to the point, informing me about a job opening at his school: an international dean, he said, and he believed I was just the person for it.

"An international dean?" I echoed, my words tinged with incredulity. My question was innocent, perhaps even naive, but wholly genuine. This was uncharted territory for me.

He indulged my confusion, his voice patient and assuring as he explained the responsibilities and the scope of the role. As I listened, another concern sprouted within me. "Am I even qualified?" I ventured, feeling as if I were digging myself into a pit of self-doubt.

But my friend remained undeterred by my apprehensions. His belief in my capabilities was unshaken. He was persuasive and confident, urging me to consider attending an interview during my next trip to France.

That unexpected call marked the beginning of a journey that would change the trajectory of my career and my life. I had no idea then what that role would bring, but I knew I was stepping onto a path that would lead me to an unimaginable adventure.

The interview was set to start at the business school, a modern architectural masterpiece with its sharp lines, its sleek glass surfaces, and an atmosphere buzzing with intellectual fervour. Every corner of the campus seemed to breathe life into the pursuit of knowledge.

Then came the elusive director of the renowned engineering school, a man who was as legendary as the institution itself. His reputation for having exacting standards and discerning judgement preceded him. He was known to be particularly concerned with age and experience—a potential stumbling block for someone like me, who often found myself underestimated because of my youthful appearance.

I met his first question, "How old are you?," with a response that echoed my American attitude: "In America, you are not supposed to ask that question."

A smirk flickered on his face, a flash of French defiance against American convention. "But we are in France!" he retorted. Our shared laughter broke the tension in the room. The chill of formality melted away, replaced with a warmth that spoke volumes about the culture of this prestigious institution.

He excused himself for five minutes, leaving me alone in the grandeur of the meeting room, my heart pounding in anticipation. Upon his return, I found his words to be as unexpected as they were thrilling.

"You have the job," he said simply, a glint of approval in his eyes. "You can start after you complete your PhD field trip to Bhutan."

I left L'École X that day with a renewed sense of purpose and confidence, knowing that I was about to embark on an exhilarating new chapter. Not only was I closer to achieving my academic dreams, but also I was poised to bring my experience and unique perspective to one of the world's most esteemed institutions. The horizon of my journey had just extended, and I couldn't wait to explore it.

1.12 Un Adieu Doux

As my time in France began to draw to a close, the City of Love seemed more beautiful than ever. The grand Eiffel Tower, the alluring Louvre, the bustling cafes, and the serene banks of the Seine all took on a bittersweet hue. Each place whispered tales of my journey, echoing with the laughter, tears, and countless conversations I'd experienced.

In the final days, I found myself traversing the labyrinth of my memories, revisiting the moments that had left a deep imprint on my heart. I remembered the first time I arrived, a bundle of nerves and excitement; the taste of my first real French wine; the intellectual discussions with the French attorney; the philosophical insights from the thrice-divorced professor; and the loyal companionship of Maxwell. Each experience was a precious treasure, a fragment of my story intertwined with the charm of France.

My journey had been much more than an academic endeavour. It had been a voyage of self-discovery, of unravelling layers of my own personality and beliefs, fuelled by the openness and dynamism of the French culture. I had arrived seeking knowledge but was departing with wisdom—wisdom about life, relationships, and myself.

As I packed my belongings, each item seemed to tell a story, bringing forth a flood of emotions. The ticket stubs, postcards, photographs, and half-empty bottles of French perfume were all pieces of a beautiful mosaic that I'd always cherish.

The anticipation of my upcoming adventure to Bhutan added a sparkle to my eyes. Though I was leaving a part of my heart in France, I was carrying with me an enriched soul, ready to embrace the next chapter.

And so, in the quiet Parisian dawn, I bid adieu to France. Not a sorrowful goodbye, but a sweet farewell, knowing that the city had left its imprint on me, as I had left mine on it. With the promise to return someday, I turned the page, the whispers of France still echoing in my heart, my mind filled with vivid dreams of the Bhutanese mountains.

1.13 Happiness Is ... Doing What You Love

In the heart of France, happiness has a different definition. It isn't measured in towering skyscrapers or impressive titles; rather, it blooms in the vineyards of Burgundy and sizzles in the kitchens of Parisian bistros.

And it was in France that I found two individuals who had found their joie de vivre, not in grand ambitions, but in the simplicity of doing what they loved.

The first was a French wine seller who left the corporate life behind to turn his passion for viniculture into a thriving business. His tiny shop, nestled in a cobblestoned alley, was brimming with bottles from the best French vineyards. Each had its own story, and he was the storyteller.

"Expansion?" he spit out, scoffing, when I asked him about his plans for a franchise. "Why would I want that? This, right here, is my happiness." He gestured around his shop, the twinkle in his eye mirroring the gleam of the glass bottles. "The smell of the cork, the sound of the pour, the feel of the glass in my hand—I love it all. I quit the corporate life for this simplicity, for this joy. And I would not trade it for the world."

There's something to be said about the French way of life—the lack of urgency, the savouring of simple pleasures, the reluctance to surrender to the cold corporate demands. It flies in the face of everything I'd learned, everything I'd taught in business school.

"I've got enough," he'd tell me, swirling the ruby-red liquid in his glass, watching it catch the sunlight. "Why would I want more?"

And I pondered that. In a world where success was often equated with size, where growth was the definitive marker of prosperity, was there space to be content living simply? Could less really be more?

The wine seller's philosophy reminded me of an old tale I'd heard, one of a Mexican fisherman and an American businessman. The American businessman had grand plans for the Mexican fisherman—expanding the fisherman's modest operation, turning it into a profitable enterprise, and building an empire, only to retire in a quiet Mexican village and live a peaceful life.

To his surprise, the fisherman had gently rebuffed his proposals because he was already living that idyllic retirement life the businessman yearned for. The fisherman had time for his family, his hobbies, and his afternoon siestas. He had happiness. He had enough.

The parallel between the vigneron and the fisherman is profound. Both are men who find joy in their work, who value the essence of living more than they do the allure of profit. Their lives are a testament to the fact that one's happiness cannot always be measured by financial success or business expansion.

Perhaps it's not always about growing bigger and getting better. Perhaps it's about finding satisfaction in where we are, cherishing the work we do, and realizing that sometimes we already have enough. That was the lesson my French wine seller friend taught me—a contradiction to the business mantras I'd known, but a revelation in understanding the art of living.

Then there was the French chef, a culinary artist who orchestrated symphonies of flavours from the freshest local ingredients. His little restaurant in the heart of Paris was not graced with a Michelin star, but that didn't faze him.

"I do not want a star," he told me one night as we sat in his restaurant long after the last customer had left. Our conversation danced between my broken French and his broken English, with laughter filling the gaps when we couldn't translate. "I want to cook, create, bring joy through my food. That is my aspiration."

I fell asleep on the dining bench amidst the lingering scents of that night's dinner, only to be awakened by the chef at four o'clock in the morning. "Come," he beckoned, a sparkle of enthusiasm in his eyes. We spent the morning at the local market picking out fresh produce and seafood for the day. Despite the early hour, his energy was contagious, his passion palpable.

Seeing the wine seller and the chef live their passions taught me an invaluable lesson: happiness isn't about scaling heights or achieving glory, it's about doing what you love, whether it's pouring wine or cooking meals, and doing it with your whole heart. It's about finding joy in simplicity and savouring the moments that make life worth living.

Happiness is when your thoughts, words and actions are aligned.

Chapter 2

ENLIGHTENMENT IN BHUTAN

2.1 A New Terrain

As the plane began its descent into Paro International Airport, I caught my first glimpse of Bhutan. Only an elite group of a few dozen pilots worldwide are authorized to guide their aircraft to the tarmac of Paro International Airport in Bhutan. The runway, situated amongst the breathtaking, sky-piercing Himalaya mountains, is a meagre ribbon of asphalt stretching unassumingly below these towering peaks. The combination of the airport's restrictive size and its daunting geographical surroundings has earned it a formidable reputation: Paro International Airport is frequently hailed as the most challenging commercial runway on the planet for pilots to navigate their landing.

Below lay a patchwork quilt of verdant hues interspersed with silver rivers and dotted with clusters of houses. The land was wild, untamed, and unimaginably beautiful. The Himalayas seemed to pierce the heavens, their snowcapped peaks shimmering in the golden light of the setting sun. It was a sight that took my breath away, instilling a sense of awe and tranquillity within my soul.

My arrival in Bhutan marked the beginning of a new chapter in my life. The Gedu College of Business Studies, where I would be teaching, was nestled amongst the mountains, seemingly part of the landscape itself. The architecture of the college buildings was striking, characterized by the traditional Bhutanese style with colourful wooden window frames, sloping roofs, and intricately designed carvings. The harmony of the design with the surroundings exuded a profound sense of spiritual and aesthetic balance.

Every day in Bhutan felt like a communion with nature. The mornings were crisp and fresh, the air rich with the earthy aroma of the damp soil and the gentle fragrance of pine. Fog would roll in from the mountains, cloaking the world in an ethereal blanket, only for it to be slowly lifted by the warming sun. As the day progressed, the sky would change from a pale, milky blue to an expanse of azure, brushed with strokes of feathery white clouds.

The weather in the Himalayas was unpredictable and fascinating. There were sudden showers, the rain falling in torrents, feeding the rivers and brooks, making them gush and roar, then there were also moments of utter serenity when the winds would stand still, the leaves would stop rustling, and all one could hear was the rhythmic chanting of the monks from a nearby *dzong* (kind of a fortified monastery).

The terrain was equally enchanting. Hiking on certain trails led me through thick pine forests, where the sunlight barely penetrated, across lush green meadows blanketed in wildflowers, and up steep mountainsides offering breathtaking panoramas of the valleys below. My weekend excursions included visits to ancient monasteries perched precariously on cliff sides, wandering through traditional Bhutanese villages with their distinctive architecture, and indulging in the rich, spicy flavours of the local cuisine at roadside eateries.

The Bhutanese architecture was one of the most fascinating aspects of my journey. Everywhere I looked, I saw a fascinating amalgamation of form, function, and symbolism. From the towering fortresslike dzongs with their massive internal courtyards and beautiful wall paintings to the humble farmhouses with their whitewashed walls and wooden shingles, each structure was a testament to the Bhutanese people's devotion to harmony, beauty, and spiritual expression.

Through every experience, every interaction, and every exploration, I found myself being drawn into the cultural and spiritual fabric of Bhutan. It was as if the majestic Bhutanese terrain was subtly reshaping me, guiding me towards a sense of peace and enlightenment I had been seeking all along.

While in Bhutan, I recalled a blustery New York day when I, armed with sheer audacity and a burning passion, found myself in front of the Bhutan Mission near the United Nations Building. The imposing structure stood tall against the steel and glass skyline of the city like an island of serenity in a sea of chaos. I was there, not with an appointment or by invitation, but because I was taking a leap of faith and had a sense of determination.

Earlier, I had written to the king of Bhutan, outlining my earnest desire to study gross national happiness, this extraordinary concept that has led Bhutan to be recognised as the happiest place on earth. Despite the energy and optimism with which I had dispatched that letter, I had received no response. But I was not one to be deterred by silence. If anything, it stoked my resolve to try harder.

So, I found myself knocking on the door of the Bhutan Mission. As I waited, my heart drummed a steady rhythm of anticipation, apprehension, and excitement in my chest. The door opened, and I was greeted by a dignified man with the warmest of smiles. I learned that he was the Bhutanese commissioner once he introduced himself.

Over a steaming cup of *suja*—Bhutanese butter tea—which the commissioner had graciously prepared, we began to talk. I laid out my aspirations, my aim to write a dissertation on gross national happiness, and my passion for understanding the Bhutanese way of life. I told him about my wish to live in Bhutan for six months to immerse myself fully in the culture, the environment, the ethos of this unique nation.

Throughout our conversation, the commissioner listened, his eyes reflecting a gentleness and attentiveness that put me at ease. He was gracious, patient, and utterly generous with his time. The glow of his goodwill made the modest office feel even more cosy, like a safe haven in the midst of an often indifferent metropolis.

Before I left, he assured me that he would do his utmost to assist me. And true to his word, he helped secure my sponsorship, facilitating my dream to live in Bhutan while teaching at the Royal University of Bhutan and consulting for the Gross National Happiness Commission (GNHC).

I walked out of the Bhutan Mission that day with my heart brimming with gratitude and optimism, the harsh New York winter suddenly feeling less intimidating. It was a moment of affirmation, a testament to the power of courage, the kindness of strangers, and the magic of serendipity.

In the end, it was not a royal response, but the kindness of the Bhutanese commissioner, that paved the way for my Bhutanese adventure. My journey was a testament to the very essence of gross national happiness, underscoring the importance of compassion, community, and the pursuit of meaningful goals—the foundations of true happiness.

As my plane stopped effortlessly on the tarmac at Paro International Airport, I couldn't help but marvel at the journey so far. It was a journey that had begun with a desire, was sustained by a spirit of resilience, and was realized through a stranger's generosity. It was a journey that affirmed my belief that happiness isn't just about the destination: it is very much about the journey itself.

About Bhutan

Bhutanese people are as diverse and beautiful as the country's varied landscapes. Steeped in history and tradition, they are deeply respectful of their heritage, which is evident in their lifestyle and cultural practices. Bhutan has managed to retain its unique identity while slowly adapting to the influences of the outside world, and this blend of tradition and modernity is captivatingly visible in its people.

The Bhutanese culture is largely influenced by Buddhism, which is evident in the Bhutanese people's daily lives. They deeply value principles of kindness, respect, and community, practising a unique philosophy known as "gross national happiness", to which I have already alluded.

This principle dictates that the country's policies and progress should contribute to the holistic well-being of its people, including their mental and spiritual health, rather than solely focusing on material wealth.

The Bhutanese people are known for their warm hospitality and genial nature. Smiles and bows are common greetings, and many of the people still wear the national dress—the *gho* for men and the *kira* for women—on a daily basis, reflecting their commitment to preserving their cultural identity.

Religion is deeply woven into the social fabric. Monks in saffron-coloured robes are a common sight, and prayer flags fluttering in the wind are an essential part of the landscape. The Bhutanese hold numerous festivals, or *tshechus*, throughout the year. These vibrant events offer a captivating display of masked dances and music, where locals gather to watch the performances, socialize, and receive blessings.

Music is integral to Bhutanese culture. It's a beautiful tapestry woven from the threads of both folk and religious traditions. Folk music, often accompanied by traditional dances, is played on indigenous instruments such as the *dranyen* (a stringed instrument), the *lingm* (flute), and the *yangchen* (a type of dulcimer). The tunes are melodious and haunting, often telling tales of love, nature, and folklore. Religious music, on the other hand, is usually heard during religious ceremonies and consists of chants and hymns accompanied by cymbals, drums, and horns.

The Bhutanese are also skilled artisans. Traditional arts and crafts known as *zorig chusum* are highly valued, including such things thangka painting, sculpture, wood carving, and weaving, all of which products carry religious and symbolic meanings. The Bhutanese people's expertise in these crafts is visible in the architecture and intricate designs found in monasteries and houses across the country.

Living amongst the Bhutanese people, learning their customs, and experiencing their unfaltering kindness and happiness is an enlightening journey. Their deep respect for nature, their strong sense of community, and the spiritual richness of their daily lives offer a unique perspective on life—one that fosters peace, mindfulness, and contentment.

Family, friendship, and work in Bhutan are all heavily influenced by the nation's Buddhist heritage and the gross national happiness principle, both of which emphasize the importance of kindness, respect, and community.

Family Values

Family is central to Bhutanese society, with households often accommodating members of the extended family. It is common for three generations to live under the same roof. Grandparents play a crucial role in taking care of the children and inculcating traditional values and customs.

The Bhutanese have a matrilineal system, meaning inheritance is generally passed through the female line. Women often inherit the family home, and men move into their wives' homes after marriage. This practice underscores the important role that women play in Bhutanese society.

Bhutanese families, irrespective of their economic status, value education and recognise it as a key to future opportunities. Parents and grandparents often share stories and legends with younger members, passing down historical and moral lessons.

Friendship

Friendship and community are considered vital elements for personal happiness and social harmony in Bhutan. The Bhutanese are known for their warmth, generosity, and hospitality. They place a great deal of value on strong social bonds and community involvement, reflecting the importance of interdependence in Buddhist philosophy.

It's common to see friends and neighbours helping each other in times of need without any expectation of return. This is often the case during house construction, farmwork, or times of personal crisis, exemplifying the strong sense of community that exists in Bhutanese society.

Work Attitude

The Bhutanese work attitude is one of dedication, respect, and harmony. They view their work not just as a means to earn a living, but also as a way to contribute to the welfare of the community and the country as a whole.

There is a deep respect for all types of work, and the dignity of labour is recognised and celebrated. In rural areas, farming is the main occupation and is seen as both a duty and a way of life.

A balance between work and leisure is also a crucial aspect of Bhutanese life. Time spent with family, participation in cultural activities, and involvement in community affairs are given an importance equal to that of work. The emphasis is on achieving a harmonious balance between material progress and spiritual well-being.

Bhutan's unique approach to life, influenced by its rich cultural heritage and the GNH principle, has resulted in a society where family values, friendships, and work attitudes are closely intertwined with the nation's core values of kindness, respect, and community.

GNH

Gross national happiness (GNH) is a term coined by Bhutan's Fourth King, Jigme Singye Wangchuck, in 1972. The concept signifies a commitment to building an economy to serve Bhutan's culture based on Buddhist spiritual values, instead of Western material-based values gauged by gross domestic product (GDP). The idea behind GNH is to strive for holistic development and recognise that the beneficial development of human society takes place when material and spiritual advancement occur side by side, complementing and reinforcing one another.

King Wangchuck believed that the existing focus on GDP was too narrow and failed to consider broader human needs, values, and well-being. The GNH Index was thus created to measure the happiness and well-being of the population. This holistic approach to development was seen as a way to safeguard Bhutan's unique culture and values in the face of rapid economic and technological change. It represented a shift in thinking about the purposes of development and progress.

The GNH Index is based on four pillars, as follows:

- **Sustainable and equitable socioeconomic development.** This includes a diverse economy and the reduction of income and opportunity gaps.
- **Conservation of environment.** The environment's health is prioritized, with the implementation of sustainable practices and the recognition of nature's intrinsic value.
- **Preservation and promotion of culture.** Bhutan's cultural heritage is valued as contributing to the national identity and ensuring continuity with tradition.
- **Good governance.** Democracy, transparency, accountability, and public service are considered crucial.

These pillars are further separated into nine domains, which include health, education, living standards, time use, psychological well-being, cultural diversity and resilience, community vitality, good governance, and ecological diversity and resilience. Seeing as the government uses the GNH Index to guide its policies, these domains help the government to analyse and understand the happiness of its citizens better and craft policies accordingly.

Bhutan's philosophy has attracted global attention, with discussions on whether the GNH model can be applied to other countries and contexts. It's considered a pioneering vision in a world searching for alternatives to uncontrolled economic development. GNH has placed Bhutan at the forefront of the debate on progress and the true meaning of development. Despite challenges in implementing and measuring the results of the GNH model, the concept continues to guide Bhutan's development policies. The kingdom's commitment to this unique principle symbolizes a dedication to holistic well-being, sustainability, and cultural preservation.

2.2 College in the Sky

In the delicate haze of waking, I was stirred by a ringing from an uncanny source—a New York number. The corporate jingle of a bank's sales call, perhaps? I dismissed it once, then again, each time finding my return to slumber blocked by the technological intrusion. With no voicemail left for me, I concluded it to be inconsequential.

As my senses came to life, I was struck by the unfamiliarity of my surroundings—a different bed, a scent to which I was unaccustomed. *Ah yes! I am in Bhutan.* The distance from home was not just geographical but also sensory.

Not long ago, I had been nestled in the stylish embrace of Paris, cradling my café crème, relishing my duck confit, and indulging in the sinful pleasure of crème brûlée. I recalled the jovial ambiance of Zagros, my preferred Parisian restaurant near Republique, where I was graced by the charming company of a friend, most handsome and *très beau.* Amidst the city's ceaseless charm, I had been bestowed an offer to serve as an international dean, a testament to the fruit of my endeavours and the result of an introduction by a friend. Leaving my beloved Paris, my third home, was something I'd done with a heart full of accomplishment.

Next was Helsinki, a vibrant city breathing warmth into the crisp autumn air, a mirror of Melbourne. The friendly faces in Finnair Lounge added a charming element to the city's song, where green trams danced on cobblestone streets.

Contrastingly, the New Delhi airport, though only a month old, wore a veil of antiquity with its unfinished construction, inactive lifts, and nonoperational toilets, its fresh façade masking the paradoxes beneath. Why, I pondered, were certain amenities such as currency exchange counters or airline lounges denied to foreigners?

Fast-forward to my arrival in Paro, Bhutan. The fact that my flight had been delayed by two hours did nothing to diminish the warmth of the Royal University of Bhutan store manager's reception. The following six-hour car ride to Gedu was filled with dramatic stunts—a road dotted with potholes, rocks, and precarious turns, demanding utmost precision lest we plunge into the abyss below. Our driver's peculiar tactic of conserving power by turning off the headlights in this challenging setting left me bemused. Thanks to the compassionate store manager, we made pit stops for comforting cups of hot milk tea and local delights such as noodles and beef *momo*, soothing my travel-worn senses.

After the forty-eight-hour journey with scarce sleep, I was no more than a somnambulant figure, struggling to retain the director's name. A gallant Indian marketing professor met me with a warm smile and introduced himself. We exchanged pleasantries, my feeble joke about marketing professors lost somewhere in the fatigue.

In the solitude of the wee hours, my conscious mind wrestling with sleep, I recalled my upcoming meeting with the elusive director. Sleep remained an mysterious siren till dawn, and by six o'clock that morning, I decided to embrace the day. Bundled in my cosiest New Zealand icebreaker gear, I felt instantly recharged.

As I soaked up the surrounding beauty of Bhutan, an adventurous impulse led me down a set of steps. A slip resulted in an embarrassing tumble—later a haunting memory of a past injury—but I carried on undeterred, my spirit untouched.

On returning to my assigned room, guilt crept over me when I saw my privileges—the private bathroom, the hot water, a comfortable abode—while my complaints about trivial discomforts echoed in my conscience. Realizing I was luckier than many, I decided to shed my foreigner's vanity.

Breakfast and the director both arrived at my doorstep at their appointed times. The day commenced with a walk to the campus, my high-heeled boots clashing with the rugged Bhutanese terrain. The director's office was the epitome of efficiency despite the chaos of Saturday morning visitors.

The day rolled on, highlighted by my connection with Professor Sangay Rinzin. Despite the exhaustion, I found myself enmeshed in delightful conversations and working on the seemingly endless research questionnaire, my quest for perfection winning out over my need for rest.

The director and I were dinner guests at the quarters of the provost of students, an affair laced with contrasting accents and conversations that I was able to comprehend only in part. An elegant Indian professor sat across from me. I was wrapped in my casual attire. The director's driving, my stylish leopard print hat, and the host's respectful restraint added further nuances to the evening.

Back at the guesthouse, I got a little rest in the afternoon, which fuelled my work into the late hours. Finally, with the perfect questionnaire at hand, I sent a reassuring text to my children back home. Thus, I bid adieu to an eventful day in Bhutan, my body and mind stirring with a strange mix of exhaustion and exhilaration.

Awakening at the ghostly hour of four o'clock in the morning, I was greeted by the stealthy crawl of time's passage. My struggle with jet lag had seen a half-hour victory, eliciting from me a silent, solitary cheer. My brain, perpetually industrious, insisted on reworking the questionnaire, a demanding undercurrent beneath my attempts at rest.

At twenty minutes to six o'clock, I found myself drawn to my journal as if the empty pages could quell my racing thoughts. As the morning matured, I descended to the dining room, intrigued by the absence of the usual breakfast summons. I stepped into an orchestrated symphony of Bhutanese conversation. The Bhutanese people's passionate engagement with their work rendered me invisible, a quiet spectator of their morning rituals.

As more Bhutanese in their traditional attire gathered, my curiosity about their delectable breakfast broke the ice. Their hospitality shone forth as they invited me to partake in their meal.

"What are you having?" I asked.

"Oh, it's an Indian breakfast with dahl. We requested it," came the answer.

The unfamiliarity dissipated as introductions flowed. The group consisted of three from the Royal University of Bhutan (RUB), including the director of academic affairs, two industry professionals, and a member of parliament. Our shared Australian education connected us by a cord of warm camaraderie.

The day flowed effortlessly. I retreated to Mr Rinzin's office, which had internet access. Lunch was a delectable Indian feast in a town about twenty-five kilometres away. Our journey back was leisurely, the driver conspicuously absent.

The afternoon saw me ensconced in the director's office, armed with his key and engrossed in refining my questionnaire. Sending off the survey link to my network of people seemed like a significant accomplishment, with the additional hope of its reaching their friends and colleagues.

Dinner was a potpourri of Indian delicacies at the marketing professor's home. The leisurely stroll back in the cool Bhutanese night air seemed delightfully feasible, our bellies satiated with the flavours of the meal. The director surprised me with a request that I deliver a speech at Monday's school assembly—a vast sea of more than a thousand students, faculty, and visitors.

The question "What should I write about?" echoed in my mind as I retired to bed, my doctoral dissertation questionnaire having been dispatched to eager participants across the globe.

At precisely half past eight the next morning, the director was waiting, a picture of patient elegance. Our breakfast was soon concluded, and we moved, I in his wake, towards the auditorium. The instant we entered, the students rose, lending an unexpected aura of prominence to the moment. Standing on the podium, I basked in the exhilaration of facing a sea of one thousand eager faces.

The speech commenced:

"Good morning, everyone. My name is KT, and just like many of you, I am also a student. I am from the United States, and presently I am pursuing an international business doctorate degree at a US-French university.

"I am sure you are wondering why I chose to come to Bhutan. The answer lies in my PhD dissertation topic, which revolves around the unique and transformative philosophy of gross national happiness (GNH).

"At present, the primary barometer of a country's prosperity is the gross domestic product (GDP). This metric emphasizes the output of a nation, often neglecting the crucial aspect of citizen well-being. Contrastingly, Bhutan's GNH philosophy provides a refreshing perspective, pivoting on four central pillars: sustainable development promotion, cultural values preservation and promotion, conservation of the natural environment, and establishment of good governance.

"What I find truly fascinating is how these pillars of GNH can be applied at the microlevel. In the global paradigm, entrepreneurial success is typically gauged by an individual's monetary net worth. My PhD dissertation boldly challenges this convention and seeks to redefine the very notion of entrepreneurial success.

"I suggest that the principles that shape an individual's success should echo those of GNH. I argue that the yardstick for entrepreneurial triumph should extend beyond monetary gains to encompass an entrepreneur's overall well-being, their adherence to ethical values, their contributions to the betterment of others' lives, and their commitment to preserving nature for future generations.

"I have named my dissertation 'The Four Pillars of Responsible Entrepreneurs'. My theory, which I refer to as 'the four E's'—empathy, earth, ethics, and earnings—is a reflection of these principles. But allow me to elaborate further ..."

Later that morning, a quick glance at my SurveyMonkey account revealed that a satisfying thirty-six surveys had been completed within a day. With a sense of accomplishment, I switched gears, preparing for a lecture on organisational behaviour with less than six hours' notice. In a spontaneous offer to be of use, I'd asked the director if I might help in his Monday class.

At a quarter after two in the afternoon, the classroom was mine till half past three. A role-play negotiation ended in an impasse, sparking laughter so infectious that tears pricked at my eyes.

At half past three, we assembled in anticipation of the Rinpoche's arrival. The guesthouse fell silent as we sat along the altar. After being served tea and rice, we partook of the quiet feast until the Rinpoche retired to his room.

At five o'clock, we accompanied the Rinpoche as he blessed the girls' and boys' dormitories. The evening concluded with a three-hour dance performance. The Rinpoche, however, retired without dinner, his presence lingering in our minds long after his departure.

2.3 My First Encounter with the Rinpoche

Today began bright and early with a trip to Sangay's office. The comforting glow of the computer screen greeted me, revealing that the SurveyMonkey count had reached fifty-five. Satisfied, I spent my morning in the director's office responding to emails.

At ten in the morning, a wave of excitement radiated from outside. The public had gathered, drawn to the campus by the presence of the Rinpoche. I seized the chance to sprint upstairs and retrieve my camera. It was a day of grandeur: the Rinpoche, having arrived with the dawn, seemed to bring the sunshine with him. The campus was vibrant and cheerful with the crowd sprawled on the grass, enjoying a communal picnic. Children frolicked freely, their laughter harmonizing with the sound of chatter as parents shared the latest news and gossip.

A student informed me about lunch's being served next to the auditorium, an opportunity for another delectable meal that I would not miss. Full and content, I spent the afternoon amidst the students, enveloped in the rhythmic cadence of the Rinpoche's chants. However, my knees, unaccustomed to the hours of sitting cross-legged, impelled me to move to the front row. The security team graciously allowed me, providing me a front-row seat as the Rinpoche began blessing individuals. To my delight, I was blessed twice!

I found myself striking up a friendship with one of the Rinpoche's assistants, who wore many hats—driver, photographer. He took a picture of me and a young boy who kept looking at me, seemingly fascinated by my blonde hair. Perhaps it was the first time he had seen a blonde Asian.

At five o'clock in the evening, just as I was about to lose myself in a swirl of conversation and the glorious weather, the director rang. He insisted I join them for tea, as his good friend from Canada was visiting.

And that's how I met Istvan, a charming Hungarian who, after marrying a Canadian, had grown quite fond of the local Bhutanese attire the gho. He seemed to have an unending appetite for conversation, making the evening all the more enjoyable. The day ended on a delicious note with dinner scheduled at half past six at the guesthouse. After a day filled with blessings and warm interactions, what could be more rewarding than that?

As morning dawned, I found myself at breakfast by seven o'clock, rubbing shoulders with the executive director of Tala Hydropower and other senior executives. A casual conversation with the dean of academic affairs ended with the promise of more when I returned.

Our day started at half past seven with the sun gently rising. It was supposed to be a half-day journey but turned into a daylong adventure. Our procession, five cars deep, trailed the Rinpoche's entourage. Rinpoche blessed three hydropower locations before ending at a secondary school. The children and locals brimmed with joy at the sight of Rinpoche, each eagerly waiting for a moment of his attention. And true to his nature, he stopped to bless everyone, irrespective of who they were or where they were from.

The lunch hosted by Tala Hydroelectric Power Plant seemed to be just a pause in a day filled with continuous activity. We then set off for Chukka to bid farewell to Rinpoche. But barely five kilometres from the school, we were halted by a blast. Rocks from a cliff had descended onto the roadside. A looming rock hung precariously, threatening to fall off the edge any second.

Following the director, I ventured to the other side of the rock. Three people were engrossed in the task of drilling. Their mission? To blast off the massive rock.

After several deliberations, it was decided that Rinpoche would walk to the other side. His spirit was unwavering as he led us across the rubble and past a line of cars. We found a resting spot nestled amongst large rocks. Here, I stole a few moments to take some photographs with Rinpoche, teasingly calling him "handsome".

From then on, we travelled mostly by car. Rinpoche's assistants seemed to have taken a liking to me, keeping a watchful eye. In a delightful turn of events, Rinpoche himself broke his silence and conversed with me in English. During a stop at a rest house, he extended an invitation that I join him at his retreat at Bumthang.

Upon my sharing of this news with the director, one of the Tala boys offered to escort me to Bumthang. A quick reminder that he needed the director's permission silenced his proposal, though he seemed persistent.

Rinpoche, who I learned would be in Australia for the next three months, shyly admitted his reluctance to speak English despite his proficiency in it. Imagine my surprise to discover that a man revered by thousands was shy to converse with me, an ordinary woman!

The day ended back at the guesthouse where I'd first savoured chow mein. We were greeted by a group of final-year students who had been waiting since eleven that morning. The sendoff was a warm gathering of these students indulging in tea and rice as they received blessings once again.

The journey back was filled with the harmonious chanting of the students, a soothing melody that coaxed me into a peaceful slumber, aided perhaps by the day's exhaustive excitement.

At half past nine, we found ourselves at the familiar Dankar Canteen. The once bumpy road to the college was now paved, a change that I had almost forgotten. Amidst the clatter and chatter, I found myself lost in dreams of my knight in shining armour.

The day concluded with a visit to the Indian professor's house, in the absence of the other professor who usually hosted Indian professors. The mix of eggs and beer had an immediate effect, and before long, the pull of sleep was too strong to resist. And so, I ended another day of this extraordinary journey.

The next day was a momentous day at Gedu College of Business Studies. It was Foundation Day! School was off for the students, but don't mistake it for a day of rest. Each residence group was required to put on three performances. The grand finale—the last group got a pumpkin!

Amidst the frenzy, the Indian professor recruited one of the girls to dress me in traditional Bhutanese attire—the kira. The moment I saw myself in it, I couldn't help but fall in love with it. Yes, vanity might be my sin, but I believe I looked rather fetching in it.

The students, young as they were, breathed life into the ancient traditions with their *beda* dances. There was an invincible kind of energy in the air, palpable and infectious. The performances stretched till four o'clock in the afternoon. At the end, the boys, ravenous, sprinted to the food hall for a well-deserved feast. Istvan was bid adieu, the director having managed to hail a private car for him—a surprisingly efficient method of travel around those parts.

Around five o'clock, with my stomach still bursting at the seams from lunch, the director informed me about dinner at another Indian professor's house. If it hadn't have been for my full stomach, I would've been intrigued at the idea of another sumptuous meal.

By six o'clock, the director announced a change in my lodgings. I was moving from Room 306 to Room 208. But here's the twist: it was the room where the Rinpoche had resided! My interest was instantly piqued.

We arrived at the professor's house, a homely abode where he lived with his father. The director humorously referred to him as a "chronic bachelor". I mused at his comment, considering I'd used the term "perennial bachelor" for some of my male friends.

One thing I learned about the director was that he had an endearing affection for walking. He once said, "People around the world pay three hundred US dollars to walk here. Why wouldn't I walk for free?" The sentences still ring in my ear. He's a man of deep philosophies, but also the one who keeps his feet firmly on the ground.

By the dawning light, I found myself at my limit: a week without internet access had become too much to bear. Mercifully, the director had a young worker escort me to the telecom office. Enthusiastically, the boy led me up a hill with an altitude of twenty-five hundred metres, a steep climb made even more challenging by my three-inch heels. But the promise of a broadband modem was an enticing enough carrot to keep me going.

The telecom office was perched like a bird's nest above Gedu College. A woman named Tara proved to be helpful, though she initially asked me to go back down to fill in the paperwork. I was stubborn, though, refusing to leave without a modem in my possession. Tara called the director, who, in his uncanny, almost mind-reading way, instructed her to assist me. I left there some forty-five minutes later with a modem in my hand and a broad smile on my face.

Back at the guesthouse, two telecom technicians were waiting to install the modem. One made an attempt to discuss the prospects of my marrying a Bhutanese man. I held my ground, making it clear that my stay in Bhutan was based on my own desires and was not a matrimonial venture.

When the technicians were about to nail the cable into the room with a four-inch nail, I protested. This room was used by the Rinpoche and other VIPs, and despite my non-VIP status, I felt it important to maintain the room's integrity. They agreed to return later with smaller nails.

Suddenly, I was online again, and it felt like being handed a tall glass of water after a long trek in the desert. When I was in the middle of a Skype call with my daughter, my local phone buzzed. Maya needed me at the college. It was time to visit the hospital for a medical certificate, and the hospital was closing at three in the afternoon.

Back down the hill I went, this time sensibly attired in jeans and hiking boots. A drive to the hospital revealed that I would need to return the next morning for a battery of tests.

Heading back to the guesthouse, I found the technicians had returned with their smaller, albeit reused, nails. They proceeded to nail the cable into the middle of the wood, which was precisely what I had asked them not to do. Resigned, I had them redo it, asking them to hide the nails and cable neatly in the crevices as I'd initially requested. It was an odd sight: used nails and a lack of hammer necessitated the use of pliers instead.

Newly connected to the world, I began responding to emails, uploading pictures on Facebook, and gazing out my window at the stunning view. In the midst of it all, I received a pleasant surprise—Sangay Rinzin managed to secure my route permit, even without the medical certificate!

The evening brought more companionship with the Indian professors and a phone call from Dasho—the director's official title awarded from the king. It seemed that "Where are you?" was his favourite opening line. We headed off to another professor's house for dinner—a home kept immaculate inside and out. Although the professor's English was challenging to decipher, his wife's dhal was a language I immediately understood, one that spoke of exquisite taste. It was a dish so delightful that I could have eaten it as soup.

The walk back was enjoyable, and I bumped into Tshering, another lecturer. She gave me Bhutanese ngultrums worth less than one hundred US dollars in exchange for three hundred US dollars, promising to pay me the rest upon my return in November. Finally, I fell into bed, basking in the pleasure of my newly arranged room and, I daresay, the sheer joy of being connected to the world again.

2.4 The Heart of Happiness

Rise and shine to another day in the Land of the Thunder Dragon. Today, Dasho presented me with a choice: to attend a soccer match down south or to travel to Lobesa with Sangay and impart some knowledge. True to my nature, I chose work. It was the least I could do after Sangay's tireless efforts to secure my route permit.

Even though we had cancelled our bus ticket in anticipation of needing to get the medical certificate, Dasho miraculously managed to flag down a Bhutan Post bus and instructed the driver to take me to Thimphu. On the journey, I met a woman named Pabi, her husband, Indra and their two adorable children. They mentioned having seen me at the Foundation Day ceremony. Both educators themselves, they extended an invitation to their home, a gesture that warmed my heart.

During a pit stop in Chukka, I shared my bag of chips with a child who seemed to be the only one without anything in her hands. Her wide smile in response was a gift in itself, a genuine human connection made.

In Thimphu, Sangay picked me up with his friend Ugyen, a partner at a private management training institute. Ugyen's chatter about the institute's benefits for overseas professors was engaging, but when the question of actual payment came up, he became as elusive as the snow leopards of the Himalayas.

Sangay wasn't looking his best, and a visit to a doctor confirmed he was suffering from low blood pressure. He was advised not to drive to Lobesa, which meant a sudden change of plans for me. I ended up staying at the Hotel Jumolhari, the same hotel I had stayed at as a tourist earlier that year.

Settling in, I found myself delighted by the Western-style toilet, the crisp, freshly ironed sheets, and the comfort of carpet under my feet. Still, I wasn't one to stay cooped up, so I decided to venture out into the city.

Thimphu, with a population of less than sixty thousand, is a peculiar blend of charm and chaos. While the city was a wonder to explore, it was also filled with a surprising amount of trash and an equally surprising number of souvenir shops. Sangay had quipped, "It's one souvenir shop per tourist."

I strolled through the three main streets of Thimphu, feasting on baby bananas for dinner, and then I returned to the hotel to indulge in an internet spree—replying to emails, making Skype calls with my children, aged ten and six, and even helping my daughter do research for a speech on Oxford.

I turned in around one o'clock in the morning, cocooning myself in the luxury of clean bed sheets. Oh, did I mention they were crisp?

There was a tiny detail I may have overlooked in the rush of the day—the bus fare. Amidst the whirl of being picked up by Sangay, I realised I might have skipped paying the bus driver. Well, it was a matter of less than five US dollars, something that slipped through the cracks of an eventful day.

As the first notes of the alarm chimed through the room at six o'clock in the morning, I nestled deeper into my dreams until seven, when I finally surrendered to the pull of the day. I awoke feeling extraordinarily rejuvenated, a stark contrast to the usual. The first order of the day, as had become the routine, was to connect my computer to the World Wide Web and disseminate my survey across various websites. After all, I was in Bhutan for my PhD research, wasn't I?

Like clockwork, Sangay called, and we arranged to rendezvous at half past eleven. True to his word, he arrived precisely on the dot. Our journey to Lobesa was a harmonious blend of picturesque sights and enlightening conversation. The two-hour drive along the partially paved road unfolded smoothly, the beauty of the landscape a soothing balm. Midway, we halted to stock up on fresh fruits—apples and bananas—and resumed our discussions about life, dreams, and entrepreneurial ideas.

Upon reaching Lobesa, we dropped our luggage at the guesthouse. The toilet, designed in the traditional Indian style, didn't exactly meet my expectations, reeking with an odour that pricked my nostrils. However, the adventurous spirit in me chuckled and chose to ignore it; I closed the bathroom door behind me until the need became too pressing to ignore the next day.

Summoning one of his students, Darjee, Sangay arranged a visit to Punakha Dzong, Bhutan's oldest dzong, famed for being the site of the Fifth King's inauguration. The majesty of the ancient structure left me awestruck. I eagerly took a plethora of photographs for posterity.

Our day wrapped up with a delightful Indian dinner at a local restaurant in Wangdue whose decor and tablecloths, and the presence of foreign tourists, hinted at its tourist-oriented nature. Generous servings of chicken filled our plates, and I relished every bite, allowing the protein-rich food to nourish my exhausted body.

The hustle and bustle of the town provoked a wave of nostalgia, reminding me of my own childhood town, Mentakab in Malaysia, where I had spent my earliest years. Sangay explained the Bhutanese government's plan to alleviate the congestion by relocating shops to a newly constructed town centre. While the government would allot the land, the shop owners would have to secure loans for the construction. Life, as I observed, was a blend of blessings and challenges here too, as elsewhere.

There was an unmistakable sense of excitement in the air as I entered my first day of teaching at the College of Natural Resources (CNR). The classroom was filled with field naturalists, seasoned professionals with fourteen to twenty years of forestry or agricultural experience. The students' insightful presentations on their marketing plans left an indelible impression, a testament to the pool of talent in Bhutan.

Focus Group

Our focus group discussion today unfolded amidst the piercing gaze of a camcorder, transforming our cosy huddle into a studio. The students, ever cognizant of the camera's unblinking eye, stiffened visibly at the outset. Their anxiety was not spoken but was palpable, a silent tension that danced in the ether and peered back at us from the camcorder's impassive lens.

Yet, as the minutes dripped away and the camera's red light became a more familiar sight, the students found their footing. The rigidity of their initial responses softened, to be replaced by a proactive engagement that resonated with authenticity and depth.

With the symphony of their responses captured by the video recorder, my duty as a researcher took centre stage. As I replayed the footage, the voices echoed through the room once again, reaffirming and redefining the contours of the conversation. This meticulous process of replaying and analysing served as firm assurance that every whisper of insight was faithfully captured and accurately interpreted.

This focus group session, with its depth and diversity, demonstrated an impressive understanding of gross national happiness (GNH) principles amongst these Bhutanese students. Their intuitive application of these principles to entrepreneurship revealed a keen insight that underscored their understanding and the unique characteristics they as entrepreneurs possessed.

Their upbringing, a beautiful mosaic of Bhutanese culture, tradition, and wisdom, served as their guiding compass, enabling them to perceive nuances that remain shrouded to those of us from other corners of the globe. The ultimate triumph of this focus group, however, was not just their understanding of GNH principles or entrepreneurial attributes, but their vision of profit-driven business models that carry the promise of shared benefits, enhancing the lives of all those touched by the venture.

Elaboration of GNH

In the warm cocoon of our discussion, I ventured the most simplistic of questions: "What is gross national happiness?" An unexpected silence billowed out along with a ripple of surprise across the room. Just as the quiet threatened to turn awkward, Mr B. B. Rei, a dignified gentleman from the Ministry of Agriculture, broke the stillness. "GNH," he said, "is our guiding star, the philosophical lighthouse that guides our country, Bhutan. It stands on four pillars."

Stoma, a veteran from Department of Revenue and Customs with fifteen years in research and communication, took the baton and began to elaborate on the four pillars of GNH: (1) environmental conservation, (2) good governance, (3) cultural preservation, and (4) equitable and social justice development.

As though passing an invisible torch, Mr Rei then ceded the floor to Dorji Stupa from the Ministry of Forestry in Bumthang. Dorji, a young executive shaped by his education at Columbia University, dove into the pillar of environmental conservation. "Our constitution," he said, "requires us to maintain 60 per cent of our land as forests." He continued painting a picture of Bhutan, nestled and vulnerable in the bosom of the Himalayas. "If we neglect our environment, then degradation and GLOF [glacial link outburst flood] become the imminent threats. They loom large and are already known globally, posing a critical danger to our country."

As the discussion moved on to good governance, Tshering Penjor from the East brought a heartfelt perspective to the table. "Good governance," he asserted, "is all about the people." He spoke of a governance that is not merely focused on the positive but is also tuned in to the well-being of the Bhutanese populace.

The third pillar, preservation of culture, found its voice in Dorji from Trashigang Dzongkhag. "Our culture is our identity," he proclaimed. His words underscored the importance of Bhutan's unique and distinct culture, which not only garners international attention but also drives tourism, a major source of income for the country.

As we approached the final pillar, equitable and social justice development, Laksmi, a former employee of the research centre in Bhutan, stepped up to the plate. She spoke fondly of the Fourth King, the originator of the GNH concept. "He believed happiness is more essential than gross domestic product (GDP). His advocacy was centred on ensuring that every Bhutanese citizen has access to all the country's facilities," she explained, putting a heart-warming end on the enlightening discussion.

Four Pillars of Happy Entrepreneurship

I began to peel back the layers of the grounded theory for my dissertation, which I refer to as the Four Pillars of Entrepreneurial Success, or 4E—a novel way to measure success, breaking away from the traditional tether of monetary net worth. My E's, serving as the yardstick for entrepreneurial success, were (1) earnings (the fruit of entrepreneurial capacity, exclusive of any inheritance), (2) empathy (gauge of societal contribution), (3) earth (an evaluation of the entrepreneur's commitment to nature through his or her business practices), and (4) ethics (the character and integrity of an entrepreneur as a measure of success, over and above mere financial accumulation).

What followed was an open dialogue, a communion of minds soaked in the culture of GNH. I laid down my queries about the applicability of GNH principles at a micro level and their feasibility. The questions hovered in the air: Are we all responsible for our environment?

As entrepreneurs, do we need to reciprocate to society beyond merely amassing wealth? Is an ethical backbone crucial for a person to have to be deemed a successful entrepreneur? Should inheritance be considered as part of an entrepreneur's earnings calculation?

As I traversed the landscape of earnings, the notion of inheritance subtraction sparked a vibrant debate. Many voices resounded with the idea that true entrepreneurial success lies in demonstrating money earned through personal aptitude, relentless effort, and hard work rather than inheriting a fortune. Such students pointed to numerous instances both in Bhutan and abroad where supposedly successful entrepreneurs who had inherited wealth had misused it or ineffectively managed it. Other voices offered a contrasting perspective, emphasizing the significance of every stakeholder's contribution, including parents or investors, to an entrepreneur's success. These students argued that every business endeavour requires seed money, and amidst this social construct, an inheritance could be a stepping stone to greater success.

In this chorus of opinions, one voice stood out, that of Mr Sangay Rinzin, the co-teacher of the entrepreneurship class, who humbly objected to the title of "professor", stating, "I'm merely a teacher dedicated to my profession"—a man who embodied the humility central to the GNH philosophy.

Sangay applauded the resonance of the 4E concept with GNH principles, thrilled to see them applied to entrepreneurship. He put forth the suggestion of a mini research project in Bhutan to discover how entrepreneurs here climbed the ladder to success.

Characteristics of Entrepreneurs

Here are the defining characteristics of an entrepreneur that I outlined after hearing the insights offered by the focus group during our discussion: risk taker, opportunist, resourceful individual, leader (helping the poor become richer), helper, investor, initiative taker, enterprising, seeking to improve the livelihoods of others, impact maker, believer, achiever, innovator (finder of new ways of doing things), invested with one's own money, creative, hard-working, time management skills, ability to stand tall (is the entrepreneur alone, or is there a mountain of people beneath him or her?), honest, sociable, charismatic, calming, knowledgeable (knowledge of his or her enterprise, products, and resources), dedicated, trustworthy, good networker (social and professional networker), bold, outside-the-box thinking, mutual understanding, receptive to feedback, energetic, team player, use of both left and right brain, passionate about his or her work, looking after the social welfare of others and meeting the needs of community, extraverted, great communicator, and a darer to do things differently.

These insights led me to conclude that entrepreneurship embodies a unique set of skills and a unique mindset, suggesting that not everyone is predisposed to thrive as an entrepreneur.

Business Profit Motive with a Social Mission Mindset

Apart from the shared ambitions and textbook entrepreneurial traits such as resourcefulness and innovation, I discerned a unique characteristic amongst these students that I'd never encountered in my professional sojourn. Each business plan they laid on the table was more than just a blueprint for profit: it was a social mission in its own right.

At the inception of the workshop, the students were asked to form groups, explore potential products, and present a marketing strategy. Each group responded with meticulously researched material, presenting a tapestry of marketable products and astute marketing schemes.

Amongst this sea of impressive strategies, several stood out, challenging conventional norms.

Take the group that offered the novel idea of using rice grains as currency. They envisioned a cooperative-run rice storage warehouse, a granary of sorts, that would lend rice grains to farmers during "rainy" seasons. The initial grain stock would come from donations, and farmers could borrow as needed. The payback? Grains and 5 per cent interest once the season ends. This unique grain currency system may be feasible within Bhutan, yet in many parts of the globe, it might throw a wrench into the works of even the simplest financial plan.

The theme of cooperatives as a business norm was prevalent too. Four of the five groups came forward with business cases centred on this model, from a group of women in the ricefields of Paro planting and selling flowers to another cooperative fishing and marketing unique dried fish in a remote village. One group suggested a fresh produce cooperative, gathering produce, marketing it, and delivering it to local hotels, streamlining the process of buying from multiple vendors. The fourth group presented the granary cooperative concept. Their choice of cooperative models was intuitive, almost instinctive, as no one could put into words why it simply made sense.

The outlier working with this theme was a group that sketched a business plan not for themselves, but for the entrepreneur. They conceived a mushroom business where they would package the product differently for extended shelf life and target the overseas Japanese market. Amidst the symphony of types of cooperatives, this solitary entrepreneur's tune was melodic in a different way.

After lunch, I delved into my presentation on the sources of funds, venture capital, and financial planning. My words echoed around the room, the students silent and receptive, and the session concluded smoothly. At day's end, Sangay complimented our collaborative dynamics. Warmed by the recognition, I echoed the sentiment. I genuinely wished to contribute to these diligent students' education, hoping that my presence here would benefit them and, in turn, contribute to Bhutan's future. These students had such hard-working spirits, and yet they gave off a sense of humility. One of the students shouldered my heavy backpack all the way to my room in the guesthouse—a kind gesture, deeply appreciated.

As evening settled in, dinner called. We meandered down to Lobesa township, where we relished some of the Bhutanese cuisine. I found myself resorting to ordering something familiar, a Coca-Cola, to quench my thirst, a minor transgression in this journey of cultural exploration.

As we dined in the humble restaurant nestled amongst the ten shops and bustling vegetable stalls of Medini township, we crossed paths with yet another forestry professor. Mr Ugyen Tenzin, formerly a professor at CNR (the Bhutanese do love their initialisms, indeed), was now working for the Ministry of Agricultural in the Forestry Division. His lively chatter filled the evening air. Interestingly, he was the tenth Ugyen and the twentieth Tenzin I'd encountered. Bhutanese naming conventions continued to intrigue me—two first names, often unisex, and some of these bestowed based on the day of birth.

A pleasant young student, Dorji, added to the charm of the evening with his delightful company.

Our journey back to the guesthouse consisted of a leisurely stroll, invigorating me to the point where I felt I could circle the township twice more. Poor Sangay, still battling his illness, bid me goodnight with a courteous wave of his hand and retired to his room just next door.

Before I turned in, Dorji's gentle reminder rang in my ears. My journal beckoned. And so, amidst the hush of the Bhutanese night, I wrote the night's entry, recording the beautiful weave of the day that had just ended.

In the muted light at seven o'clock the next morning, I stirred from my slumber. The day's tasks already prickled at the corners of my consciousness. Sangay and I were due to depart from Lobesa for Thimphu after class, but the weight of an unresolved accommodation issue hung on my shoulders. As I dialled the numbers of various hotels in Thimphu, my frustration mounted. Seven hotels all echoed the same dreaded phrase: *fully booked*.

As I stewed in my predicament, I glimpsed Mr Ugyen Tenzin, the former professor, ambling past my window. With an urgency born of desperation, I hailed him, asking, "Ugyen, do you know of any hotels in Thimphu? All seven I've tried are fully booked!" My voice carried an undertone of anxiety.

Ugyen, ever the picture of calm, casually offered a solution that both surprised me and relieved me, "You can stay at my house. It's just my wife and me in a three-bedroom apartment," he said. The generous invitation sent a wave of gratitude washing over me. I thanked him profusely before turning my attention to the day's teaching agenda.

Today's lecture hinged on the practical aspects of business—the crafting of a financial plan for the students' business proposals. Sangay and I divided our attention amongst the student teams—two for me, three for him. By midday, it became apparent that the students needed more guidance. Sangay, demonstrating an unwavering dedication, decided to extend his stay by a day to assist the students further.

Once again, Ugyen stepped in as my saviour, graciously offering to drive me to Thimphu.

Interview with the Vice-Chancellor of the Royal University of Bhutan

Ugyen, my guide, escorted me to the Royal University of Bhutan (RUB). A few meters into our drive, he realized he had forgotten his ceremonial scarf, a mark of respect needed to enter official buildings. He didn't even need to turn the car around before the young lad he'd summoned arrived, panting, scarf in hand. He said, "Good exercise for the lad."

RUB's modern structure stands in contrast to the surrounding residential district. Its halls were echoing with silence at half past nine o'clock in the morning. By a quarter to ten, the director of academic affairs, Mr Yangka, greeted me with a firm handshake and a warm smile. This Oxford scholar was the epitome of composed professionalism.

We discussed the educational needs of Bhutanese youth, and he expressed his interest in the idea of offering microfinancing from kiva.org to the winners of business plan presentations at each respective RUB college. He even proposed designating someone to be the liaison for Kiva's on-site coordinator.

Next, I met with the administrative manager, Mr Pema Wangdi, who diligently handled my visa extension, route permit, and work permit. An unassuming building that would hardly qualify as an immigration office anywhere else played host to us. After examining my visa and supporting documents, he told us that a work permit was necessary.

Throughout these procedures, Mr Pema was swift and efficient. Afterwards, I had a conversation with another director, a woman with a warm smile, the one who had forwarded my résumé to the Gedu director.

From a hilltop, Ugyen and I had admired the commanding visage of the RUB building while observing a gentleman alight from a four-wheel-drive below. He was donning a red *kabney* and was assisted by his driver, a visual marker of his status in Bhutanese society. Different colours represent various titles here—yellow for the king, orange for ministers, olive green for judges, and red for Dasho, this last being an honour akin to knighthood. In this intricate assemblage of titles and ranks, one thing remained universal: respect for service to the nation.

Gingerly, I navigated my way down the hill, a precarious journey in my three-inch heels and over wet, muddy terrain. Despite rain-soaked land, the requirement of formal attire remains uncompromised when entering any official building. My kabney was snug around my neck, a sign of my respect for Bhutanese customs.

Upon meeting, I addressed Dasho Pema Thinley with his title, introducing myself as a visiting professor at Gedu College. With a twinkle in his eye, he asked, "What took you so long to get here?" Then, displaying true Bhutanese hospitality, he graciously invited me to his office.

As we ascended the stairs, I apologized for any confusion about his proper title. With an air of humility that seemed to personify him, he assured me, "My name is Pema Thinley. Just call me that. It will be sufficient." I couldn't help but think, *What a refreshingly humble man.*

In his office, he requested that a witness accompany us, finally settling on the director of research. Over the span of two engaging hours, we delved into conversations about my life, my work in Bhutan, his vision for RUB, and possible ways I could lend my expertise to the university. There, with our shared aspirations resonating, I felt the magical intertwining of individual destinies and a collective dream.

At the helm of this singular university in this small kingdom is

Dasho Pema Thinley, the vice-chancellor of the Royal University of Bhutan (RUB). He served under the benevolent reign of the Fifth King, Jigme Khesar Namgyel Wangchuck, the figurehead of RUB. Appointed by the Fourth King, Jigme Singye Wangchuck—the bringer of the gross national happiness (GNH) philosophy to the global stage—Dasho Pema Thinley is a fervent advocate of entrepreneurship anchored in GNH principles.

Since its inception in June 2003, RUB has expanded into ten constituents that are scattered across the country, including the College of Natural Resources (CNR), the College of Science and Technology (ST), and the Gedu College of Business Studies (GCBS), amongst several others. These establishments offer courses in diverse academic fields such as teacher education, business and management, engineering and physical sciences, and Dzongkha language and literature, to name a few.

The RUB maintains a robust network with prestigious international universities such as the University of New Brunswick in Canada and the University of Delhi in India. They collaborate in multiple areas, such as with student exchange programmes and faculty internships.

In this enlightening encounter, Dasho Pema Thinley outlined his intention to implement the theme of "GNH-Enabled Education" across all RUB colleges. In the serene tranquillity of his office, he conveyed enthusiasm for finally having a discussion merging business and GNH principles. When presented with the idea of the four E's (empathy, earth, ethics, and earnings) of happy entrepreneurship, he expressed full support and commissioned a comprehensive textbook that would be accessible to all Bhutanese students.

As a testament to the significance of entrepreneurship to Bhutan's economic development, most students would take "entrepreneurship" classes as part of their curriculum. Gedu College of Business Studies took the reins in creating the Entrepreneurship Development Centre for the RUB, which is aimed at college students, corporate managers, executive managers (offering them workshops), and community leaders (to focus on community development).

The execution of the entrepreneurship programme was to occur in a sequential order across the colleges, starting with Gedu College of Business Studies. This concept of GNH-principled entrepreneurship aligned seamlessly with Bhutan's philosophy of living happily by living responsibly.

After my meeting with Dasho Pema Thinley, I caught up with the director, assuring him I was alive and well. I told him about my plans to be in Thimphu for most of the following week before jetting off to Paris.

I then phoned Sonam at the Bhutan Orchid Restaurant to let her know I might not be able to drop by in the morning. She confessed that her schedule was just as hectic. I adored her even more for her candour.

The following afternoon, Ugyen picked me up from the hill. The ascent was noticeably less strenuous this time around, and I found a new passenger in the car, Dechen Zam, who worked at the Gross National Happiness Commission. She was eager to meet me, having heard about me from her cousin Karma.

Through Dechen's connections, I found myself anticipating a meeting with the secretary of the GNH Commission. The rest of the day was a whirlwind of activity as the research department scrambled to secure appointments for me with various officials and prepare for their upcoming annual council meeting.

As I stepped into the main dzong, a wave of nostalgia washed over me. I was reminded of my first visit, back in March 2010, recalling a captivating photograph I'd taken of pigeons soaring up to feed on a monk's offerings—a moment so picturesque that a friend had suggested I send it to *National Geographic*.

Waiting outside the secretary's office, I was fraught with nervous anticipation. Upon meeting Secretary Karma Tshiteem, I showed him his GNH letter accepting my application, and he handed me his business card in return—simple and elegant, bearing his name without the "Dasho" title.

Our planned fifteen-minute meeting evolved into an hourlong engaging conversation. As our discussion drew to a close, the secretary expressed his desire to introduce me to the Prime Minister and invited me to his meetings with some consultants from McKinsey the next week—an unexpected but exciting proposition.

Interview with Karma Tshiteem, Secretary of the Gross National Happiness Commission (GNHC)

In Bhutan, a tapestry of tradition and progress unfolds with the inception of the first socioeconomic development plan in 1961. A decade later, in the year 1971, His Majesty the late king Jigme Dorji Wangchuck lit a flame of pioneering by instituting the Planning Commission—an autonomous body put at the helm of modernization. Appointed by then crown prince HRH Jigme Singye Wangchuck, as chairman, and by HRH Ashi Dechen Wangmo Wangchuck, as vice-chairperson, the thirteen-member Commission was a convergence of voices, including those from representatives of His Majesty, those from the National Assembly, those of ministers, those from the Royal Advisory Council, and even those of advisers from the government of India and also from the development and finance sectors.

The Commission, a fulcrum for overall development strategies, five-year plans, aid management efforts, and interministerial development, was also a keen observer of the macro-level progress of any programmes and a vanguard for ensuring timely completion of plans as per the specified objectives and priorities.

Come 2008, a fresh chapter unfolded with the erstwhile Planning Commission's being rechristened as the Gross National Happiness Commission, taking upon itself additional responsibilities to propagate and firmly integrate the principles of gross national happiness (GNH) into the policies and implement them.

At the heart of this transformative endeavour was Dasho Karma Tshiteem, the secretary of the GNH Commission, a member of the Planning Commission, and a trusted adviser to the Prime Minister's Office. With an illustrious career that began in 1989 and educational credentials including a master's degree in business administration from the University of Canberra, Australia, and a bachelor's degree in commerce from Sherubtse College in Bhutan, he was entrusted with the mammoth task of breathing life into GNH philosophies and implementing them within all governmental agencies.

The GNH Commission stands on four robust pillars—development of a dynamic economy for a vibrant democracy, harmonious living aligned with tradition and nature, effective and good governance, and recognising the nation's people as the greatest asset. Their work is marked by an exhaustive screening process, which filters out policies and projects with an eye towards GNH, ensuring that all government agencies adhere to practices promoting the nine domains of GNH, from psychological well-being to governance.

During this particularly memorable meeting on 21 October 2010, I was fortunate enough to share the 4E approach with Dasho Karma Tshiteem. He saw it as a "logical way of new thinking to incorporate GNH at an entrepreneur level", a perspective that felt very timely with Bhutan opening its arms to foreign direct investment in the near future.

Bidding farewell to the GNH Commission, I was overcome by a rush of exhilaration as I embraced Dechen, my guide throughout this journey. The evening beckoned, and my friends Nann, Ugyen, and Rinzin awaited me at home. Once I was there, after we all had shed our official garb and stepped into pyjamas, the stories poured out of us, filling the space with excitement and laughter.

Later, the night led us to a local haunt where Budweiser beer for the men and chicken and sweet corn soup for the women was in order. As we indulged in ribs, Bhutanese noodles, and fried vegetables at the AMA Restaurant, I was caught off-guard when the men insisted on paying for the meal. I learned it's a Bhutanese tradition for the inviter to foot the bill—a cultural nuance Ugyen remembered having learned the hard way on a trip to the UK. After we had laughed at his anecdote, I promised to treat them at our next outing—a little fusion of cultures that felt perfectly in sync with the Bhutan I'd come to know.

Interview with Mr Phub Tshering, Bhutan Chamber of Commerce and Industry

At eleven o'clock the next morning, the door to my meeting room opened to admit a man whose presence seemed to occupy more space than his did physical form alone. This was Mr Phub Tshering, a representative from the Bhutan Chamber of Commerce and Industry. He carried about him an air of assurance and calm, much like the country he hailed from.

In his presence, I felt an immediate sense of respect. Here was a man who was helping to shape the economic future of a nation while ensuring that it stayed true to its values founded on gross national happiness. Mr Tshering had the challenging task of balancing modern economic needs with ancient wisdom and tradition, a task he seemed to undertake with both pride and personal responsibility.

After we exchanged pleasantries, we soon found ourselves immersed in a deep conversation about Bhutan's unique approach to commerce. Mr Tshering was a wellspring of knowledge, his thoughts and insights shaped by his vast experience and deep love for his country. With each word he spoke, I found myself drawn deeper into the fascinating tapestry of Bhutanese commerce and industry, an arena where profit wasn't the only measure of success and where businesses were as concerned about their impact on the community and environment as they were about their bottom lines.

As Mr Tshering shared his experiences and observations, I could not help but admire this man. He was not just a figurehead in the Bhutanese business community, but also a guardian of the nation's ethos. His dedication to his work, his commitment to the values of his country, and his vision for a future where business and happiness could coexist harmoniously all served as a testament to the spirit of Bhutan.

As the conversation drew to a close, I was left with a renewed sense of admiration for the Bhutanese approach to business and a deeper understanding of the complexities and challenges involved in balancing economic growth with social and environmental well-being.

My meeting with Mr Phub Tshering was not just an exchange of ideas, it was a lesson in balance, in harmony, and in the possibility of a different, more compassionate way of doing business. As I bid him farewell, I knew I would carry the insights from our conversation with me long after our meeting, a priceless keepsake from my Bhutanese journey.

Interview with Ms Kunzang Lamu and Dorji Penjore

At half past two o'clock, in the afternoon, the air in the room seemed to still in anticipation as Kunzang Lhamu of the Gross National Happiness Commission (GNHC) walked in. There was something about her that commanded attention, not through sheer force or authority, but because of her gentle, almost tangible aura of wisdom and serenity.

Her name, I learned, means "all good and pure" in Dzongkha, Bhutan's national language. As we spoke, I realized that it was not just her name, but also her very essence, that seemed to reflect this purity and goodness. Here was a woman deeply connected to her work at the GNHC, a role that seemed to her less like a job and more like a purposeful mission.

As we delved into our conversation, Kunzang painted a vivid picture of Bhutan's approach to development, one that was holistic, balanced, and deeply respectful of both the environment and the well-being of the nation's citizens. Her words resonated with me as she spoke not just with her mind, but also from her heart. She was like an ambassador of Bhutan's unique philosophy, carrying the message of gross national happiness with grace and conviction. She embodied the values of this philosophy—the importance of mental well-being, ecological conservation, cultural preservation, and sustainable development.

Listening to her speak, I found myself humbled and inspired. She spoke not just about policies or strategies, but also about the very essence of what it means to be human—about happiness, fulfilment, and the pursuit of a good life. The passion with which she spoke, and her belief in the potential for a different kind of development, was contagious.

In her presence, I found that gross national happiness was not just a theoretical concept, it was a lived reality, a tangible aspiration that was guiding an entire nation towards a future that promised not just economic wealth, but also true well-being. I found this to be an incredible testament to the power of a vision, a philosophy, and a way of life.

As the meeting with Kunzang Lhamu drew to a close, I was left with a profound sense of gratitude for the opportunity to have met such an inspiring individual, for the chance to learn about a different way of looking at progress, and for the possibility that we too, in our own ways, could contribute to a happier, healthier world.

In the field of research and understanding of gross national happiness in Bhutan, one figure stands tall, enigmatically illuminating the world with wisdom: Dorji Penjore. As the senior researcher and the right hand to the president of the Centre for Bhutan Studies, Dasho Karma Ura, Dorji has an expansive set of duties far beyond the task of publishing the annual GNH Index. Dorji's mastery of the language of numbers, his dexterity with the quantitative and statistical realm, has led his work to garner much recognition from distinguished publications.

The Centre for Bhutan Studies, an intellectual bastion in its own right, dances to the tune of social science and public policy research. A phoenix risen in 1999, it serves as the solitary lighthouse of its kind in this kingdom, guided by the Council for the Centre of Bhutan Studies. Within its embrace, researchers delve into the rich tapestry of Bhutan's economy, history, religion, society, and culture, unearthing the stories it weaves and giving voice to its silent narratives.

The Centre has been at the vanguard of a remarkable quest to understand, promote, and deepen the concept of gross national happiness. Its devotion to the cause resonates in the three tomes it has birthed on the subject and in its multidimensional objectives. Beyond performing evaluative studies and offering feedback on government programmes, it kindles the spirit of research within government agencies in Bhutan, hosts special lectures and seminars, and publishes invaluable journals and research papers.

I asked Dorji Penjore, the eloquent scholar, whether he thought the GNH philosophy could be woven into the fabric of the business world. His response was nuanced, insightful, and peppered with wisdom: "We Bhutanese embrace GNH as a beautiful philosophy," he began. "Yet our biggest challenge lies in truly embodying compassion in our actions, despite understanding its profound importance."

He presented an argument as intriguing as it was profound. "Business often signifies competitiveness, being the best, outdoing the others. However, does this mean it must be at odds with compassion? Must these ideals stand on opposing sides of a divide?" He invited me to question traditional notions of success, suggesting that Bhutan need not necessarily follow the US model of individualistic success, which often fractures rather than nurtures familial bonds.

With an earnest gaze, he shared his interest in the 4E approach proposed by my dissertation, emphasizing the need for GNH to be adaptable to businesses in light of the imminent impact of foreign direct investment (FDI). "FDI corporations," he insisted, "should merge global templates with local sensibilities within a GNH context."

He painted a picture of a future where businesses benefitting local economies and societies were imbued with the principles of GNH. He passionately argued that GNH was not a philosophy resisting globalization, but rather one that sought to engage and localize it. Mr Dorji advocated for a balance between Western best practices and Eastern GNH principles, emphasizing the importance of education in cultivating creativity, analysis, rationality, and problem-solving skills.

Dorji concluded our rich dialogue by reaffirming the need for GNH principles in business practices as he envisioned a society where ethical businesses would be driven by customers who valued, not just product quality and price, but also the moral fabric of the producers, a world where GNH was not anti-moneymaking, but an instrument to harmonize the growth of society. As he offered these insights, I couldn't help but feel like a participant in a profoundly transformative conversation, one that had the potential to shape the future of Bhutan and the world.

Conference with Mr Karma Tshiteem, Gross National Happiness Commission

The hands of the clock aligned themselves to indicate the tenth hour of the morning, as if the universe itself was in sync with our scheduled presentation. Mr Karma Tshiteem, the esteemed commissioner of the Gross National Happiness Commission (GNHC), was about to take the stage. The room was pulsating with energy, a delightful cocktail of anticipation and curiosity filling the air. Nearly two hundred pairs of eyes—an intriguing blend of business representatives and international attendees, along with a handful of locals—were fixated on the dais.

Amidst this tableau of intent faces, one stood out—a young woman, a reporter. Her features were as sharp as the pencil she was twirling between her fingers, and her eyes sparked with an audaciousness that seemed to challenge the norm.

As the presentation unfolded, it was she who had the first question. Her query was astute, pushing the boundaries of conventional wisdom, a question that challenged the commissioner yet that was asked with a sense of earnestness that spoke volumes about the woman's professionalism and intellect.

In response, Mr Tshiteem unexpectedly grinned. Rather than deflecting the question or succumbing to defensiveness, he leaned into it. His reply was tinged with cheekiness, easing the tension and infusing the room with warmth. The audience responded with hearty laughter, their faces brightening in delight at his light-hearted banter.

This was not your average business conference, sterile and constrained by formalities. This was a Bhutanese gathering, congenial, sincere, and even a bit cheeky—a place where challenging questions were met with good-natured humour, where differences were bridged by shared laughter, and where serious discussions were flavoured with the joy of human connection.

The presentation continued, but it was this moment—a surprising exchange between a curious reporter and a cheeky commissioner—that stayed with me. It was a testament to the Bhutanese spirit, a reminder that business and pleasure, seriousness and light-heartedness, can indeed coexist. This was Bhutan, where even a business conference was imbued with gross national happiness. The experience was, simply put, refreshing.

BCCI—Social Business Conference

Originating in the vibrant heart of Utrecht in the Netherlands, the corporation Context International has provided a new tool for those in the field of impact measurement. The tool, named the "social return on investment" (SROI), beckons us to pause, to ponder, and to look deeper into the repercussions of our actions.

SROI stems from a profound realization that our actions, like pebbles thrown into a pond, send ripples throughout the world, altering the fabric of our shared reality. We create, we add, we modify, and we destroy value in ways that go beyond just the financial realm. Yet, often we let ourselves be blinded by the hard, cold numbers, forgetting to acknowledge the myriad other forms of value generated.

SROI is an exploratory lens, a holistic approach that measures the contours of change across the social, environmental, and economic realms and possibly other realms. It seeks to define value by looking through the kaleidoscope of stakeholder experiences and perceptions, then expressing these in financial terms to facilitate comprehension. By transforming these indicators into monetary values, SROI offers a common language that transcends sector boundaries, portraying the social and environmental returns in monetary terms.

The crown jewel of SROI analysis is the SROI ratio. Imagine, for instance, a ratio of 3:1, indicating in this case that each euro invested yields three times its value in benefits to the nation, whether economic, social, or environmental. However, the use of SROI extends beyond just this ratio. It helps create a narrative of value creation, providing enrichment through quantitative, qualitative, and anecdotal accounts. This vivid narrative further elucidates the SROI ratio and shines a spotlight on values that were unable to be monetized during the analysis.

Though diverse methodologies exist, a typical SROI analysis embarks on a nine-stage journey: defining boundaries, identifying stakeholders, formulating a theory of change, determining inputs and results, determining valuation, calculating the SROI ratio, undertaking verification, and finally, crafting the narrative. By passing through these stages and collecting qualitative and quantitative data, a comprehensive SROI report is fashioned, bearing testament to what truly matters to the project's stakeholders.

As I continued my journey, my path intertwined with those of several remarkable women in Bhutan. In hushed whispers, I spoke of Kiva's need for a champion from Bhutan. An enigmatic female reporter who seemed to have a special bond with Karma Tshiteem volunteered.

Karma Tshiteem, as it happened, ferried me back to my place of stay. When he learned of my need for an early morning taxi, his kindness painted a smile on the dawn—he arranged for his driver to take me to Paro. As I embraced the morning chill, I could only reflect on the enduring beauty of human connection and the shared values that had brought us together.

2.5 Bhutanese Hospitality

Early in the morning, I was greeted by a cheerful face, that of Karma, Ugyen's best friend's wife. Her spontaneous compliment, likening my beauty to that of a queen, brought me a moment of warmth and caused me to blush in modesty. I smiled and expressed my gratitude, recalling a light-hearted comment from the Indian professor that he wouldn't be surprised if I were to become the queen of Bhutan.

After I'd met Ugyen's charming wife, Nann, I overheard her immediately sharing with Ugyen the same observation, in a hushed tone as I headed to the restroom, echoing Karma's compliment: "She is so beautiful!" I couldn't help but attribute the praise to the wonders of Bhutan's crisp fresh air and my stress-free existence here, which worked miracles for my skin and my overall demeanour.

Morning in Bhutan began with breakfast, graciously prepared by Nann, whose rank as a police officer, equivalent to a lieutenant, warranted her a paid maid, who was in fact a constable. I found it intriguing that in a place like Bhutan, where crime is virtually unheard of, the excess constables are put to use doing domestic chores for seniors.

After lunch, Ugyen was tasked with driving me to get a medical fitness certificate. In another government building, I met Gyem Tshering, the CEO of Natural Resource Development Corporation Ltd (NRDCL). At first, he seemed cautious, but he relaxed as he realized our visit was a friendly one. The conversation blossomed, and he even invited me to spend a weekend with his family.

The day took us from official buildings to hospitals and tailors, and even to a local restaurant. At Bhutan Orchid Restaurant, the owner, Sonam, recognised my name from her friends' book—a surprising coincidence, or perhaps not.

The day ended with a festive dinner at Nann's friend's house: delicious food, warm company, and heartfelt conversations—the epitome of Bhutanese hospitality. Plans were hatched for a journey to Bumthang for the coming weekend to witness the renowned "naked dance". With that prospect in mind and a grateful heart, I retreated for the night, eager for the days ahead in this enchanting land.

The next morning unfolded gently as Nann, with her unceasing hospitality, prepared yet another flavourful breakfast of scrambled eggs with chillies; chickpeas; yoghurt; and toast and jam. I couldn't help but observe a thread of chauvinism weaving its way through the fabric of Bhutanese life. Even a UK-educated scholar like Ugyen Tenzin unconsciously upheld this weighty tradition, expecting his wife to cater for his needs.

On the fourteenth day, a Friday, a tide of change swept over my life. I bid farewell to the loving confines of Ugyen and Nann's home. A summons to Punakha had come calling for Nann, whose departure left only Ugyen and me in the house. It was a situation where for propriety's sake, considering Bhutanese society, and out of respect for Nann's feelings, I was compelled to move out, despite Ugyen's reputation as an honourable man.

I had sensed a twinge of jealousy in Nann whenever Ugyen spent time with other women. And a thread of tension ran through his and my relationship, his clandestine meetings with me and the unspoken agreement that Nann would remain in the dark about these. It was a dance I was no longer willing to partake in, preferring honesty over convoluted pretence. So, I decided to step back, to refrain from seeing Nann altogether and decline Ugyen's Facebook invitations. Oh, the liberating sigh of relief that issued from my lips! I enjoyed this splendid affirmation of my status as a single woman on a journey that, I just then realized, was free from such nuanced entanglements.

My next home took the form of the Royal College of Health and Science (RCHS), a place that was spartan in amenities, lacking hot water, but rich in the warmth of its inhabitants. Here, I heated my water with a heating rod, an adaptation of the simplest kind that was in this environment a luxury.

A luminous moment of kindness graced my time at RCHS—a young girl named Pema gifted me her mother's bag. Her action, a balm for my displacement, was a reminder that home isn't always four walls and a roof. Sometimes, it is a mere gesture, or a gift passed down from mother to daughter or given by one stranger to another stranger, forming a connection that speaks nothing but the language of compassion.

2.6 India Rendezvous

In the early morning hours, as the sun began to cast a gentle glow over the Paro airport, I found myself facing an unexpected obstacle. The gate to the airport was locked, seemingly barring my path to the awaiting driver who would transport me to my next destination. Undeterred by the barrier, I summoned my determination and, with a mix of agility and audacity, leaped over the gate, determined to reach my ride.

The journey continued as I embarked on a flight from Paro to Calcutta. Little did I know that my encounters in this latter bustling city would be both humbling and enlightening. As I ventured out into the vibrant streets of Calcutta, I found myself in need of a restroom. But the taxi driver who approached me saw an opportunity to take advantage of my situation. He demanded a fee in exchange for allowing me to use the facilities of a nearby hotel. This event was a reminder that even in the midst of travel, I must remain vigilant for those seeking to exploit me.

Within the bustling city of Calcutta, amidst the teeming crowds and busy streets, lies a haven of compassion and love—Mother Teresa's house. This sacred space serves as a testament to the unwavering dedication and profound impact of one extraordinary woman.

Mother Teresa, known as the "Saint of the Gutters", devoted her entire life to caring for the poorest of the poor. With boundless empathy and an unyielding spirit, she established the Missionaries of Charity, an organisation that would come to embody her mission of serving the marginalized and forgotten.

As I entered the doors of Mother Teresa's home, I was enveloped by the serene atmosphere. The air was filled with a sense of profound peace and quiet reverence. The walls, adorned with images of and quotations from Mother Teresa, spoke volumes about her profound wisdom and unwavering faith.

I made my way through the corridors, witnessing the selfless work being carried out by the dedicated volunteers and nuns who were following in Mother Teresa's footsteps. They moved with grace and purpose, tending to the sick, comforting the dying, and offering solace to those in need. The spirit of love and compassion permeated every corner of the home, creating a sacred space where the forgotten and neglected could find refuge.

As I visited the rooms where the sick and destitute were cared for, I was struck by the immense humility and love that radiated from the dedicated souls who worked there. They embraced the suffering of others as their own, offering solace, comfort, and dignity to those who had been cast aside by society.

Mother Teresa's legacy extends far beyond the walls of the house in Calcutta. Her tireless efforts to alleviate poverty, combat disease, and provide education and shelter touched the lives of countless individuals worldwide. She received numerous accolades for her humanitarian work, including the Nobel Peace Prize in 1979, yet she remained steadfastly focused on her mission, never seeking personal recognition or fame.

Through her profound acts of kindness and unwavering commitment, Mother Teresa embodied the essence of selfless service. She once said, "Not all of us can do great things. But we can do small things with great love." Her life was a testament to the transformative power of love and compassion, showing us that even the smallest acts of kindness can create ripples of change in the world.

As I left Mother Teresa's home, I carried with me a renewed sense of purpose and a deep admiration for the extraordinary woman in whose footsteps I had hoped to follow. Her life's work continues to inspire countless individuals to this day, reminding us that in the face of adversity and suffering, love and compassion can transform lives and bring hope to the darkest corners of our world.

In the late evening, as the sun began to set, I boarded a flight from Calcutta to Delhi. In anticipation of this new chapter, I was filled with a mix of excitement and trepidation. Little did I know that the journey ahead would present unforeseen challenges and unexpected joys. But for now, as the plane took off and soared into the night sky, I let the hum of the engines lull me into a contemplative state, ready to embrace the next adventure that awaited me in Delhi.

In the early hours of the morning, as the city of New Delhi slept, my longtime travel companion Debbie and I found ourselves in a dingy hotel room, exhausted from a long day of sightseeing. The room was dimly lit, and the creaky beds seemed to whisper tales of countless previous guests. Despite our weariness, we couldn't help but feel a sense of unease, unsure of what awaited us in this unfamiliar place.

Memories of past adventures flooded our minds, reminding us of the times when we embarked on journeys without proper preparation. There was the trip to Africa, where we ventured into the wilds of Zambia without even getting malaria shots and stayed in a rustic tent camp next to hippopotamuses. The thrill and the risk intertwined as we embraced the raw beauty of the African wilderness. Then there was our journey to the Middle East, exploring the ancient wonders of Israel, Egypt, and Jordan. In Jerusalem, we marvelled at the rich tapestry of history that unfolded before our eyes. But it was our bus trip through Egypt, amidst heightened security after a car bombing, that truly tested our resilience. Escorted by an Egyptian police force, we continued our journey, knowing that even in the face of adversity, there was still magic to be found.

One such moment came when we arrived in Wadi Rum, Jordan. As the sun set, we found ourselves surrounded by the magnificent desert landscape with its towering sandstone cliffs and vast expanses of sand. Our noses guided us to settle on one camping ground. That night, we slept under the stars in the largest tent we could find, gazing up at the twinkling heavens. It was a moment of awe and serenity, where the grandeur of the universe felt palpable.

And now, in the heart of New Delhi, Debbie and I found ourselves once again faced with uncertainty. The discomfort of the hotel room and the fear of unseen fleas reminded us of the unpredictability that often accompanies travel. But in the midst of these challenging moments, we also knew that they held the potential for unexpected beauty and unforgettable experiences.

As we lay in those beds, our hearts filled with a mix of apprehension and anticipation, we knew that the journey ahead would be filled with both triumphs and tribulations. And just like those previous adventures, we were ready to embrace the unknown, knowing that amidst the challenges, we would experience moments of sheer magic that would leave an indelible mark on our souls.

With a sense of determination and a spirit for adventure, we drifted off to sleep, ready to awaken to a new day of exploration and discovery. For in the world of travel, it is often in the most unexpected moments and the most unconventional circumstances that the true essence of a place reveals itself. With that thought in mind, we eagerly awaited the dawn of a new adventure in the bustling streets of New Delhi and Agra.

The next day, we found ourselves standing before the Taj Mahal, a mesmerizing symbol of love and a feat of architectural brilliance. As we marvelled at its majestic beauty, we couldn't help but be drawn into the enchanting story of its creation, a tale that has captured the imaginations of romantics all over the world.

Legend has it that the Taj Mahal was built by the Mughal emperor Shah Jahan as a tribute to his beloved wife Mumtaz Mahal. The story goes that Mumtaz Mahal was Shah Jahan's soulmate, his confidante, and his constant companion. They shared a love that was deep and profound, one that transcended time and space.

Tragically, Mumtaz Mahal passed away while giving birth to their fourteenth child. Devastated by her loss, Shah Jahan vowed to honour her memory in the most extraordinary way possible. He commissioned the construction of a mausoleum that would be unparalleled in its beauty, a monument that would stand as a testament to their eternal love.

For more than twenty years, thousands of skilled artisans, craftspeople, and labourers worked tirelessly to bring Shah Jahan's vision to life. The Taj Mahal was built with exquisite white marble, meticulously carved and adorned with intricate designs and precious gemstones. Its shimmering reflection in the surrounding pools and the delicate interplay of light and shadow add to its ethereal allure.

As Debbie and I wandered through the grounds of the Taj Mahal, we were captivated by the stories and anecdotes shared by our guide, a young boy with an infectious enthusiasm. His words evoked memories of the movie *Slumdog Millionaire*, where a reflective fountain was humorously portrayed as a swimming pool. It reminded us that even in the face of poverty, joy and creativity can thrive.

Later that evening, after a long drive, our local driver led us through the meandering streets of Jaipur, where we found ourselves venturing into unfamiliar territory. The bustling city gradually gave way to a maze of narrow lanes and humble dwellings—the slums. Our driver seemed to have a plan of his own, taking us to a small home and instructing us to stay in a room.

As Debbie and I entered the room, a sense of unease washed over us. We felt vulnerable and unsure of our surroundings. Our fear and helplessness was palpable. In that moment, we knew we had to trust our instincts and prioritize our safety. Gathering our belongings, we made the difficult decision to leave and seek the solace and comfort of a hotel.

As we retired to our hotel room, thoughts of the Taj Mahal and its timeless love story lingered in our minds. We reflected on the grandeur and beauty of the monument, a testament to the enduring power of love. The Taj Mahal, with its intricate architecture and captivating history, had left an indelible mark on our hearts, reminding us that amidst the unpredictable nature of travel, love and beauty can still prevail.

In the vibrant city of Jaipur, known as the Pink City, we embarked on a whirlwind tour of the many remarkable sights and attractions. Each place we visited had its own unique charm and historical significance, taking us on a captivating journey through time.

Our first stop was the magnificent Amber Fort, a grand fortress that stands majestically atop a hill. As we ascended the fort's ramparts, we were transported back to the days of the Rajput kings and their opulent lifestyles. The intricate carvings, stunning palaces, and sweeping views of the surrounding landscape left us in awe of the architectural marvel before us.

Next, we ventured to the City Palace, a sprawling complex that showcases the rich heritage and grandeur of Jaipur. Within its walls, we explored the beautifully adorned courtyards, intricate frescoes, and ornate gateways that bear witness to the city's royal history. The palace's museum offered a fascinating glimpse into the lives of the maharajas with its collection of artefacts, artworks, and royal regalia.

We couldn't miss the iconic Hawa Mahal, also known as the Palace of Winds. Its unique façade, with its intricately carved windows and balconies, served as a stunning testament to the architectural genius of the past. As we stood before the palace, we imagined the royal women observing the bustling streets below while remaining hidden from view.

Jaipur's bustling bazaars beckoned us with their vibrant colours and high energy. We immersed ourselves in the vibrant chaos offered by numerous bazaars. Johari Bazaar, where shops overflowed with glittering jewellery and precious gemstones, stands out. Then there was the aroma of spices filling the air at the bustling markets of Bapu Bazaar, tempting us with their array of flavours. We found ourselves irresistibly drawn to the textile shops of Nehru Bazaar, where artisans showcase their exquisite fabrics and traditional crafts.

Our stay in Jaipur, however, took an unexpected turn when our hotel reservations were altered after we had refused to stay at a private home. Despite the change in plans, we remained determined to make the most of our time in this captivating city. We sought accommodation in a different hotel, embracing the unexpected with open hearts.

Later, as Debbie and I bid farewell to Jaipur, we knew that we would be carrying away with us memories of its majestic forts, palaces, and bustling markets. The city had painted for us a vivid portrait of Rajasthan's rich cultural heritage, a city that was a particularly poignant part of our journey. Jaipur had reminded us of the resilience and adaptability that travel often demands, and we embraced those lessons with gratitude and a sense of adventure.

Back in New Delhi, we found comfort in the familiarity of the bustling streets and the vibrant energy that permeated the city. As we strolled through the crowded markets and admired the architectural wonders, we couldn't resist indulging in a cold, refreshing Coca-Cola, a beverage that we had come to associate with our travel adventures—a taste that brought back memories of far-flung destinations and the joy of discovery.

Sipping on our Coca-Colas, Debbie and I marvelled at the way this ubiquitous drink had become a symbol of global connection. In a world where cultures and traditions varied immensely, there was something reassuring about the consistency and reliability of the familiar taste of Coca-Cola. We savoured each sip with the knowledge that the drink had been bottled according to strict hygiene standards, which provide us with some comfort and reassurance as we navigated through new environments.

As we bid farewell to New Delhi, our hearts were filled with gratitude for the experiences we had enjoyed, the friendships we had forged, and the memories we would carry with us forever. In the spirit of adventure, Debbie and I raised our Coca-Cola bottles high, toasting the journey that had brought us here and the ones that lay ahead.

2.7 Getting Reacquainted with Gedu

Come morning, I was on the move again, this time destined for Paro, Bhutan. As the plane sliced through the clouds, I felt a sense of exhilaration. I was closing in on my destination, inching closer to the new role that awaited me and to the challenges and triumphs that lay hidden in the folds of the future.

By afternoon, I had touched down in Paro, the gateway to Bhutan. The descent into Paro was a spectacle in itself, a magnificent dance of precision and skill, a testament to the extraordinary in the ordinary. From there, it was a short journey to Thimphu. My final stop for the day was Hotel Galingkha, a warm sanctuary nestled amidst the enchanting landscapes of Thimphu.

Journeying to Bhutan is akin to embarking on a pilgrimage, an expedition to one of the farthest corners of the world. It is a test of one's will and perseverance, a dance with unpredictability, an exercise in embracing uncertainty. Not unlike the flight of a mountain bird, the flight on the way to Bhutan is lined with jagged edges and precipitous drops, but it is this very ruggedness that makes it an adventure worth pursuing.

Indeed, Bhutan is not the easiest country to reach. The path that leads to it is strewn with a myriad of obstacles. One must navigate the tricky flight routes, traverse the awe-inspiring yet treacherous Himalayan terrain, and patiently adhere to the strict tourism policies. It feels like a path less travelled, a challenge reserved for the most earnest of seekers.

But the moment you cross the threshold into the Land of the Thunder Dragon, you realize that every single effort, every hiccup, every seemingly insurmountable obstacle, was worth it. Because once you arrive, the reward is not just immense, it is transformative.

You are greeted by vistas so breathtaking, they seem to have been conjured up by a particularly imaginative artist. Verdant valleys, towering mountains, ancient monasteries clinging precariously to cliffs—Bhutan is a visual symphony that plays on an endless loop.

The air is different here. It's purer, crisper, imbued with a quiet sanctity that whispers in your ear the stories of centuries gone by. The people are different too. Their smiles are genuine; their hearts, brimming with warmth; and their lives, in beautiful harmony with the rhythm of nature.

Being in Bhutan is like being in a waking dream, where each moment is imbued with an ethereal quality. It's a place where gross national happiness is valued over gross domestic product, where spirituality permeates daily life, where the pace is slow and life is savoured one breath at a time.

Once you are in Bhutan, you don't just visit a country, you step into a different reality—a reality where materialism takes a backseat, where mindfulness is a way of life, and where happiness is a collective pursuit. And therein lies the true reward—the wisdom that Bhutan offers, the perspective it grants, and the transformation it inspires.

So yes, the journey to Bhutan is not easy. But then again, the most meaningful things in life rarely are. But as you stand on a mountaintop with the wind whispering ancient secrets and with the world spread out at your feet, you can't help but feel that every challenge was merely a stepping stone to this moment of immense reward.

With the break of dawn, I found myself embarking on a journey to Gedu, cradled within the heart of Bhutan's ethereal landscape. The bus hummed rhythmically through the winding mountain roads, mirroring the heartbeat of this country—steady, tranquil, full of soul.

As the bus halted its journey, I found myself in Gedu again, before the welcoming façade of the GCBS guesthouse. The air was rich with the scent of earth, the undulating hills crafting a canvas of serene beauty that left my soul feeling profoundly moved.

With the Gedu College of Business Studies being nestled high in the Himalayas, one can instantly see why it has been affectionately dubbed "the College in the Sky". Sitting at an elevation of more than two thousand metres, the campus looks over lush valleys and the majestic peaks of the Himalayas. This breathtaking panorama imbues the college with an air of tranquillity and inspiration, almost as if education here takes place closer to the heavens.

The architecture of the college reflects the vibrant Bhutanese culture, incorporating traditional motifs and construction techniques. Buildings are characterized by the Bhutanese style with bright wooden window frames, intricately designed carvings, and sloping roofs. The central building at GCBS, housing the library and the administration, is reminiscent of a Bhutanese fortress, or dzong, with its massive structure and high-reaching tower.

On my first day there, I was struck by the sight of professors and students alike wearing traditional Bhutanese outfits: men wearing the *gho*, a knee-length robe tied at the waist, and women wearing the *kira*, an ankle-length dress, accompanied by a light outer jacket known as a "tego". This practice of dress, which is encouraged by the government to preserve and promote Bhutan's unique cultural identity, made the atmosphere at the college an enchanting blend of traditional and academic.

During the college festivities, the campus came alive with colour and music. Students performed traditional Bhutanese dances and songs. They wore vibrant costumes with intricate designs, their movements precise and graceful, in harmony with the rhythm of the music. These performances were not just an expression of joy and celebration, but were also an essential part of preserving and passing down the cultural heritage of Bhutan.

I found a friend in the director of the college, a wise and affable man who had spent many years dedicated to the field of education in Bhutan. He shared stories about the founding of the college, its evolution, and the challenges and successes they had faced over the years. I found his company enlightening, his insights shaping my understanding of Bhutan's educational landscape and the unique balance the country seeks to achieve between modern education and traditional Bhutanese values.

This unique blend of academia, culture, and friendship amidst the setting of the awe-inspiring Himalayan landscape made my time at Gedu College an experience that transcended the realms of ordinary academic life. It was an education, not just of the mind, but also of the soul.

When I arrived at the faculty housing, I was welcomed with exceptional warmth and generosity. The Bhutanese culture of hospitality is deeply ingrained and a matter of national pride, and this was evident in the treatment I received from my fellow faculty members and the college staff.

I was given the largest room in the guesthouse again, a generous space with a panoramic view of the stunning landscape. The room was simple, reflecting the Bhutanese ethos of minimalism, yet it was thoughtfully arranged with essentials—a comfortable bed, a study table, and a shelf of books, which included both academic texts and works of Bhutanese literature.

The living room was adorned with traditional Bhutanese décor, including thangkas, or religious scroll paintings, and intricate wood carvings. Despite its simplicity, there was a subtle grandeur to the place that was indeed befitting of a Rinpoche or a king, emanating a sense of peace and serenity.

Every morning, I would begin my day with a humble breakfast served by the college staff. I would receive two pieces of toast, a perfectly fried egg, and some jam and butter. The simplicity of the meal was characteristic of the Bhutanese way of life, promoting contentment in simplicity.

One serene morning as the sun began to paint the skies with hues of gold, I wandered into the kitchen of Gedu College's humble abode. To my surprise, I found the chef, a diligent and resourceful soul, squatting on the floor next to a small, unassuming heater. With great care and ingenuity, he was toasting two pieces of bread for me, a simple yet very generous gesture that touched my heart.

As I savoured the delectable warmth of those two pieces of toast, I couldn't help but ponder the intricacies of life in this distant corner of the world. It was during one of my serendipitous explorations of the local market that I stumbled upon a remarkable revelation: eggs, a breakfast staple in Western countries, are a precious commodity in this charming town. Here they were being sold individually, not by the dozen, reflecting how highly they were valued.

In a place where every resource is cherished and every offering holds profound significance, I came to realize that the breakfast served at Gedu College was reserved for dignitaries like me. The chef's earnest efforts to make my breakfast special in his own endearing way touched my soul, highlighting the essence of hospitality and warmth that emanated from every corner of this enchanting land.

In this distant land, where simplicity and appreciation for life's little joys intertwine, I felt a deep sense of gratitude. The realization that every small gesture is crafted with intention and love, from having slices of bread toasted for me on a modest heater to my being offered a prized egg, left me humbled and in awe of the beauty found in simplicity.

As I immersed myself in the charm of Gedu College and its surrounding wonders, I learned a profound lesson about embracing life's modest blessings. In a world where abundance often blinds us to the true value of things, this humble corner of the world reminded me of the beauty of scarcity and the magnificence of heartfelt gestures.

Gedu College, with its caring chef and dignitary-worthy breakfasts, became a sanctuary where I found myself appreciating every simple nuance of life. It is in these unexpected moments and chance discoveries that the true essence of a place and its people is unveiled, as happened for me, leaving me with memories etched in my heart.

In the evening, dinner was a communal affair, often shared with other faculty members, including Bhutanese and Indian professors. These dinners were a delightful culinary and cultural journey. The meals usually included a mix of Bhutanese and Indian cuisine, ranging from *ema datshi*, a Bhutanese dish made of chilli peppers and cheese, to Indian classics such as dal and curry.

These shared meals gave me an opportunity to engage in enlightening discussions with fellow professors as we talked about everything from academic subjects, the nuances of Bhutanese culture, and our shared experiences as educators. It was a melting pot of ideas and perspectives, the conversations often extending late into the night.

The hospitality I experienced at the faculty housing was not limited to ensuring my physical comfort. It was an all-encompassing experience that made me feel at home in a new place, building a sense of community and camaraderie that transcended cultural differences. My time in Bhutan was not just about teaching at a college; it was also about being part of a larger family, experiencing Bhutanese life in its most authentic form.

I recall when I first walked into the classroom at Gedu College: there was an electricity in the air, an undercurrent of anticipation and curiosity. I was met by a sea of young faces, vibrant and eager. Clad in their traditional Bhutanese attire, the *gho* for boys and the *kira* for girls, my students were a vision of cultural pride and youthful enthusiasm.

Every day, as we delved into lectures and discussions, I couldn't help but marvel at their insatiable appetite for knowledge. The world outside Bhutan—a world filled with rapid advancements, diverse cultures, and complex socioeconomic dynamics—was an enigma to them, an abstract painting waiting to be deciphered.

Each lecture was an exploration, a voyage into the unfamiliar terrains of global trends, socioeconomic theories, and cultural shifts. Their eyes sparkled with intrigue as they soaked up information about the world beyond their mountains. They asked questions, probing and insightful, pushing the boundaries of their understanding.

And it wasn't just in the academic realm that they showed their curiosity. They were equally enthusiastic about the subtler nuances of life in the outside world—the everyday practices, the music, the food, and the languages. They yearned to understand not just the what but also the why behind the multitude of human experiences and expressions.

Despite their enthusiasm for the world outside, they were firmly rooted in their Bhutanese values and traditions. They spoke with reverence of the principles that guided their lives—respect for all forms of life, a deep commitment to community and family, the pursuit of spiritual growth, and a profound sense of contentment.

As their teacher, I became their guide into the unknown, their bridge to the outside world. It was not a one-way journey, though. While I offered my students glimpses of the world beyond, they unveiled to me the beauty of their culture, the wisdom in their simplicity, and the wealth in their contentment. It was an exchange, an intersection of worlds, where learning flowed like a two-way stream.

Through their eyes, I began to see the world anew. Their enthusiastic exploration of the unfamiliar made me reassess my own assumptions and preconceptions. Their pure curiosity and eagerness to understand served as a gentle reminder of the joy of learning and of the thrill that comes with diving into the unknown.

In the hallowed halls of Gedu College, nestled in the Bhutanese mountains, we journeyed together. We explored the vast landscapes of knowledge, traversed the winding paths of culture, and navigated the intricate labyrinth of human experiences. And in that journey, amidst textbooks and traditions, lectures and laughter, we discovered the essence of education—the quest for understanding, the thirst for knowledge, and the joy of discovery.

2.8 Unexpected Lifelong Friends

In the midst of settling back into these familiar surroundings, I received a call from Pabi, as melodious as a bird's morning song. I couldn't help but smile that she had remembered I'd be arriving "home" that day. The warmth and inclusivity of the Bhutanese culture was evident in the people's ease of inviting a stranger into their home. It felt less like an act of charity and more like a testament to our shared humanity, a norm that felt incredibly humbling.

After my arrival in Gedu, I was graciously invited into the warm embrace of Indra and Pabi's humble abode. Both were esteemed secondary school teachers, and their home radiated with a sense of familiarity and belonging.

As I stepped through their doorway, I was greeted by the tantalizing aroma of Bhutanese delicacies wafting from the kitchen. The air was filled with laughter and the gentle chatter of their children, creating an atmosphere of pure joy and togetherness.

We gathered around a table adorned with traditional Bhutanese dishes, each dish a testament to the rich culinary heritage of this extraordinary country. As we indulged in the flavours and shared stories, the boundaries normally surrounding people who are strangers to one another dissolved, to be replaced by the feeling of being kindred spirits connected by the simple act of breaking bread together.

Indra and Pabi's hospitality was as boundless as the mountain vistas surrounding their home. They shared tales of their experiences as educators, providing me with glimpses of the transformative power of education and their unwavering dedication to shaping young minds.

Time seemed to stand still as we laughed, savoured the delectable

Bhutanese cuisine, and immersed ourselves in the warmth of genuine human connection. It was a dinner that transcended cultural differences, forging bonds that I will forever cherish.

Leaving their home that evening, my heart was brimming with gratitude for the kindness and generosity bestowed upon me. Indra and Pabi had opened their doors, not merely as hosts, but as true ambassadors of Bhutanese hospitality, making an indelible mark on my journey through this enchanting land.

Lead Life Skill Trainer, Ministry of Education

Pabi, a dedicated high school teacher at Gedu Secondary School in the college town of Gedu, shone as a lead life skill trainer and played a vital role in shaping the future of Bhutan's teenagers. Selected from amongst her peers, Pabi had been entrusted with the important task of training other teachers in essential life skills to ensure that the nurturing hands of educators reached every corner of the nation.

The government of Bhutan, recognising the immense potential held by its teenagers, understands that their mastery of life skills is paramount to the country's success. Since 1994, in collaboration with UNICEF, Bhutan's Ministry of Education has actively incorporated life skills education into the high school curriculum and extracurricular activities. By 2005, an impressive nineteen thousand students between the ages of twelve and eighteen had received training in life skills thanks to the concerted efforts of organisations such as the Bhutan Scouts. Manuals and training programmes were developed to equip teachers and scout leaders with the necessary tools to impart these vital skills to the youth.

In my interview with Pabi, I sought to delve deeper into how Bhutan instils its unique gross national happiness (GNH) culture in children. I posed two important questions: Will the characteristics of these young adults shape their traits as future leaders? And if future leaders were to possess entrepreneurial traits as advocated by academia and industry experts, how and when should these traits be nurtured?

With unwavering enthusiasm, Pabi responded positively to both questions. She emphasized the need to instil values and cultivate the development of life skills in children from a tender age. As a dedicated schoolteacher, she had travelled extensively throughout Bhutan, imparting knowledge and wisdom to principals, teachers, and trainers and underscoring the significance of life skills education.

The Royal Government of Bhutan places great importance on this endeavour, recognising that adolescents between the ages of ten and nineteen constitute a significant portion of the country's population. Endorsed by the Ministry of Health and Ministry of Education, life skills education aims to equip young individuals with the capabilities and positive behaviours necessary to navigate the challenges of everyday life. It aligns perfectly with the holistic philosophy of gross national happiness.

Life skills education encompasses a range of abilities that promote physical, mental, and emotional well-being, enabling young people to thrive in the face of life's realities. The desired outcomes of life skill interventions include enhanced self-esteem, assertiveness, effective communication, goal-setting, and the acquisition of knowledge relevant to specific contexts. These skills fall into three broad categories: social, thinking, and emotional, all of which types of skills align harmoniously with the principles of GNH.

Pabi passionately asserted that by equipping future leaders with these essential life skills, Bhutan was cultivating a generation of well-rounded and empathetic individuals who would shape a brighter future. As she imparted her knowledge and showed her dedication to her students and fellow educators, Pabi gave me confidence in the transformative power of education by making a profound impact on the lives of Bhutan's youth.

2.9 Through the Veil of Fog

Gedu hummed with its customary activity as the rhythm of life carried me through another eventful day. I found myself immersed in the world of teaching, guiding two captivating Organisational Behaviour (OB) classes. The energy in the room was palpable as I shared insights and wisdom, sparking curiosity and encouraging growth in the eager minds before me.

Collaboration became the heartbeat of the day as I joined forces with Sangay Rinzin and Sherab on a visionary project—the Entrepreneurship Development Cell. Together, we crafted a comprehensive plan that aimed to empower budding entrepreneurs and cultivate a culture of innovation within our community. The creative synergy flowed effortlessly as each idea sparked the flame of possibility.

As the day wound down, I found myself drawn to the warmth and comfort of Rupa's house. Rupa, a beloved cafeteria lady, welcomed me with open arms and a table brimming with delectable dishes. It was a feast not only for the body but also for the soul. As we ate, we shared stories and laughter, a memory of being with her that I cherish.

Seeking solace in nature's embrace, I embarked on a three-kilometre hike along the path leading to the Bhutan Telecom Tower. The serenity of the surroundings and the rhythmic cadence of my footsteps provided a respite from the bustling world. Later, I ventured upon the road to Thimphu from Zero Market, accompanied by the introspective and kind-hearted Indian professor. As we walked, the Indian professor revealed the profound impact I had made on his life. His struggles with alcohol and depression had weighed heavily on his spirit, but through our encounters and shared conversations, he found renewed purpose and a glimmer of hope. We delved into the profound mysteries of existence, exploring the depths of philosophy and the wonders of human connection.

In the midst of my adventures, a pang of longing for Paris tugged at my heart. I confided in the Indian professor, expressing the inner turmoil I felt being away from the enchanting allure of the Marais area. The longing was almost unbearable, but I reminded myself of the strength that resided within me, urging myself to persevere in the face of temptation.

Later that afternoon, the director, the Indian professor, and I embarked on a unique expedition. Our destination: Phuentsholing, the bustling border town of Bhutan, adjoined to the Indian town of Jaigaon. The purpose of our trip was rather mundane, to purchasc a washing machine for the director's wife. But, as I was soon to discover, even the most ordinary undertakings can lead to extraordinary adventures in Bhutan.

We navigated our way through the steep mountainous roads that lay between Gedu and Phuentsholing. The one-and-a-half-hour drive was both thrilling and mesmerizing. The winding roads, the sheer drops, and the panoramic views of the Himalayas were nothing short of breathtaking. The journey was interspersed with the sight of prayer flags fluttering in the wind, waterfalls cascading down the mountains, and occasional groups of yaks grazing peacefully.

Upon arriving in Phuentsholing, I was instantly hit by the different energy of the place. The orderly tranquillity of Bhutan made way for the chaotic vibrancy of this border town where the Bhutanese and Indian cultures meet and meld. There was a certain vivacity in the air, a buzzing fusion of sounds, sights, and scents that was markedly different from the serene ambience of Gedu.

After securing the washing machine, we began our return journey to Gedu. However, nature had a different plan for us. A thick blanket of fog had descended, reducing visibility to near zero. The mountains, which had been a sight to behold in the morning, now seemed like looming shadows.

The fog was so dense that the Indian professor had to take on a role akin to that of a pioneering explorer. He bravely ventured out of the car and ran ahead, carefully guiding us through the enveloping white haze. His presence ahead of us was often the only indicator that we were still on the right path.

What was initially a one-and-a-half-hour journey extended to a four-hour odyssey. It was an arduous and nerve-racking drive, filled with suspense and adrenaline. Yet, in the spirit of Bhutanese resilience, we made it back to Gedu safely.

As I look back on that day, I realize that it is a true reflection of life in Bhutan—a blending of peace and chaos, tranquillity and adventure, the mundane and the extraordinary. Every journey, no matter how small or large, carries a story within it, a narrative of the unique tapestry that is Bhutan.

My experiences in Gedu continued to unfold, bringing both challenges and moments of profound connection. Through the ebb and flow of daily life, I remained open to the lessons and gifts that awaited me, knowing that each encounter had the power to shape not only m journey, but also the lives of those around me.

2.10 Echoes of Simplicity

A female student named Pema invited me to visit her dormitory. As we walked along the campus pathways, I admired the radiant smiles and energetic laughter of the students around us, their youthful spirits in harmony with the serene Himalayan backdrop.

Pema's dormitory was a picture of simplicity and organisation. A single wooden bed, a study table with a lamp, and a shared wardrobe was all that the room contained. Pema opened her portion of the shared wardrobe to reveal her belongings—seven pieces of neatly folded clothing. The modest collection consisted of a few *kira* sets, the traditional Bhutanese attire for women; a coat for the colder days; and a couple of everyday outfits.

As I observed this minimalistic wardrobe, Pema shared some wisdom passed on to by her grandmother, who had told her that she had too many clothes and, in essence, needed only two outfits—one to wear and one to wash. This principle was grounded in the Bhutanese belief in simplicity, sustainability, and contentment with what one has.

For me, this was a poignant moment, underlining the contrast between the cultures I was accustomed to and the way of life in Bhutan. It illustrated the deep-seated Bhutanese values of simplicity, nonmaterialism, and sustainability, highlighting how these values are not just preached but also practised, even by the younger generation.

In a world often characterized by consumerism, Pema's modest wardrobe and her grandmother's wisdom served as a powerful reminder of the potential for contentment in simplicity and the joy of living within one's means. I found in this simple situation a profound wisdom that transcended beyond clothing to the very essence of Bhutan's culture and way of life.

2.11 In Pursuit of Wisdom

With a sense of accomplishment, I closed the final phase of my questionnaire, a testament to my dedication and perseverance thus far. The responses had poured in, reaching a resounding count of 303, precisely the number deemed essential by my esteemed chancellor. It was a milestone in my research journey, the collective voices having generously contributed to my quest for knowledge.

As the weight of responsibility settled upon my shoulders, I immersed myself in the realm of academia, embracing the arduous task of completing my dissertation. The days were long, and at nights I stayed awake into the early hours as I delved deep into the realms of theory and analysis. The pages before me were the culmination of years of study, the culmination of a profound intellectual journey.

The ticking clock reminded me of the impending deadline, urging me forward. The finish line beckoned, and I vowed to meet it before the turning of the year. I was pursuing a PhD not merely to acquire a title; it also represented my profound commitment to knowledge and was a testament to my unwavering passion for learning.

Amidst the whirlwind of research and writing, I found solace in the dance of words and ideas. Each sentence, each paragraph, became a brushstroke on the canvas of my intellectual odyssey. I navigated the labyrinthine corridors of academia, drawing inspiration from the wisdom of scholars who had paved the way before me. It was a sacred endeavour, a pilgrimage of the mind and soul.

The path ahead was illuminated by the flickering flame of curiosity, which guided me through the intricate maze of literature and analysis. The words flowed from my fingers, forming a tapestry of insight and discovery. The mere act of writing became an act of liberation, a cathartic release of thoughts and ideas that had taken root within me.

As the year drew to a close, I carried the weight of my aspirations and dreams, mindful of the importance of crossing the finish line. The final days of December held the promise of completion, of celebrating the culmination of my intellectual pursuit. With unwavering focus and a heart filled with determination, I embraced the challenge that lay before me, ready to embrace the title of a PhD scholar.

The journey to the finish line was a testament to the resilience of the human spirit, an ode to the transformative power of knowledge. As the final pages of my dissertation came together, I knew that I had embarked on a voyage of self-discovery, one that would forever shape the trajectory of my life.

So, with pen in hand and with a heart alight with purpose, I remained immersed in the world of academia, eager to carve my name in the annals of knowledge before the page of the calendar was turned.

2.12 The Rinpoche's Wisdom

It was a day filled with anticipation, as the phone call from Lobzang, Namkhai Nyingpo Rinpoche's assistant, filled me with excitement and spoke of opportunity. An invitation to the monastery had been extended to me. Without hesitation, I eagerly accepted.

News of my upcoming visit quickly spread, and I found myself caught up in a whirlwind of preparation. Calls were placed, arrangements were made, and the path to Bumthang began to take shape. Pema Wangdi, ever friendly and playfully sarcastic, played a crucial role in securing my Bumthang route permit. His amusing enquiry as to my whereabouts at the market reminded me that work called, even amidst the excitement.

Thursday arrived, and with it came the long-awaited permit, delivered via fax. Sangay and I discussed the details, and thanks to his resourcefulness, I reserved a seat on a bus to Thimphu and purchased a ticket to Bumthang. The director, a pillar of support, extended his kindness by arranging my stay in Bumthang. His trusted friend would soon guide me from the hotel to the monastery.

Returning to the vibrant city of Thimphu, I found solace within the walls of the charming Hotel Galingkha. Nestled amidst the bustling streets and their vibrant energy, it served as my sanctuary during this leg of my journey. The city hummed with life, offering a tapestry of colours, scents, and sounds that awakened my senses.

As I settled into my room, I couldn't help but be captivated by the panoramic views that stretched beyond the window. The cityscape unfolded before me, a testament to the harmonious blending of tradition and modernity that defined Thimphu. Each passing moment held the promise of new adventures and new discoveries that awaited me in the heart of Bhutan's capital.

The days in Thimphu were a symphony of experiences, a blend of old and new that resonated within my soul. I wandered through the vibrant markets, where the scent of spices mingled with the chatter of locals and the vibrant hues of traditional textiles adorning the stalls. I immersed myself in the rich tapestry of Bhutanese culture, eagerly exploring the city's ancient monasteries, intricate temples, and awe-inspiring dzongs.

In the evenings, the city came alive with the rhythmic beats of traditional music and the infectious laughter of locals gathering to celebrate life's simple joys. I revelled in the warmth of their company, engaging in conversations that bridged the gaps of language and culture. Through shared experiences, I discovered the profound beauty of human connection, a reminder that despite our differences, we are all united in our quest for happiness and fulfilment.

At the Hotel Galingkha, I found respite from the exhilarating pace of the city. Its tranquil ambiance provided a haven where I could reflect on the wonders I had witnessed and the lessons I had learned. The staff greeted me with genuine warmth and hospitality, ensuring that my stay was not just comfortable but also infused with Bhutanese grace.

As the days turned into nights, I marvelled at the vibrant tapestry that Thimphu wove, each thread adding depth to my understanding of this captivating land. And as I bid farewell to the Hotel Galingkha and Thimphu, I knew I'd be carrying with me memories that would forever be etched in my heart—a testament to the enchanting allure of Bhutan and the indomitable spirit of its people.

As the director's friend and his wife pulled up in their minivan, I couldn't ignore the familiar pang of motion sickness that threatened to dampen my spirits. Swiftly, I reached for a motion sickness tablet, hoping it would tame the effects of the roller-coaster journey that awaited us. At midpoint, Rinpoche's driver, Karma met me.

Though the small Suzuki car may have seemed unassuming, the driving prowess of Karma, who coincidentally crossed my path, made all the difference. With his skilful navigation, we traversed the roads with ease, leaving behind the trials of the earlier drive.

Oh, the relief that washed over me as we arrived in Bumthang unscathed! Along the way, we had stopped for lunch at a mountaintop restaurant, surrounded by breathtaking views. A pause in Trongsa for coffee added another layer of tranquillity to the journey. Seeing as we were accompanied by six young monks, the atmosphere was imbued with an indescribable sense of serenity and sacredness.

The sight of the grand monastery left me in awe, its majesty standing as a testament to Rinpoche's vision and dedication. The guesthouse, far from the "dirty" image Rinpoche had painted, exuded pristine beauty. Though lacking in heaters, the presence of hot water and cleanliness brought me comfort and provided me with a sense of home.

Lobzang, my gracious guide, led me through the monastery's intricate architecture, igniting my curiosity about its funding. Thirteen years in the making, Rinpoche's labour of love had manifested as an extraordinary haven of spirituality and splendour.

Rinpoche's journey, from being chosen by a Tibetan Rinpoche at the tender age of four to his training under Khentsen Rinpoche, unfolded before me in a captivating way. The monastery housed hundreds of devoted monks, their presence a testament to Rinpoche's profound impact and the wisdom that emanated from his teachings. The realization struck me—Rinpoche was not only a Rinpoche, but also an extraordinary entrepreneur. This was a revelation that piqued my curiosity and fuelled my desire to interview him.

Lobzang, entrusted with the task of accompanying Rinpoche's guests, shared tales of his previous journeys, such as taking Taiwanese visitors on a ten-day exploration of the country. As I marvelled at the serendipitous circumstances that had led me here, pondering the reasons behind Rinpoche's choice, I couldn't help but smile at Ugyen's playful suggestions. Perhaps it was my karma and charm that had opened this extraordinary door.

Rinpoche, in a rare departure from his retreat policy, had agreed to see me for lunch the following day. Lobzang would be my guide once again, arriving in the morning to whisk me away. Overwhelmed with gratitude, I promised to join the monks in prayer at six-thirty in the morning. Surreal as it may seem, this journey felt like a dream turned into reality, an experience beyond the realms of ordinary existence.

In the midst of this extraordinary encounter, I couldn't help but marvel at the intricate dance of fate and destiny. Bhutan had woven its magic around me, guiding me along a path towards profound connections and experiences. As I prepared myself for the rendezvous with Rinpoche, a sense of wonder and awe enveloped me, reminding me that sometimes dreams do come true—and in the most unexpected of ways.

Dawn broke with a chorus of roosters and whispered early morning conversations drifting through the air. The darkness still enveloped the world outside my guesthouse. I glanced at the clock to discover it was half past five o'clock. With an hour left to sleep, I decided to seize the opportunity to get a little more rest.

At precisely half past six, I mustered the strength to rise from my bed, quickly gulping down some hot water to wet my parched throat. Rushing out the door, I forgave myself for neglecting my toothbrush, knowing that at such an early hour, there would be no one to detect any morning breath. I was still dehydrated from the previous day's journey as I had purposely refrained from drinking too much to avoid inconvenient pit stops out in nature. Memories of my travels in Africa flooded my mind, reminding me of the challenges and growth I experienced.

If I could navigate Africa digging holes for my souvenirs in the desert using a paper cup, then I believed I had the power to explore any corner of the world.

With my curiosity piqued, I peered through the curtain door, to be greeted by the mesmerizing sight of about twenty young monks immersed in melodic chanting. As I stepped into the main temple, all eyes turned towards me, the gazes reflecting a mix of astonishment and curiosity. I pondered how many blonde Asian women the monks had encountered before, suspecting the answer to be few, if any.

The minutes passed, and my ageing bones began to protest because of the demands of the continuous chanting. Regrettably, the session concluded sooner than I had hoped. Outside, Lobzang awaited me with patience and warmth.

Enchanted by the ethereal beauty surrounding me, I fervently took a great many photographs with the magnificent monastery as a backdrop. The clouds delicately hugged the mountains, painting a picture of a dreamlike shangri-la. Unable to contain my enthusiasm, I snapped away as Lobzang guided me through the sprawling twenty-seven-acre monastery. Rinpoche's visionary spirit materialized in the structures he had built within a mere thirteen years, with ongoing expansions hinting at his unwavering dedication. With three hundred and eighty students, four Khenpos (abbots), more than twenty teachers, and a junior Rinpoche, the monastery stood as the largest of its kind in Bhutan.

Lobzang must have thought me a restless American woman as I relentlessly pushed forward. Even after the morning tour, when offered respite, I suggested venturing into town. Unfortunately, a devastating fire had ravaged half the town just weeks earlier, but its people, along with three hundred army soldiers who came to help at the order of the Fourth King and the Fifth King, worked diligently to rebuild the homes and businesses. I couldn't help but jest with Lobzang about the "traffic jam" in Bumthang when we encountered parked cars in the middle of the town's one and only main street.

After a refreshing shower, I ascended to meet Rinpoche for lunch. In the kitchen, I observed the chef monk preparing our meal while

Lobzang attentively supervised. Posters of Indian women adorned the kitchen area, with the name Kareena gracing four life-size images, two of which were prominently displayed at the entrance. I pondered whether Rinpoche approved of this unusual decoration, but when he entered the kitchen and appeared to be comfortable, no one made an effort to hide the posters—at least not while I was there.

Rinpoche graciously invited me to dine in a separate room. Unshaven, he wore a merino wool jacket over his monk's attire and the same Croc shoes that had sparked conversations amongst my friends in previous encounters. He seemed genuinely happy to see me. And when Lobzang enquired about booking a bus ticket for the following day or the day after, Rinpoche intervened, suggesting that I extend my stay. Who was I to argue with Rinpoche's wishes? I eagerly accepted his invitation, anticipating the continuation of this extraordinary journey.

Our lunch conversation delved into the intriguing aspects of Rinpoche's journey and the inner workings of the monastery. Curiosity sparked within me, I couldn't resist posing a question originating from my business-oriented mindset.

"In the business world, Rinpoche, I would call you an entrepreneur. How did you manage to build this remarkable monastery?" I enquired, genuinely curious about the financial aspects.

Rinpoche's response carried a touch of humility. He said, "I don't know. I simply engage in dharma activities, and people offer their support. The more dharma I share, the more offerings I receive. It's not about dictating amounts; individuals give whatever they can afford. And I utilize all the offerings for the construction and expansion of the monastery. Surprisingly, I've managed to accomplish all this without any sponsors. Many doubted my ability to achieve such progress independently.

"The monastery initially housed just twenty people when I first joined. I purchased twenty-seven acres of land from the Bhutanese government at a nominal price and gradually built one structure after another," Rinpoche explained, revealing the seeds of his grand vision.

Curiosity compelled me to ask, "Isn't it a tremendous responsibility to oversee more than five hundred monks, especially considering none of them earn a living or pay fees for their Buddhist studies?"

Rinpoche responded with a heartfelt laugh, saying, "The more students I have studying Buddhism, the happier I am. Their commitment to learning and practising the teachings brings me immense joy."

Eager to be given more understanding on the financial aspects, I enquired about the means by which Rinpoche raised funds. "Mostly through offering prayers and teaching the local Bhutanese," Rinpoche shared. "However, I also endeavour to raise funds from overseas. Regrettably, we receive no financial support from the government."

At this point, I recalled Lobzang's earlier suggestion about attracting more overseas contributors. "Lobzang mentioned that you need more international support for fund-raising. How do you typically engage people to contribute?" I asked.

"It's becoming increasingly challenging to raise funds overseas for the monastery," Rinpoche admitted. "People are more inclined to give for education and healthcare initiatives as overseas governments don't provide support in those areas. When I am abroad, I offer dharma teachings and prayers. I particularly enjoy conducting these activities overseas because I can pray without any disturbances, as anonymity provides me solace."

Teasingly, I proposed, "Perhaps I should write a book about you. That would make you truly famous. And then you could hide away in Alaska!"

With a touch of modesty, Rinpoche replied, "I am not among the most famous Rinpoches. I would consider myself somewhere in the middle. It's a difficult question to answer. But truthfully, I have no strong desire for fame."

I interjected, reminding Rinpoche of the overwhelmingly positive reputation he held amongst the one hundred individuals I had spoken to about him. "Every single person I've spoken to describes you, the Namkhai Nyingpo Rinpoche, as the purest and most respected Rinpoche in Bhutan. Consequently, they are more inclined to offer generous contributions during pujas," I said.

Rinpoche graciously accepted the sentiment, expressing his gratitude. "Thank you. I simply strive to do what I believe is right," he humbly acknowledged.

Both Karma and Lobzang had previously mentioned Rinpoche's adherence to strict Tibetan teachings and disciplines, which set him apart from other Bhutanese Rinpoches. The monks in his monastery upheld standards of cleanliness, proper monk attire, vegetarianism, and abstinence from drinking, smoking, and *doma* (fermented betel nut). They practised full chastity, and each elder monk had assigned responsibilities. Students were not to leave the monastery without permission, with the Khenpo and teachers ensuring their presence on the grounds at all times.

During Rinpoche's retreat periods and his absence from the monastery to offer dharma teachings, the Khenpos and teachers took charge of running the monastery. They held regular meetings to discuss matters, with Rinpoche occasionally joining them. This hands-off approach showcased Rinpoche's visionary leadership style.

To maintain the monastery's vegetarian values, Rinpoche decided to make the guesthouse exclusive for friends and relatives of the monks. In the event of overflow, there was the Mepham Guest House operated by local family and named after a great master. This family would rent Rinpoche's guesthouse, provide meals for their guests, and pay rent to Rinpoche, ensuring the guesthouse remained occupied.

As our conversation continued, I shifted the focus to how I could contribute effectively despite not being a Buddhist and having limited Buddhist connections. "In what way do you believe I can assist you in raising funds?" I enquired, genuinely interested in providing meaningful support.

Rinpoche's response emphasized the importance of a long-term approach, aligning with my own expectations. "Perhaps you could help me find sponsors in the USA. That would significantly aid our fund-raising efforts for the monastery," he suggested.

Acknowledging the long-term commitment required for such endeavours, I replied, "I see. That's certainly a long-term plan, and I don't envision myself achieving it within the next few months."

"Indeed, it is a long-term undertaking," Rinpoche affirmed, reinforcing the idea. The conversation had transitioned into a businesslike exchange, yet beneath the surface, it remained rooted in Rinpoche's deep spiritual journey.

"Please feel free to use my house and car whenever you visit Los Angeles," I offered, extending a gesture of friendship and support.

Rinpoche expressed gratitude, adding, "There are only a few Bhutanese living in Los Angeles."

Recognising the need to broaden my understanding of Buddhism and Rinpoche's offerings, I shifted the conversation towards learning more about his teachings and exploring avenues where I could assist in promoting his services.

With our lunch conversation drawing to a close, Rinpoche invited me to join him for another meeting the following day. Overwhelmed by a sense of privilege and awe, I couldn't help but marvel at the extraordinary journey I had embarked upon.

Feeling the need to shift the conversation to deepen my understanding of Buddhism and Rinpoche's spiritual offerings, I decided to steer the discussion towards his remarkable journey as a Rinpoche.

"So, Rinpoche, how were you chosen as the great Rinpoche?" I enquired, eager to learn about the divine circumstances surrounding his selection.

Rinpoche's eyes sparkled with a hint of nostalgia as he began to recount his childhood encounter. "When His Holiness Gyalwa Karmapa Rinpoche travelled to Trashigang, on the eastern side of Bhutan, I was merely a three- or four-year-old child, riding behind my mother's backpack," he began. "Amidst the sea of people, His Holiness Gyalwa Karmapa Rinpoche spotted me and asked a police officer to lift me onto the stage. I sat on his lap for a brief moment, but I couldn't stop crying. Eventually, he handed me back to the police, who returned me to my mother.

"The following day, my grandfather was summoned by the police to take me to see His Holiness Gyalwa Karmapa Rinpoche," Rinpoche continued. "As I stood before His Holiness, he looked at me and remarked,

'What an old man.' Although I was too young to recall these details, my grandfather later shared this extraordinary encounter with me. The only vivid memory I have is drinking a cup of tea offered by Rinpoche, which I found tasteless compared to our Bhutanese tea, which is usually sweetened. It turned out to be Chinese jasmine tea."

Rinpoche's destiny took a more profound turn when His Holiness Gyalwa Karmapa Rinpoche arrived in Bumthang. "He contacted the disciples of the sixth Namkhai Nyingpo to investigate this young child in Trashigang," Rinpoche revealed. "The disciples travelled to Trashigang and confirmed that I, as a four-year-old, was indeed the reincarnation of Namkhai Nyingpo. When I was seven, my parents sent me to Bumthang, where I grew up in two separate temples before embarking on the journey to build this very monastery."

The monastery, aptly named Kharchu Monastery, meaning "where the sky meets the river", offers an enchanting view of Bumthang that justifies its poetic name.

After our enlightening lunch, as I prepared to bid farewell, I encountered Rinpoche's younger brother. He had travelled all the way from the east to visit Rinpoche and would soon be departing on a bus. Although they were brothers, I couldn't discern any familial resemblance. Rinpoche possessed a fair complexion and baby-soft skin, whereas his younger brother bore a darker complexion, suggesting a life spent toiling in the fields.

"How did you come to know Dzongsar Khyentse Rinpoche?" I asked, interested in uncovering the bonds that connected these revered spiritual figures.

"We both studied under the same Khenpo, Kuenga Wangchuck," Rinpoche explained. "Khenpo Wangchuck also served as the Dalai Lama's Khenpo, making him a highly respected teacher. In fact, even the Dalai Lama would prostrate to him in a sign of deep respect." Lobzang informed me that Rinpoche and Dzongsar Khyentse Rinpoche shared this remarkable teacher.

Continuing with a sense of reverence, Rinpoche added, "I also received profound teachings from another esteemed master named Dilgo

Khyentse. He was a Tibetan monk who resided in Nepal after the Chinese invasion. I learned invaluable lessons from him."

As Rinpoche's stories unfolded, I couldn't help but marvel at the intricate web of connections that shaped his spiritual path, which left me in awe of the profound knowledge and wisdom he had acquired along the way.

As I walked away from our enlightening lunch, a sense of clarity washed over me. I had gained a deeper understanding of the factors contributing to Rinpoche's remarkable success. He was a man of uncommon modesty and unwavering discipline, and it was through his steadfast commitment to these values that he had earned the respect and admiration of those around him. In contrast to other Bhutanese Rinpoches, who indulged in worldly pleasures, this Rinpoche exuded a sense of grace and refinement. He adhered to the principles of classic Tibetan Buddhism with unwavering dedication, and this adherence had attracted a loyal following.

But Rinpoche's accomplishments extended beyond his religious pursuits. He possessed a keen entrepreneurial spirit and was always quick to recognise opportunities when they presented themselves. When he met me and other foreigners, he saw the potential to raise significant funds in a shorter span of time than would be possible in Bhutan alone. His genuine hospitality and generosity, inviting me to his guesthouse and even meeting with me during his retreat when he typically refrained from seeing anyone other than his fellow Rinpoche, demonstrated his belief in the power of genuine connections. It became clear to me that I owed him a referral in the United States, where I could help raise awareness and support for his noble cause.

Rinpoche embodied resourcefulness, dedication, and innovation, setting himself apart as a true leader. He surrounded himself with exceptional teachers and administrators who could ensure the smooth functioning of his monastery even in his absence. It was remarkable to witness how a naturally shy individual could command such influence and build an empire day by day, quietly but resolutely, leaving an indelible mark on the world.

Later, Lobzang kindly took me to a handicraft shop, where I indulged myself in purchasing *tego* and *wangju*, elegant Bhutanese women's jackets. I decided to exchange the kira I had bought in Thimphu for a more exquisite hand-woven kira from here, despite its considerable cost of USD 165. Though I was thinking I might only wear it on a few occasions during my time in Bhutan, I felt it necessary to fully immerse myself in the beauty and traditions of this extraordinary land. I couldn't help but feel a sense of certainty that this journey to Bhutan was just the beginning and that it would not be my last.

The next day, I woke up before my alarm had a chance to chime, feeling invigorated by the crisp mountain air. The roosters, ever eager to showcase their vocal talents, had already filled the morning with their boisterous crowing. But their enthusiastic serenade didn't disturb my tranquil state; in fact, it only added to the charm of this enchanting place. I slipped on my shoes and was tempted to dash off to the morning prayer, but the lack of fibre in the Bhutanese cuisine reminded me of a pressing matter. I spent the next ten minutes in the solitude of the bathroom, attending to my bodily needs.

The melodic chanting of the monks drew me into a dreamlike state as I entered the temple. I could have listened to their harmonious voices for hours, losing myself in the transcendental rhythm of their prayers. Alas, like all beautiful moments, it came to an end, leaving me longing for more.

As if on cue, Lobzang was awaiting my presence in the dining room, ready to embark on our day's adventures. There were couples seeking the blessings of the Rinpoches, asking for prayers to be offered for their ailing parents. Just last night, two gentlemen from Thimphu had sought the Rinpoches' puja to honour their departed father. In Bhutan, death is referred to as "expiration", a gentle way of acknowledging the impermanence of life.

Our next stop was the Bhutan National Bank, where I gathered all the leftover currencies from my wallet. To my dismay, Chinese renminbi were not accepted. What had I been thinking? With a heavy heart, I reluctantly parted with my last US hundred-dollar bill and exchanged what euros I could spare, ensuring that I had enough cash to cover my stay in Thimphu and the bus fare. Once I reached Gedu, my expenses would dwindle to a minimum, mostly consisting of water and snacks, each worth a mere fifty cents.

I handed over ten thousand ngultrums—Bhutanese currency—to Lobzang, apologizing for the modest offering. I couldn't be sure if he was impressed, but it was the best I could manage. I tried to rationalize my purchase of kira, tego, wangju, and a pin totalling seven thousand ngultrums, having resorted to using my credit card. Rinpoche later reassured me that the offering was unnecessary, emphasizing that he had extended the invitation to have me present as he was grateful for my company. A warm smile formed on my face as his words sank in.

While waiting at the bus station, I had the pleasure of meeting the owner, whose daughter graciously mended my kira that had begun to unravel. This man once had been a prominent figure in Bumthang, renowned even by the Fourth King. Miraculously, his shop had remained unscathed during the devastating fire that ravaged half the town, a phenomenon he attributed to his personal mantra. He was a legend in his own right, proud to share that he had eighteen children: nine with his devoted wife, and another nine with various mistresses. To his surprise and delight, his wife not only approved of his extramarital relationships, but also even had introduced him to some of his paramours. He claimed that he was still in the honeymoon phase with his wife—in my view, she had a unique approach to keeping her man content. Such revelations made me contemplate the merits of becoming a nun.

While I was browsing the wares in the shop, Captain Kinley approached me, excitement radiating from his every pore. He eagerly recounted how Dechen and I had brought joy to the young boys during the archery match, igniting a competitive spirit within them. As a captain, he held the esteemed position of being third in command over the reconstruction efforts after the fire. Above him stood a colonel and a major, who were overseeing the monumental task of rebuilding the charred shops. Captain Kinley then proceeded to demonstrate the intricate process of making Bhutanese bricks: mixt mud, water, and pine needles, mould it together, and leave it to dry under the rays of the sun. These remarkable bricks were known to last an astonishing twenty-five years. Instead of relying on imports from India, the king had wisely chosen to produce bricks locally. The construction work, despite the limited equipment, was a testament to the Bhutanese craftsmanship.

Lobzang revealed that I had been invited to share another lunch with Rinpoche. Filled with eager anticipation, we ascended the uphill path to the Rinpoche's abode. This time, Rinpoche emerged from within, his countenance radiating joy. Seizing the opportunity, I promptly requested to capture the moment in a photograph, assuring him that it would be my personal keepsake alone, a cherished memento of this extraordinary encounter.

During our lunch, I eagerly described the essence of my PhD research to Rinpoche—the concept of the four E's. As I elucidated the principles of empathy, earth, ethics, and earnings, Rinpoche's face lit up with recognition and approval. He concurred that such a message deserved wider dissemination, expressing that even if a mere two out of ten individuals were to heed its call, that would be a cause for celebration.

Despite Rinpoche's modesty regarding his command of the English language, it became evident to me that he grasped the essence of our conversation. The gentle cadence of his voice, as his trusted assistant Lobzang Drakpa interpreted, lent an air of profundity to our exchange.

"The essence of your dissertation aligns beautifully with the dharma I strive to spread," Rinpoche mused. "It is fundamentally about doing good, a topic that has been contemplated for ages. At long last, a connection has been forged between the teachings of dharma and the realm of business."

He further expounded, "Buddha teaches us that in order to find true happiness, we must cultivate contentment, irrespective of wealth or poverty. Many individuals contribute to the deterioration of our world precisely because they lack this essential quality of contentment.

"Earning a livelihood is an integral part of life," Rinpoche said, "but we must undertake this endeavour with unwavering adherence to ethical principles.

"People often mistake dharma for the mere act of beating drums and ringing bells," he shared. "These rituals serve as reminders for us to engage in virtuous deeds. True dharma lies in guiding one another towards wise thoughts and benevolent actions. Regrettably, even some esteemed figures, like a senior person in Bhutan preoccupied with governmental affairs, misunderstand dharma, claiming they lack the time to engage in such practices.

"Dharma encompasses intention, action, and the action's impact on others," Rinpoche emphasized. "Buddha teaches us that every action which benefits sentient beings is an act of dharma."

With a warm smile, Rinpoche focused his attention on me and remarked, "KT, you are already immersed in the practice of dharma." His laughter reverberated in the room; he was brimming with satisfaction.

"Some individuals attempt to justify their harmful deeds by claiming they benefit others," I interjected. "In the business world, for instance, affluent individuals may exploit child labour, offering meagre wages, while justifying their actions as being beneficial to consumers." Rinpoche nodded in agreement, asserting that whatever causes harm to others is unequivocally condemned by Buddha.

He recalled an intriguing encounter with an English teacher in Barcelona who posed a question about the minds and feelings of flies. Rinpoche's response illuminated his compassionate wisdom—every living being, be it human, animal, or insect, possesses a spark of life and should therefore be spared from harm. In response to Rinpoche's teachings, the teacher pledged never again to harm an insect, choosing instead to relocate them from her home while delving into the profound teachings of Buddhism.

"Even in relation to nonliving entities such as grass and trees," Rinpoche elucidated, "Buddha urges us to refrain from indiscriminate cutting. Even when we must prune, we should replant to safeguard the well-being of future generations and protect our precious earth. Residing in the embrace of the Himalayas, we keenly perceive the changes in weather patterns—the palpable effects of global warming. Bumthang, once graced by snowy winters and frozen rivers, now witnesses the absence of a single snowflake throughout the season."

Rinpoche reiterated that he was merely a messenger of Buddha's teachings, humbly stating, "All the dharma spoken by Buddha has been documented as science and is supported by evidence. Buddha himself never intended for his speeches to be worshipped or blindly respected. Instead, he encouraged individuals to analyse his teachings and discern their truth for themselves. If one believes in their validity, then one can embrace, practise, and personally experience them."

He emphasized the transformative power of skilful engagement with dharma, expressing, "If you become skilful and immerse yourself in the study of dharma, you will become an invaluable asset to the world."

Rinpoche's tone turned unexpectedly stern as he addressed the role of visiting professors, particularly within the context of the Royal University of Bhutan. He expressed his concern, saying, "Nowadays, young people tend to listen more to foreigners like you. As a visiting professor, you have considerable influence over these students. Your responsibility should not be taken lightly." Although I politely objected to his comment, he remained firm in his belief.

It was during this conversation that I shared with Rinpoche the request from the university to write a book on GNH-enabled entrepreneurship. He nodded approvingly and agreed that it would be a worthwhile endeavour. He also granted me permission to incorporate some of his teachings into the book, reiterating that everything he said was merely a repetition of Buddha's teachings.

With a serious expression, Rinpoche said, "Business is interconnected with dharma. Even the larger and more powerful countries can learn from your four E's. Bhutan, as a small country with profound philosophies, holds great potential. If the USA, China, and India were to adopt policies aimed at curbing pollution, the positive impact would be immense. It would cascade down to smaller countries like Bhutan, influencing them to follow suit. But, of course, this is just my opinion." His laughter filled the air, lightening the intensity of the conversation.

"Even the Dalai Lama advocates for environmental preservation and peace, promoting a world without war," Rinpoche added.

Rinpoche looked out at the expanse of Bhutan's valleys and mountains, shrouded in the quiet mystery of the middle of autumn with its cool air. He remembered a winter from his childhood that seemed to extend itself into eternity.

"The winter would arrive and the snow would fall, covering everything in a blanket of white," Rinpoche began, his eyes glazed over with the film of reminiscence. "I was perhaps ten or eleven, and I remember the cold that would creep in: it seemed almost to touch your soul. But there was beauty in it, a stillness that only winter could bring. We children would play in the snow, fashioning our games and stories around it. It felt like winter lasted forever."

His gaze shifted, looking towards the future, but tied to the past. "Now, thirty years later, the winters are not the same. They're shorter, less intense. The snow falls late, melts early. The beauty, the stillness, it feels"—he paused—"diminished. It is a tale of loss that only those of us living here, living with the rhythm of the seasons, can truly understand."

Rinpoche sighed deeply, the corners of his eyes crinkling. "Climate change is not a debate for us. It is not a theory, not a far-off possibility. It is our lived reality. We see it, feel it, and experience it every single day. And it is not just in the change of seasons or the melting of our snow. It's in the shrinking of our glaciers, the change in our wildlife, the unpredictability of our weather."

He looked directly at me then, his gaze intense and his voice firm. "We are the witnesses and the victims, living on the frontlines of a world that is changing before our eyes. But we are also the messengers. We carry a warning from the heart of the Himalayas to the rest of the world."

His gaze softened—he the elder statesman, the spiritual teacher, the voice of the Himalayas—becoming clear. "There is an urgent need for the world to act. It is not just our Himalayas that are at risk. It is our planet. It is our future. And it is our responsibility.

"We in Bhutan have long understood the balance of happiness, living not just for today, but also for tomorrow. In our gross national happiness philosophy, the environment is a key pillar. We understand that we cannot have happiness without harmony with nature.

"Climate change is a challenge for all of humanity," Rinpoche concluded, "and it is one that we must face together—for the sake of our planet, for the sake of our future, and for the sake of the happiness of all living beings."

We shared a joyous laugh before delving into other topics of discussion. It was evident that my informal interview with Namkhai Nyingpo Rinpoche had been a resounding success.

To express my gratitude and contribute to the ongoing construction of Kharchu Monastery, I left an envelope containing three hundred US dollars for Rinpoche.

Following the meeting, Lobzang kindly took me on a tour of one of the oldest monasteries in Bumthang. As my gracious guide, he shared fascinating insights. However, my true intention was to meet his family. Lobzang revealed that he had been sent to the monastery at the tender age of ten, destined to walk the path of a monk. There was a touch of sadness in his eyes as he mentioned that fewer young people nowadays aspired to be monks, opting for alternative paths such as marriage and secular employment.

As we embarked on our journey, I glanced at my watch and casually asked Lobzang, "Does your mother live far from here?"

With a furrowed brow, he responded, "No, she's just around the corner."

A mischievous smile spread across my face as I suggested, "How about visiting your mum now?"

Overjoyed, Lobzang replied, "Why not!" And with that, the car accelerated.

In a matter of minutes, Lobzang abruptly halted the car in the middle of the road and began engaging in a spirited conversation with a vehicle heading in the opposite direction. Despite the absence of bustling traffic akin to that in cities such as Los Angeles and New York, the sudden stop created a small stir. Eventually, a woman and a young girl entered the backseat. Lobzang introduced them, saying, "This is my mother and my niece. They were on their way to the monastery …"

Such serendipitous encounters were commonplace in Bhutan!

We arrived at Lobzang's brother's house, where we were greeted with customary Bhutanese hospitality in the form of a warm cup of milk tea and biscuits. Lobzang graciously showed me around, guiding me through each room. The living room exuded an undeniable coziness, the furniture centred around a customary fireplace. I couldn't help but wonder if the children ever came into contact with the scorching copper or steel chimney, but then again, children are remarkably astute in avoiding anything burning hot.

Before bidding farewell, I discreetly slipped some money to Lobzang's mother, mindful of conserving some cash for my return trip to Thimphu.

2.13 A Checkpoint in Bhutan

At half past five in the morning, Lobzang's polite knock on my door marked the start of our day. It was time to catch the six-thirty bus, and to my surprise, the bus driver treated me with utmost respect and hospitality throughout the seven-hour journey. He ushered me to the best seat and even invited me during one stop to have lunch in a separate VIP room, away from the other passengers. At another stop, he kindly paid for my snacks.

As I was marvelling at the unexpected special treatment from the bus driver, a phone call interrupted my thoughts. It was the handsome captain, checking to ensure I was being well taken care of. Suddenly, it all made sense—a moment of realization.

As we approached the first of several checkpoints around six o'clock in the evening, the driver instructed me to present my papers. Stepping off the bus, I inhaled the refreshing evening air. The checkpoint police scrutinized my documents and uttered the unwelcome words, "You can't proceed. This paper is invalid."

Bewildered, I argued, "But I entered this district legally. Why else would I have stopped here to prove my legitimacy?"

The police sternly replied, "You can't go." Unsurprisingly, just when

I needed my mobile phone to work, the battery chose that moment to die on me. *Great!* Filled with frustration, I rushed back to the bus and began rummaging through my belongings to find my mobile phone charger. Plugging it in, I anxiously waited for my phone to regain power. Once it did, I dialled the captain, desperate for assistance. Reluctantly, he chose not to get involved—an understandable decision as we had only met after my arrival in Bumthang.

My best bet lay with the director. Dialling his number from the checkpoint's phone, I anxiously awaited an answer. No response! Disheartened, I pleaded silently, *Pick up the phone, Dasho!* Meanwhile, the checkpoint officer dialled the Ministry of Immigration office. Unfortunately, the assistant minister of immigration couldn't help as the minister had already left for the day—a major setback! The officer then reached out to the couple who had initially driven me to Lobesa, but they denied any involvement and directed him to contact my director.

Meanwhile, curious heads peered out from the bus, observing the unfolding situation. Some passengers grew agitated, likely expressing their frustration to the bus driver, who appeared anxious, unwilling to leave me behind.

Finally, my mobile phone displayed a glimmer of reception—a single bar—and the battery held on with just a sliver of power. Seizing the opportunity, I called the director, who answered immediately. "Director, I need help. Can you please speak to the checkpoint police in the Punakha district?" I implored.

His response came gently: "What trouble has found you this time?" Without answering, I handed the phone to the police officer. When my phone was returned to me, the director assured me, "I will call the minister of immigration now. Hang in there."

Those five minutes felt like an eternity, but eventually, my mobile phone and the checkpoint phone rang simultaneously. We answered simultaneously as well. The director conveyed, "The minister of immigration will grant you passage this time as the problem is due to an oversight that is not your fault. Please refrain from getting yourself involved in such incidents in the future, OK? Now, get home safe and in one piece."

By the time we reached Thimphu, it was close to nine o'clock at night as we had been delayed by two hours thanks to me, an unruly foreigner. However, the other passengers displayed kindness and refrained from commenting on the delay. I hopped into a taxi for a two-minute ride to Hotel Galingkha, where I found solace—a slice of heaven.

Just as I settled in, my mobile phone rang. It was half past ten at night, and Pema from the Royal Institute of Health Sciences wanted to meet with me. Unfortunately, I was scheduled to take the two-thirty bus back to Gedu.

Next morning, Pema greeted me with a warm smile, revealing her straight, pristine white teeth, as I invited her into my room. I sensed that she had never been to a hotel catering specifically for foreigners, and she appreciated the gesture. Although she politely declined my offer of breakfast, she surprised me with a hand-knitted bag made by her mother. Its vibrant colours and intricate patterns mirrored the bags I had admired in Bumthang and other tourist destinations. The fabric was coarse, but I could feel the love that had gone into every stitch.

Taking the bag from her hands with caution, I noticed the calluses adorning her palms, a testament to her years of toiling on her family's farm. Expressing my gratitude, I embraced her in a heartfelt hug. Unsure of what to offer in return, I gifted her three bracelets I had purchased during my time in India.

At nine o'clock in the morning, Khandu from the Prime Minister's Office arrived, exuding an impeccable sense of style. We engaged in a discussion about my background and PhD dissertation. She eagerly seized the opportunity to arrange a meeting with the Prime Minister. However, after days of meticulous organisation, it turned out that he would only be available on 17 December, a few days after my departure from Bhutan. With teaching commitments awaiting me in Paris, I reluctantly let go of the chance to meet the legendary and beloved Prime Minister.

Following Khandu's meeting, I hopped into a taxi en route to the campus of the Royal Bhutan Police for Nann's promotion ceremony. The ceremony took place in the grand reception hall on campus, but unfortunately, the taxi driver took a wrong turn, leading me astray. Just as I began to feel a bit lost, a girl I had met at Nann's house spotted me and waved with enthusiasm. Without hesitation, I exited the taxi and joined her in front of the reception hall.

Nann's promotion ceremony was a ritual-filled affair. She received blessings from a Rinpoche and numerous superiors before being acknowledged by her friends. After indulging in some snacks at the reception hall, I excused myself and swiftly returned to the hotel to collect my luggage. From there, I headed to the bus station, mindful that I hadn't paid the taxi driver earlier, as he had agreed to pick me up for my journey to Gedu at two o'clock.

2.14 Amidst the Shangri-La

After days of subtly hinting at his feelings, the Indian professor finally revealed that he had developed an attachment to me. The intensity of our past few days together had left me too emotionally immersed to continue writing in my journal, yet the experience felt undeniably magical.

Since returning from Bumthang, the Indian professor and I had grown exceptionally close. We spent practically every day in each other's company. Whether it was strolling to the shops to buy bottled water or topping up our Tashi mobile phone cards, we found joy in even the simplest of activities. We rekindled the fire in his front yard, embarked on a trek up the hill to the telecom tower, and engaged in intriguing conversations with the chatty locals we encountered along the way.

Our connection extended beyond surface-level interactions; we delved into discussions about philosophy, shared stories from our pasts, and divulged our dreams for the future. Conversation seemed to flow effortlessly between us, and even after I had left his house and retired to bed, he would call me around midnight just to continue our enthralling dialogues. However, it had become evident that our friendship had evolved into something more—an undeniable mutual attraction.

During one of our walks along the National Highway, the Indian professor mentioned that he had never ventured beyond a particular rock. Intrigued, I asked why he had never gone farther. He responded with a simple yet revealing statement: "There was no reason to go beyond that rock."

I turned to him, a playful smirk on my face, and encouraged him to challenge himself. I urged him to take steps beyond his comfort zone, even if it was just a few extra paces. The significance lay not in the distance covered, but in refusing to settle for the status quo. He nodded in agreement, acknowledging my words with a heartfelt, "Yes, Professor."

On one of my final days in Gedu, I called the Indian professor and asked him to accompany me as I returned some books to Pabi. As we walked downhill, I miraculously located Pabi's house amidst the cluster of residences. Pabi greeted us warmly, inviting me inside and offering tea. She playfully tried to convince me to stay for lunch, knowing full well that I longed to savour her delectable culinary creations. Renowned as one of the best cooks in Gedu, Pabi's culinary skills had earned her some well-deserved recognition.

During our conversation, Pabi shared that the director had informed them about the need for additional housing to accommodate incoming students next year. Consequently, she and her family would have to move. Despite recently purchasing a brand new Suzuki car, their finances were tight, leaving them with limited resources to build a new home on the land they had bought a couple of years ago—a picturesque hillside location overlooking the college.

Curiosity got the better of me, and I enquired about the estimated cost of building a house. Pabi mentioned that if Indra were to build it himself, it would likely amount to less than one lakh, equivalent to a hundred thousand rupees. In a spontaneous moment, I offered to lend them the money to construct their dream home on their land. Pabi gazed into my eyes with her own, which were filled with a mixture of surprise and gratitude. She insisted that it wasn't the reason she had shared their predicament with me. Undeterred, I reassured her, saying, "It's OK, I know. I genuinely want to do this for you."

Excitedly, Pabi shared my offer with Indra upon his return home.

To my surprise, Indra's initial response was anger. He vehemently protested, insisting that they couldn't possibly accept such a generous offer. However, I persisted, assuring them that it was a loan, not charity. I reminded them that both their sons would have a place to live and that they could repay me when I returned to Gedu. After a moment of contemplation, Indra relented, his scepticism giving way to acceptance. He made it clear that they would repay the loan as soon as they had saved enough, promising to do so within a year, well before my next visit to Gedu.

With smiles on our faces, we shook hands, then sealed the deal over a joyous lunch. As the time for my departure approached, we embraced one another tightly. I could see tears welling up in Pabi and Indra's eyes, mirroring the emotions swirling within me. I quickly turned away, attempting to hold back my own tears. The Indian professor and I walked back together in silence, the weight of the moment hanging in the air.

The Indian professor broke the silence, acknowledging the inevitable. "You're not coming back, are you?" I smiled, choosing not to respond directly. His nod conveyed understanding as he uttered, "Hmm, you are a very special person."

The day stretched before me, offering ample time to immerse myself in the task of writing in my journal and summarizing the insightful interviews I had conducted for my PhD dissertation. Deep down, however, I couldn't deny a slight inclination to avoid encountering the Indian professor.

As I settled into my writing, the words flowed from my pen with ease, capturing the essence of my experiences and reflections. Each sentence etched onto the paper served as a testament to the profound moments I had shared with the people I had encountered on this journey. The stories unfolded, revealing insights that transcended the boundaries of academic research.

Time seemed to slip away unnoticed as I poured myself into my work. With each passing hour, I delved deeper into the analysis of the interviews, deciphering the nuanced meanings behind the words spoken and the things that had been left unspoken. The weight of my research mingled with a subtle unease, as if a part of me were seeking to keep a safe distance from the complexities that had arisen between the Indian professor and me.

But the persistent whisper of his presence lingered in the back of my mind, nudging me to confront the reality that had unfolded. The undeniable connection we shared had kindled a flame, one that I couldn't easily extinguish. As much as I wanted to retreat into the solitude of my writing, the pull of our shared experiences tugged at my heartstrings, demanding acknowledgement.

With a sigh, I set my pen aside, thereby momentarily setting aside the task at hand. I allowed myself a moment to reflect on the journey that had brought me here to this crossroads, where my academic pursuits intersected with matters of the heart. The emotions swirled within me as I sat staring at the ink-stained pages of my journal.

In the end, I knew that avoidance would only delay the inevitable. To truly understand the depths of my experiences and find solace in their lessons, I had to face the complexities head-on. With renewed determination, I closed my journal and prepared to seek out the Indian professor, ready to navigate the intricate path that lay before us.

Another impulsive day unfolded before me as I followed my inner urgings to float down the current of my curiosity. No longer able to resist the urge, and without a second thought, I reached out to the Indian professor, my confidant in this journey. "Hey, do you happen to know any entrepreneurs in Gedu?" I asked, my voice filled with anticipation. "I would love to interview them for my doctoral dissertation."

True to his nature, the Indian professor responded with his characteristic enthusiasm, assuring me that he had just the right connections. "Of course!" he exclaimed. "Meet me at the market in ten minutes."

As I approached the bustling market, I couldn't help but marvel at the Indian professor's knack for understanding my needs. He had carefully considered the individuals who would be most suitable for the interviews, selecting those with a strong command of the English language. His thoughtfulness set the stage for a successful day of engaging conversations and enlightening insights.

After the interviews drew to a close, we made our way to the Indian professor's humble abode for a well-deserved meal. As we sat around the dinner table, a sense of contentment filled the air. Apparently there were lingering questions in the Indian professor's mind. "There's one thing that puzzles me," he began, his voice taking on a hint of uncertainty. "The director kept asking me if I would stay in Gedu. My contract is coming to an end."

It was unusual to see the Indian professor, an ever-wise and caretaking soul, grappling with a decision. His words hung in the air with a weight that deserved attention. I listened intently, understanding the weightiness of the choice that lay before him. I spoke softly, allowing the words to weave their way into his contemplation: "What would you regret most when you are lying on your deathbed, not amassing more wealth or not pursuing your PhD?"

In that moment, the power of introspection enveloped us. The Indian professor took a deep breath, his gaze drifting towards the vast expanse of the Bhutanese mountains as if seeking solace and guidance. Gratitude filled the space between us, unspoken yet palpable. "Thank you, KT," he finally murmured, his voice tinged with a new-found sense of clarity.

We sat there sipping our tea, enveloped by the beauty that surrounded us. The mountains stood tall, their majestic presence a reminder of the vastness of life's possibilities. In that quiet moment, we both found solace and inspiration as the mountains whispered their eternal wisdom.

The next day, we hailed a taxi at the early hour of eight o'clock on the winding National Highway en route to Phuentsholing. This was my golden opportunity to interview entrepreneurs and delve deeper into their stories. A pang of regret washed over me as I kicked myself for my disorganisation. Why hadn't I initiated these interviews earlier, rather than leisurely traversing the country at my own pace?

As we journeyed towards Phuentsholing, I noticed the Indian professor stealing glances at me from the corner of his eye. I chose to divert my attention and look towards the enchanting beauty of Bhutan, my heart yearning to absorb every last detail. During a brief pit stop, the Indian professor mustered the courage to ask the driver if he would move to the front passenger seat. A silent understanding passed between me and the Indian professor. No further words were necessary. I knew what he meant.

It was essential to maintain our boundaries, as nothing should transpire between him and me. I staunchly reaffirmed this conviction within myself, determined to safeguard the sanctity of our connection.

One evening on the phone when the Indian professor expressed his desire to visit my quarters, I swiftly replied, speaking with utmost respect for his children, his wife, and his family. "I cannot allow anything to happen between us," I declared firmly.

His response was a simple "I understand," then we hung up.

After I had successfully conducted interviews with three corporate entrepreneurs, the Indian professor and I realized the urgency of withdrawing some money from the ATM at the Indian border. As time was of the essence, we hurriedly embarked on an adventure in a vehicle reminiscent of an Indian tuk-tuk. With a touch of humour, I noted that Indian men and women seemed to possess smaller bottoms than mine, the vehicle effortlessly accommodating four individuals on a seat I deemed suitable for two. Showing his kindness, the Indian professor settled himself in the middle, allowing me to occupy the edge. Thus, with determination and balance, I clung on, determined not to succumb to any mishap.

Our pursuit of completing our financial transactions led us on a scramble through various Indian banks equipped with ATMs. The Indian professor's fluency in the local language proved invaluable, opening doors and facilitating our quest. Finally, we managed to withdraw eighty thousand rupees, although we were still short by forty thousand rupees.

In consultation with Indra, we devised a plan to return to Phuentsholing the following day, just before my last bus to Paro. As the day drew to a close, I diligently packed my belongings, preparing for the next leg of my journey.

Indra arrived at the guesthouse promptly at six o'clock, his silhouette visible in the soft morning light. As the Indian professor and I clambered into his car, the familiar terrain of the Phuentsholing highway unfolded before us. Our conversation was replaced with a reverent silence, as if we were collectively gathering ourselves after yesterday's whirlwind adventure.

We arrived at the bank just as the clock struck nine o'clock. The humdrum of morning activity was already in full swing. I managed to withdraw another forty thousand rupees. Success was in the air—a tangible, palpable entity that seemed to follow us as we drove to the largest enterprise in Bhutan for my interview with the general manager.

As the minutes slipped past, our conversation with the general manager wove an enchanting tapestry of shared experiences and insights, also illuminating the magic that is Bhutan. Another successful interview had been added to the narrative of this extraordinary journey.

With the clock striking ten, we climbed back into Indra's car, our sights set on Gedu. But we didn't set out for there before Pabi, with her characteristic warmth, insisted that I eat before embarking on the bus journey. We ate in hurried gulps, our laughter echoing in the room as we cleaned our plates. In front of the imposing façade of the GCBS, we captured our final moments in a few photographs—snapshots of an unforgettable time.

As I was boarding the bus, an avalanche of emotion overcame me. I cried. I wept openly, my tears those of the child within me bidding farewell to her parents and her hometown. But even as the tears streamed down my face, I made a silent promise: *I will be back.*

My journey took an unexpected turn when I flew to Delhi. The bureaucratic arms of immigration denied me entry, leaving me in a strange state of limbo. However, serendipity had a card to play, and I found myself in the company of the prince.

2.15 HRH Prince of Bhutan of the Royal Family

My fortuitous encounter with HRH Prince Jigyel Ugyen Wangchuck, a member of Bhutan's esteemed royal family, unfolded after I was denied entry at the New Delhi airport. Druk Air had no choice but to take me back to Bhutan as the prince was waiting for me, I was told. As we found ourselves in the luxurious first-class cabin, I couldn't resist the opportunity to engage in an impromptu interview with the prince. It turned out that he had just completed his royal duties representing his brother at the Commonwealth Games in New Delhi, adding an air of significance to our conversation.

HRH Prince Jigyel Ugyen Wangchuck, the heir presumptive to the throne of Bhutan until 2016, when his nephew was born, had received his education at prestigious institutions, including Yangchenphug Higher Secondary School and Choate Rosemary Hall in Wallingford, Connecticut, USA. He further pursued his studies in history and politics at St Peter's College, Oxford, in the United Kingdom. Notably, the prince shared responsibilities with his siblings, often representing the king at official ceremonies worldwide, including the Thirteenth Olympics Congress in Copenhagen and the Nineteenth Commonwealth Games in Delhi. In addition, both the prince and his sister, Princess Sonam Dechan, served on the executive board of the Tarayana Foundation, an organisation founded by their mother, Queen Ashi Dorji Wangmo, dedicated to combating poverty in Bhutan.

Seated in the elegant surroundings of Seat 1A on the Drukair flight, Prince Jigyel exuded a sense of ease despite the delay caused by my presence as a researcher. When I approached him with a request that he share his insights on the principles of gross national happiness (GNH) and its implications for entrepreneurship, he graciously accepted. After a brief interaction with his bodyguard, he settled comfortably into his first-class seat, ready for our conversation.

Throughout the interview, HRH Prince Jigyel Ugyen Wangchuck remained composed, imparting his personal perspective while clarifying that his opinions were distinct from those of the Prime Minister and his father, the Fourth King. He explained, "GNH serves as a set of guiding principles that can only be fully realized in certain countries. For instance, it may be too late for countries like India, the USA, and the UK to implement GNH, as it would necessitate significant environmental changes. However, certain regions in China, the Maldives, and Nepal could potentially embrace the GNH principles."

Expounding further, the prince highlighted the importance of good governance as a crucial component of GNH, also expressing concern about the misdirection observed in many Western countries. He cautioned against political promises of delivering GNH concepts, as these could be misleading. According to the prince, the need for specific indicators to measure progress towards GNH is debatable. He suggested, "When moving from point A to point B, one should focus on understanding the path towards the destination rather than incessantly measuring one's position." As GNH had garnered significant media attention, the prince noted that countries like Canada and France were currently striving to embodying GNH ideals.

Undoubtedly, further research is required to explore the feasibility of implementing GNH philosophies in various countries. It is through such exploration that entrepreneurs can potentially harness the power of the four E's to drive their individual contributions to society and the broader world. The intersection of GNH and entrepreneurship holds promising possibilities, warranting deeper investigation and thoughtful consideration.

The prince's warmth and generosity led me to stay at a Drukair employee's house, a refuge from the storm of uncertainty. From there, my journey took me from Paro to Bangkok, then on to Hong Kong and finally to Charles de Gaulle Airport in Paris. As I traced my path across the globe, I realized that each location was not merely a geographical point, but a chapter in my story—a testament to the unpredictable, exhilarating, sometimes heartbreaking, but always enlightening adventure of life.

2.16 Happiness Is ... Living in the Present

Bhutan, where the monasteries whisper ancient secrets to the winds, where the landscape undulates like a divine dream, cradles a humble haven—Kharchu Monastery. Here, spiritual wisdom blooms like rare blue poppies amidst the mountains. An accidental entrepreneur, I found myself within this oasis of tranquillity, entwining the path of my odyssey with the teachings of a Rinpoche whose words evoked both the brilliance of the present moment and the imperatives of conscientious living.

"Harmony with the now," the Rinpoche shared, "is the secret wellspring of happiness." As I sat under the flickering glow of butter lamps, the Rinpoche's words danced through the monastery. "Your heart yearns for what it already holds, not for what remains elusive in the ever-moving ether of tomorrow." His voice, a chorus with the hymn of the wind, embedded itself in the chambers of my heart.

We are all, as he suggested, masters of our present. Not of the unseen future, not of the fading past, but of the tangible, living, pulsating present. Our minds may dream of a time to come or may regret a time that has passed, but our existence, our very being, is rooted in the here and now. It is in the quiet mindfulness of our current state and in appreciating our current resources, our current circumstances, that we can find true satisfaction and true happiness.

And, as this Rinpoche implored, we must recognise that our environment, Mother Earth, is an integral part of our present. It offers us solace, nourishment, and beauty; it demands our respect, our care, and our appreciation. The changes he spoke of—the shrinking winters, the milder seasons—are cries from the heart of our planet. We who bask in moderate climates may overlook these subtle shifts, but they echo with growing intensity elsewhere in the world.

Fifty years ago, the winters of Bhutan were a dazzling spectacle of crystal clarity and biting frost. Today, the winters hum a softer tune. Our planet speaks to us through these changes, reminding us of our responsibility, our duty as its custodians. "The desecration of nature," Rinpoche warned, "is a callous disregard of our present, an ignorance of the delicate balance between living and simply existing."

As the sun painted the sky with the hues of its departing glory, I was left with these pearls of wisdom. To live in the present, to appreciate what we have, to recognise the subtle shifts of our environment, to understand our role in the cosmic ballet of existence—this is the path to true happiness. This is the path that unfurls within the shadow of the Kharchu Monastery, guiding lost souls and accidental entrepreneurs towards a fulfilling, conscious life.

In the following days, I carried the Rinpoche's words with me, mulling over each syllable like a prayer bead between my fingers. Each moment was a gift, an opportunity to fully inhabit the present. And as I moved through my days, I noticed the unique rhythm of Bhutan, a tempo set by the heartbeat of Mother Nature herself. Here, I realized, I was truly living in the present, alive to the spirit of every fleeting moment, every shifting cloud, every chorus of the wind.

I began to realize the expansiveness of gratitude. In Western culture, we're often consumed by the desire to obtain more in a relentless pursuit of the next big thing. But here in Bhutan, the Rinpoche reminded me to be grateful for what I already had. I started to see my life from a different perspective, to appreciate the ordinary miracles that graced my daily existence. And what I found was an untapped wellspring of joy, a profound contentment that transcended the materialistic confines of conventional notions of happiness.

But the teachings of the Rinpoche did not stop at personal happiness and gratitude. He urged me to understand my place in the world and my relationship with the environment, the living, breathing entity that cradles us all. He spoke of Bhutan's shortened winter, of the changes that the past fifty years had brought. In a world seemingly distanced from the consequences of climate change, the leader's words served as a poignant reminder that every corner of the earth is feeling the impact. Every creature, every tree, every river—they are our brothers and sisters in this grand tapestry of existence, and they are suffering.

Bhutan, with its majestic peaks and ancient forests, reminded me of the silent language of nature. Every fluttering leaf, every snowcapped mountain, and every whispering brook told me a story of harmony and balance, of respect and reverence, of love and care. Yet, we are slowly losing this language. We are gradually forgetting how to listen, how to understand, how to respond.

It struck me then that happiness, true happiness, is not simply a personal quest: it's a collective journey that we must embark on as inhabitants of this beautiful planet. It's about embracing the present, cherishing what we have, and recognising our responsibility towards our shared home. It's about understanding that our well-being is intrinsically linked to the health of our environment.

As I sat in the heart of the Kharchu Monastery, under the gentle gaze of the Rinpoche, I knew I had discovered a new blueprint for living. It was a map to a richer, more fulfilling existence, drawn not in grand ambitions and material pursuits, but in mindful presence, heartfelt gratitude, and compassionate stewardship of our precious earth.

Day by day, the teachings of the Rinpoche at Kharchu Monastery continued to unravel. Each word was like a stitch that brought about a more profound understanding of life, revealing patterns of wisdom previously obscured. Each phrase revealed a different facet of happiness. An accidental entrepreneur I may have been, but a purposeful student I was becoming.

In the monastery's solemn chambers, the morning sun penetrated through ancient windows, casting a warm glow on the maroon robes of the monks in silent prayer. As their chants reverberated through the cool mountain air, I recognised another lesson: silence, a profound silence that allows the heart to listen, the mind to observe, and the soul to absorb the wisdom that is omnipresent.

This silence, I realized, is not merely the absence of sound, but the presence of an attentive, engaged awareness, an awareness that enables us to appreciate the beauty of the present, to express gratitude for the riches we often overlook, and to tune into the symphony of nature, which is growing fainter with each passing day because of our actions. In the silence, I understood that happiness is not the pursuit of an ever-receding horizon, but the realization and the cherishing of what is right here, right now.

In our hyperconnected world, we often find ourselves disconnected from our surroundings, detached from the beauty of the present moment, and estranged from the intricate ballet of nature that sustains us. As the Rinpoche shared stories of Bhutan's changing climate, of winters softened and altered over the decades, I realized the severity of our disconnection, the depth of our forgetfulness.

Our existence on this planet is not solitary but shared; our journey, not independent but intertwined. Our happiness, thus, is not an individual endeavour but a collective aspiration. It depends on our relationship with our environment and on our understanding and respect for the delicate interplay of life on earth.

To care for the environment is not merely to secure the future. It is to appreciate the present, to recognise our symbiotic relationship with the world around us, and to understand that our actions today ripple into the well-being of tomorrow. This mindfulness and responsibility towards our environment, our actions, and our present is the cornerstone of sustainable happiness. The teachings of the Rinpoche reminded me that we are, indeed, the caretakers of this present moment and of our shared home.

Thus, as I roamed the sacred halls of the Kharchu Monastery, the Rinpoche's wisdom danced in my mind. I began to see happiness not as a destination to be reached, but as a path to be walked, one made up of the stepping stones of presence, gratitude, and compassionate stewardship. I found a deeper resonance, a richer symphony of existence, and a more genuine understanding of my place in the cosmos right here in the heart of Bhutan under the guidance of a humble Rinpoche.

Tiger's Nest

My lungs felt thin as the air atop the cliffside where the Tiger's Nest Temple—or as the Bhutanese call it, Paro Taktsang—clung with a tenacity and tranquillity that was nothing short of divine. From the base close to the Paro airport, it looked like a white speck tucked into the emerald canvas of Bhutan's formidable mountains, intimidating and fascinating in equal measures.

My tour guide, Tenzin, had eyes full of mirth as he told me of a time when he guided a ninety-two-year-old woman up to the temple. "It took us nine hours," he confessed, "but she did not complain even once. She took it as a pilgrimage, a journey for her spirit as much as for her body." His gaze then turned to me, teasing yet earnest. "Now, why would a healthy person like you not even consider something as meaningful?"

His question left a poignant echo in my heart, an echo that began to fill my soul with an unspoken yearning. Why wouldn't I? Why was I letting the intimidating nature of the steep mountain terrain overshadow the profound journey that could potentially unfold?

So, I decided to do it. Not to prove something to Tenzin or even to myself, but to embark on a journey that symbolized so much more than a simple trek. It was a metaphor for life itself—intimidating and demanding, yet brimming with beauty and meaning.

As we started our ascent, my heart pounded in my chest as if it were attempting to break free. The first hour was a struggle against my own doubts and physical limitations. But as we progressed, something inside me began to shift. With every step I took, every puff of breath I released into the cool mountain air, I began to feel a sense of connection with the ground beneath my feet, with the nature around me, and with the very act of living.

The journey became a meditation, a communion with the present moment. I savoured the symphony of birdsong, the rustle of leaves in the wind, and the feel of the rugged terrain under my boots. I became acutely aware of the subtle changes in my body—the stretch of my muscles, the rhythm of my breath, the beating of my heart. It was as if I were discovering a new language—a language of existence, of being present, of living one step at a time.

My destination was the Tiger's Nest, but the journey ... the journey was life itself. It was an exercise in cherishing the moment while keeping an eye on the goal, namely, of living out values while seeking purpose and of realizing that the path to happiness lies not just in reaching the destination, but also in enjoying the journey.

As I stood before the majestic Tiger's Nest Temple, gasping in the thin air and basking in the sense of achievement, I realized this was the most profound lesson Bhutan had offered me. I was overcome not just by the country's grand temples or serene landscapes, but also by the wisdom and humility of its people, their respect for nature, and above all, their understanding of the delicate dance between purpose and the preciousness of the present.

Happiness, I realized, is indeed a place. But that place is not a physical destination, it is a state of mind. Living in happiness, not merely pursuing happiness, is a way of journeying through life.

Chapter 3

LOVE AND STRIFE IN CHINA

3.1 The Dragon's Embrace

It was January 2011. I found myself standing in the heart of Shanghai, the city known as the Dragon's Head for its pivotal role in China's economic prosperity. This city was now the new compass of my life, guiding me as the international dean of an international masters' of business administration (MBA) programme at a Chinese university.

There was a bite in the air, a hint of a winter past its prime, retreating reluctantly. A few snowflakes meandered down from the steely sky, adhering to the concrete underfoot. I was about to take my first steps onto the campus of Chinese university.

There is a grandeur to this place. The architecture, impressive in its size but modest in its austerity, embodies the spirit of relentless progression coupled with respectful remembrance of the past.

I found myself lost, but not in a bad way. There was a sense of wonder in getting lost within this sprawling labyrinth, giving me a chance to stumble upon untold stories hidden in each corner. Each building, each lecture hall, held a wealth of knowledge with eager students brimming with aspiration and professors armed with wisdom.

Once I stepped out from within the comforting walls of the campus, the city of Shanghai, one of the largest megapolises in the world, was a sight to behold. From the towering heights of Pudong's skyscrapers to the bustling streets of the Bund, it's a city of stark contrasts and the harmonious coexistence of tradition and modernity.

My last visit to China was in 2000. Since then, the country, and Shanghai in particular, had undergone a transformation that left me in awe. The pace of change was nearly tangible, like a heartbeat thrumming through the city streets. There was an air of entrepreneurial spirit, audacious and ambitious. High-flying entrepreneurs were making waves, injecting new ideas, and driving growth.

Gone were the days when the state was the main actor. It was now the orchestrator, providing the rhythm for a symphony made up of a diverse ensemble of private enterprises. The balance had shifted, and the state had taken on a supporting role, masterfully guiding this market economy while allowing individual talents to shine.

From the neon-lit billboards advertising the latest technology to the humble noodle shops serving recipes passed down through generations, Shanghai is a testament to the extraordinary transformation China has undergone. The city stands proudly, looking towards the future while carrying its past gracefully. As I prepared to play my part in this dynamic ecosystem, I couldn't help but feel a shiver of excitement, punctuated by the falling snowflakes.

So here I was, at the beginning of a new chapter in my life, ready to immerse myself in this vibrant landscape. Shanghai, with its beautiful complexity and paradoxes: I was here. Here's to new beginnings, to new experiences, and to the myriad stories waiting to be written.

The snowflake, on its solitary journey down to the ground, does not stop to wonder whether it is fit for the role of winter's ambassador. It simply is. But I, a mere mortal, was caught in an existential snowstorm, sifting through thoughts and doubts, questioning if I was the right person for this monumental task.

It had all happened in such a whirlwind way: the offer, my immediate acceptance. There had hardly been a breath of hesitation. But now, in the quiet aftermath, my heart was brimming with doubt. Was I the right person for this job? The role was akin to a bridge, linking two distinct cultures, two different academic systems. I was no academic, my résumé not one showing the typical pedigree one might expect of a university dean.

The director of L'École, with his soothing voice, was a balm to my doubts. "You are exactly the person we want," he had said, his words filled with a conviction that I had yet to accept. The role was not that of a mere cog in the academic machine, but was an ambassadorial position. I was to represent the French side in this Sino-French collaboration, working hand in hand with the Chinese university.

As I mulled over the director's words, I couldn't help but see the truth in them. I was a patchwork quilt of experiences and skills. My corporate background, consulting expertise, and teaching stint were threads of vibrant colours. My PhD credentials and my fluency in Mandarin were the intricate patterns woven through my quilt. My persona, my essence, was the backing, the binding that held all the pieces together. As the director had said, I possessed all the right ingredients.

As I looked out at the snow-covered campus, I saw the path laid out before me. I realized I was not an impostor stepping into the unknown. Instead, I was a bridge-builder, using my unique blend of experience to link two different worlds. I would draw on my past, leveraging my corporate nous, my academic rigour, my linguistic skills, and my personal tenacity to shape this role.

I found myself comforted by this realization. There was a shift in perspective, a tectonic movement in my understanding of myself and the role I was about to undertake. The initial doubt gave way to a new-found resolve. I would pour all of myself into this role. I vowed to bring every thread of my varied tapestry to this task, weaving a rich, beautiful, and enduring bridge between two nations.

Like the snowflake that doesn't question its journey, I accepted my path. With such resolution, the snowflakes ceased to be mere winter ambassadors, transforming instead into affirmations from the universe, guiding me, reassuring me that I was indeed on the right path.

The news was as sharp and unexpected as the chill of the January wind. The MBA programme was standing on the edge of a precipice. The glow of its glory seemed to dim in the face of an accreditation review that had not gone as hoped. Without the anchor of a globally recognised accredited status, the very foundations of the programme were at risk of crumbling. The *Financial Times* ranking as one of the top fifty MBA programmes in the world, a badge of honour the programme had worn proudly for the past decade, would vanish if accreditation was lost.

With each passing day, I could feel the heavy weight of this responsibility and the collective hope of the university community resting on my shoulders. Yet even though the task was enormous, I felt a faint flicker of excitement. A challenge, however formidable, was after all an opportunity, a chance to create and to cause change.

I stood at the helm of this rocky ship, armed with an arsenal of experience from my past. My background in compliance, business process engineering and standardized systems was the key. The past was a treasure chest full of wisdom and tools, ripe for the picking.

But this was not merely about ticking boxes and conforming to standards. It was about restoring faith, about proving that the MBA programme deserved its place among the world's top-ranked programmes. This was about not merely meeting standards, but exceeding them, setting new benchmarks and leaving an indelible mark on the global education landscape. It was about making the programme a model of consistency, quality, reliability, and validity. And above all, it was about infusing the programme with the spirit of international excellence, fostering a culture that would resonate in classrooms, faculty offices, and the hearts of our students.

In the quiet stillness of my office, I found myself contemplating this challenge, absorbing its magnitude. My heart echoed with the rhythm of resolve. With every pulse, I was reminded that this was not a task to be undertaken lightly. It required not just my skills and experience, but also my passion and commitment.

I resolved to dive headlong into this endeavour, to treat each day as a step towards our collective goal. As the international dean, my role was not just to guide, but also to inspire, and not just to enforce standards, but to embody them.

So I pledged to put every ounce of my expertise and heart into turning the tide. I was not just saving a programme; I was preserving a legacy, safeguarding a reputation, and creating a beacon for the students of tomorrow. The task was daunting, yes, but as I looked out my window at the snow-covered campus, I was filled with an unwavering determination. This was my calling. This was my mission. And I was ready.

Each day brought a new revelation, illuminating a new facet of my role that added richness to my understanding of this programme. The aspiring students, with their bright eyes and minds aglow with dreams, were my North Star. They were not just students, they were the heart and soul of this endeavour, the reason why I was here doing what I was doing.

As I delved deeper into the academic workings, I discovered an intriguing tapestry of cultures that coloured our programme. The Chinese faculty and their non-Chinese counterparts, both incredibly skilled in their respective realms, painted two vastly different pictures of academic thought and practice.

It was as though I were looking at two sides of a coin—one deeply rooted in the rich heritage of China, the other influenced by the global landscape of knowledge. The two groups had different research methods, varying teaching styles, and a distinct method of delivery. The contrasts were stark, a testament to the enduring influence of cultural and political ideologies spanning decades, if not millennia.

Yet, within this diversity, there was a need for consistency. For an international programme like ours, consistency was not just a necessity, it was our hallmark, our beacon. But how do you ensure that? How do you find the common ground amidst the complex interplay of culture, history, and ideology?

My mind spun like a compass needle, seeking the direction that would lead us to our goal. It wasn't just about having a consistent methodology on paper; it was also about weaving that consistency into the very fabric of our programme. It was about creating an academic environment where differences are celebrated, but never at the expense of the programme's unity and integrity.

I realized that my task wasn't about enforcing a rigid framework or erasing cultural imprints. No, it was about conducting a symphony that resonated with the unique notes of each culture while retaining a consistent melody. It was about striking a balance between honouring the individuality of each academic practice and nurturing a shared commitment to excellence.

The answer lay not in diluting the differences, but in using them to enrich our programme, to make it a mosaic of global academic practices unified by a shared vision. The onus was on me to facilitate a dialogue, a fusion of ideas, that would give rise to a teaching philosophy that was dynamic yet consistent, innovative yet grounded, diverse yet unified.

And so, I found myself standing at the crossroads of culture and consistency, history and the future, individuality and unity. This was my quest, not just to maintain the accreditation status, but also to breathe life into an academic vision that celebrated diversity while championing consistency. It was a task that required not just skill but also sensitivity, not just knowledge but also wisdom. But as I looked into the hopeful eyes of our students, I knew it was a quest worth embarking on.

In Shanghai, my days took on a rhythm of their own. They were a dance, a delicate ballet of obligations, encounters, and revelations that kept me constantly on my toes. From the moment I opened my eyes in the morning, I was swept up in the flow of the day, every step I took echoing the purpose and potential of my new role.

The soft morning light filtered in through the hotel window as I awoke, pulling me gently into the dawn of a new day. I started my morning routine with a mug of warm tea, cradling the cup in my hands, feeling the warmth seep into my bones, into my consciousness. It was a small ritual, a moment of quiet before the day began in earnest.

With the tea warming my veins, I reached for my device, then begin immersing myself in a sea of emails. As I read through the messages, my mind was a whirlwind, planning, strategizing, absorbing. The morning hours in the hotel, amidst the quiet solitude, were when I felt most connected to the global network in terms of my work.

As I arrived at the MBA office, the digital world receded, replaced by the vibrant bustle of campus life. Here, I was not simply a dean but a mentor, a friend, a listener. My time was not spent behind a desk but on my feet, walking around the campus, engaging with students and potential students. These interactions, brimming with youthful vigour and curiosity, fuelled me. The palpable energy of ambition and dreams was invigorating.

The afternoons often found me sipping tea with faculty. Over lunch, we navigated through the academic labyrinth, addressing issues, celebrating victories, and brainstorming solutions. The meal was not merely sustenance for the body, but a nourishing blend of ideas and camaraderie for the soul.

As the day faded into evening, the city of Shanghai, bathed in the warm glow of twilight, played host to a different set of engagements. My evenings were a carousel of scheduled events, a whirl of meet-and-greets, discussions, and networking. Chambers of commerce, alumni, international faculty, guest speakers—each encounter was a chance to learn, to build bridges, to strengthen the fabric of our programme.

Dinner often saw me in the company of Chinese business leaders, their insights as enriching as the exquisite flavours on my plate. I found myself not just eating but feasting, not just on the food, but also on the wisdom, the stories, and the shared experiences that were offered.

Through it all, I was constantly learning, constantly evolving. Each email, each conversation, each meeting, was a thread in the vibrant tapestry of my Shanghai experience. As the day wound down and I retreated back to the tranquillity of my hotel room, I found myself reflecting on the day, the lessons learned, the connections made. And with the city of Shanghai quietly humming in the background, I readied myself for the dance of another day.

3.2 In the Throes of Power

I have always fancied myself a bit of a five-star hotel connoisseur, someone who appreciates the finer details, the understated elegance, the flawless service. With this being the case, it was a considerable jolt to me when I swallowed the bitter pill of reality: academics, I was told, only stay at three-star hotels. Even the presidents of universities—the captains of these academic ships—at best graduated to a four-star berth.

It wasn't about the luxury or the lack thereof. It was about adjusting my expectations and recalibrating to accommodate for norms. It was a little like walking a mile in well-worn shoes after years of wearing bespoke ones. I was no longer just a visitor but an inhabitant of this world—the world of academia—that had its own unspoken rules and subtle hierarchies.

When night fell over Shanghai, I'd retreat to my less-than-five-star sanctuary. Alone in my room with the hush of the city outside my window, I turned to my unlikely companion—the television. It was not for entertainment, but for understanding, for grounding myself in the realities of the world outside the university campus.

On my first night, I happened upon a news story. A truck driver, it was reported, had been caught without a valid vehicle registration during a routine check at a toll road. A small violation, I thought, perhaps deserving of a small fine or a reprimand.

The second night brought a startling revelation: the truck driver was not just fined but also sentenced to jail for the offence. I blinked at the screen, taken aback by the severity of the punishment.

The third day brought a flurry of public outcry, a wave of dissent against what many deemed to be an unjustified punishment. I could feel the city's pulse and its collective heart beating with indignation.

And then on the fourth day, there was an unexpected twist. The same judge who had delivered the harsh sentence had been reassigned to a remote region. I sat back in my chair, a silent spectator of this unfolding drama, with each day a new act, a new revelation.

It wasn't just a news story. It was a window into the landscape of

Chinese politics and law, a nuanced dance of power, perception, and public sentiment. It was an education in itself, a lesson taught, not in a classroom, but through the flickering screen of a television.

I turned off the TV that fourth night, a sense of comprehension settling in. I realized I had just witnessed a play of power and punishment, with public outcry and retribution. I felt an understanding seeping into me, a realization of the intricate dynamics of this new world I was part of. But also understanding that this was only one aspect of a multifaceted society, I resolved to focus on my mission—the university, the students, the academic bridge I was to build.

From that night on, I never again turned on the news in China. The television returned to being just an object in the room, and I, a visitor in this land, returned to my purpose—academia. I left the drama of the news to play out without me. I had my own story to write, my own part to play. I was no longer merely a spectator; I was an actor on this academic stage, a player in the grander scheme of international education. And I was ready to give it my all.

One day, my wanderings took me to the heart of the city, to People's Park. The morning sun cast long, playful shadows on the park's manicured lawns and quiet corners, with the soft hum of city life reverberating in the background. There, amidst the tranquil greenery, I stumbled upon an unexpected spectacle—a curious gathering of elders, each holding a sign.

Intrigued, I drifted closer, drawn in by the quiet intensity of the scene. Each sign bore a photo of a young man or woman, usually somewhere between late twenties and early thirties. Realization dawned upon me as I began to read the information meticulously listed below each photo: academic qualifications, home ownership, car ownership, monthly salary. It was like peering into a personal advertisement, a résumé for life—a different kind of park activity, indeed.

This was a live Chinese matchmaking show right in the heart of People's Park. Not one conducted by a television crew for the glossy TV screen, but one done out here, under the open sky. It was a captivating, poignant testament to the social changes that had been sweeping the country.

I watched the scene unfold, reflecting on China's one-child policy as I read the placards. These singles, both blessed and burdened their unique status, found themselves navigating the complex terrain of companionship. Without siblings to spar with or with whom to learn the art of give-and-take, many of them struggled to cultivate those fundamental skills in their relationships.

Beyond the personal realm, the social structure added to the complexity. Spaces for social gatherings were few and far between because of the regulations placed on large groups of people, and the gruelling work hours left little room for pursuing personal connections.

Standing in the People's Park amidst the quiet desperation of these matchmaking elders, I felt a surge of empathy. I was witnessing not just a matchmaking spectacle, but also a social panorama, a human tableau borne out of policy, culture, and generations of tradition.

As I walked away, the park resumed its placid demeanour, the morning sun bathing it in a golden hue. But the images stayed with me, a poignant reminder of the country's journey, of the personal narratives woven into the fabric of Chinese society. The matchmakers of People's Park had given me a glimpse into a world not often seen, offering a perspective not often shared. And for that I was grateful.

Pudong, the vibrant hub of Shanghai, hums with an energy all its own. A lively jumble of bars, hotels, and restaurants, its skyscrapers punch through the sky with assertive certainty. Yet, if you look closely, you see that a hint of the West appears in its modern architecture, whispering stories of the time when foreign powers held sway over the Chinese economy at the turn of the twentieth century.

But these stories, much like the architecture, are layered, complex. For a period of time, Shanghai's history with foreigners turned dark, like a summer day suddenly overtaken by a menacing thunderstorm. From a dance of commerce and culture, it devolved into a battle of power and pride. The Chinese, once a proud civilization with a rich history, were derogatorily referred to as the "sickness of the East", a title that stung and caused both humiliation and resentment.

Then there was opium, a tool of control and subjugation introduced by foreign powers. It flowed through the streets of China, seeping into homes and lives, leaving in its wake a trail of addiction and despair—an episode that left deep scars on the Chinese psyche, serving as a reminder of a time when the Chinese people were not masters of their own destiny.

Yet, like a phoenix rising from its ashes, China overcame these dark times. With the advent of the current communist government, there was a noticeable shift. Western concession regions in Shanghai were renamed with Chinese names as if to rewrite a history that had been penned by foreign hands—an act of reclaiming, of restoring, and of healing, a conscious effort to wipe away the reminders of foreign occupation as if washing away the remnants of a bad dream.

On this day, as I walked through the bustling streets of Pudong, I was surrounded by the energy of a city that had moved beyond its past without forgetting it, a city that had learned from its history, using it as a stepping stone to leap into a future of its own making. The foreign echoes remain, but they are mere footnotes to a story that is now undeniably, unapologetically Chinese. The architecture tells a tale, but it is no longer a story of occupation. It is a story of resilience, of transformation, of a city and a nation that stood up and took control of its destiny.

Across the waters of the mighty Yangpu River, another spectacle emerged in the form of Puxi. Dotted with sky-kissing high-rises, this was the financial district, the beating heart of China's pulsating economy. The modern architecture, imposing and unyielding, stood as a determined eraser, scrubbing away any trace of a Third World past. Instead, it heralded the birth of a new economic and financial titan.

This was a place of transformation and a symbol of ambition and progress. It is a testament to China's metamorphosis, a caterpillar-turned-butterfly, resplendent and undeniably powerful. As a Chinese descendant, I couldn't help but feel a surge of pride swelling in my chest, a pride that every Chinese person should rightfully possess. Shanghai, in all its modern majesty, was the epicentre of this new China, and it was awe-inspiring.

One day, under the cloudy skies of Shanghai, I decided to share this spectacle with my French colleagues, including the director. I wanted them to witness first-hand the prowess of this resurgent giant, to stand in the shadows of its architectural marvels and feel the palpable energy of ambition and progress.

As we traversed the bustling streets of Puxi, the sky opened up in a gentle drizzle. Rather than seek shelter, I found myself irresistibly drawn towards the rain. Like a child unburdened by conventions, I started to dance. The raindrops, cool against my skin, were a symphony of renewal, each one a testament to the rejuvenation of my ancestral land.

As I twirled and swayed, drenched and carefree, I felt a profound connection to this place and also a love interwoven with respect and admiration. My heart swelled with a joy that was as profound as it was ineffable. It was a feeling of belonging, of pride, of witnessing something much bigger than myself.

I danced under the Shanghai rain, my heart beating in rhythm with the city's pulse. This was my ancestors' heritage, vibrant and full of life, echoing through the high-rises of Puxi. No words could capture the depth of what I felt at that moment. In the rain-soaked streets of Shanghai, amidst the towering monuments to progress, I celebrated my Chinese roots, my heritage, my lineage. I was home, and it was magnificent.

There are places in Shanghai where the international hum is particularly loud. Xin Tian Di is one such area, a popular haunt for expats and tourists alike. The old French Concession, which has since shed its colonial name, is another one, a charming district brimming with character and history.

One Saturday night after a late dinner with my Australian and French colleagues, I encountered a scene that would haunt me for many days to come. As we left the restaurant close to midnight, a group of children materialized from the shadows, their tiny hands reaching out, their innocent eyes filled with a despair far too mature for their age. They hugged my legs, their fragile bodies pressing against me, begging for money.

A surge of sadness washed over me. These little souls, barely older than my own children, should have been at home tucked safely into their beds, dreaming of school and play and all the innocent pursuits of childhood. Instead, they were out here in the cold night, their tiny hands outstretched, their childhood stolen.

Anger bubbled up within me, an angry mama bear provoked. I rounded on the adults who hovered at the periphery, their faces impassive. With a shout, I demanded to know why these children weren't in bed, why they weren't preparing for school like every other child their age.

But before I could say more, my friends, one on either side, took firm hold of my arms. Ignoring my protests, they steered me towards a waiting taxi, their faces grim. As they hastily bundled me into the vehicle, they shared a piece of harsh reality—those adults were thugs, cruel manipulators who used these helpless children as tools to extract money from empathetic tourists. They were dangerous, not to be crossed.

The car door shut with a final thud, cutting me off from the heart-rending scene. As the taxi sped away, tears streamed down my face, each drop a silent accusation of the unjust people in the world. The images of those begging children etched themselves into my mind, a painful reminder of a harsh reality lurking beneath the glittering veneer of Shanghai's progress.

And so, I cried. I cried for the stolen childhoods, for the innocence lost, for the world's injustices that are too often hidden in the shadows. It was a night that profoundly shook me, a raw encounter with a reality that I wished did not exist. But exist it did, and it was a truth I could not, would not, turn away from.

In the midst of Shanghai's ultramodern façade, I found myself yearning for a glimpse of something intrinsically Chinese, a touch of the past, a moment of connection to a time and a culture that seemed increasingly obscured by towering skyscrapers and glinting glass façades. I sought a place where I could savour the richness of Chinese history and culture, which had been carefully woven through the centuries. And that's when I found myself at the gates of the enchanting Yu Garden.

Conceived by Fuson, a Chinese conglomerate, Yu Garden is an enchanting paradox nestled amidst the urban sprawl of Shanghai, a slice of tranquillity carved out in the chaos, a pocket of history in a city forever sprinting towards the future. This is where Shanghai's soul lives—not in the high-rises, but in the quiet corners, where the past is lovingly preserved.

The garden's architecture is a marvel, harking back to the Ming dynasty style. It is a labyrinth of winding pathways leading through a number of pavilions, rockeries, ponds, and chambers, each corner revealing a new vista, each turn a different perspective. No space is wasted; each inch is thoughtfully designed to house either delicate flora, or a serene water feature, or a traditional Chinese structure.

And then there are the walls, the famous "dragon walls". Serpentine and grand, they stretch across the garden, seeming to both protect and enclose the serenity within. Encrusted with ceramic shards, they portray vivid dragons, symbolizing the power and grandeur of the imperial family.

Even more impressive is how the garden came about. It was a labour of love, a father's gift to his son. Pan Yunduan, a Ming dynasty government officer, spent nearly two decades and all his life savings to create this garden as a peaceful retirement abode for his father. This place, then, is not just a garden; it is a testament to filial love and respect, a tangible manifestation of a revered Chinese virtue.

The garden's attractiveness lies not just in its beauty, but also in its resonance. It sings a silent song of the old world, a melody composed of culture, history, and tradition. Amidst the water lilies, the graceful arches of the bridges, and the serpentine walls, one feels an unspoken dialogue between the past and the present, an intimacy that whispers stories of yesteryear.

In Yu Garden, I found what I had been yearning for: a place where I could touch the past, where the pulse of ancient China still beat strong. Amidst the relentless march of modernity, Yu Garden stands as a sanctuary of Chinese culture, a serene testament to a rich and vibrant past. It is a reminder that while Shanghai's skyline may be ever changing, the nation's soul remains rooted in its history.

Tibet

In search of more profound cultural experiences, I took a flight that carried me away from the bustling metropolis of Shanghai and into the heart of Tibet. The altitude took hold of me as soon as I stepped off the plane, making me feel dizzy and a bit disoriented. There was an ethereal quality to the air, a thinness that, combined with the grandeur of the surrounding mountains, made me feel both insignificant and part of something much greater.

A Tibetan woman, our guide, and a man, our driver, greeted me with warm smiles, their faces weathered by the mountain sun and the harsh Tibetan winds. They whisked me away to my hotel, situated on a historical street that had seen both life's simplest joys and its most profound sorrows. It was here on this very street where Tibetan monks had set themselves ablaze, their desperate cries for freedom echoing off the mountain peaks.

The week I arrived marked the anniversary of this tragic event, and there was a feeling of solemnity in the Tibetan air, which seemed to carry the echo of the monks' sacrifice, their bravery, and their unyielding demand for freedom. It was a hushed reminder that amidst Tibet's stunning natural beauty was a heartbreaking history.

Before my trip, I had been warned not to bring any books into Tibet related to the Dalai Lama. Despite the years that had passed, the presence of the Dalai Lama, the Tibetan spiritual leader in exile, still stirred up deep emotions and tensions in the region. The topic was taboo, a reminder of a political wound that was yet to fully heal.

The act of self-immolation by Tibetan monks, which had occurred on this very street, was a heart-wrenching testament to their struggle. This wasn't a mere protest; it was an act of desperate defiance, a cry for help that was both terrifyingly personal and powerfully political.

These monks, adorned in their maroon- and saffron-coloured robes, doused themselves in gasoline before striking a match. Their bodies ignited in a horrific blaze, a macabre spectacle of searing pain and resolute determination. Their faces, usually calm and serene during their meditations, contorted in agony, but their cries weren't just of physical suffering:

they were an outcry against the oppression they felt, a desperate plea for the world to acknowledge their plight, a yearning for the return of their spiritual leader, the Dalai Lama.

To see this street where such tragic events had unfolded brought a wave of solemn respect and aching sadness. To be in a place of such sacrifice, to tread where those monks had once walked, lent a stark reality to the struggle that still exists in Tibet.

In the crisp Tibetan air, beneath the watchful gaze of the towering mountains, I found myself humbled. I was a witness to a history both incredibly beautiful and deeply scarred and was walking on ground sanctified by the ultimate sacrifice of monks whose only crime was their yearning for freedom. The magnitude of their sacrifice and of their courage spoke poignantly of their indomitable spirits and their enduring call for peace and liberation.

Having successfully checked in and quickly stowed my bag in what was said to be the best hotel in town, I felt an urgent need to acclimate to my new environment. The high altitude of Tibet was already making its presence known, the effects slyly creeping into my body. My guide, sensing my discomfort, suggested we try a local remedy: Tibetan tea and dumplings, known to soothe altitude sickness.

Once I returned to my room after the meal, a foreign object caught my eye. Sitting in the otherwise pristine ashtray was a used cigarette butt. My heart fluttered in alarm, and I immediately rushed to check my belongings. Passport—untouched. Money—intact. Relief swept over me, but it left a lingering trace of unease.

Earlier, I had been elated when the hotel manager mentioned that I had been upgraded to one of the most spacious rooms. A rare treat. Yet, as I looked around, my delight began to wane. The room was undoubtedly generous in size, but it felt oddly exposed. It was situated in such a way that it faced another, taller building across the street, its large, wraparound windows making me feel as if I were on display.

Throwing caution to the wind, I threw open the curtains, ready to embrace the view. That's when I saw them—two small, jagged openings in the glass, stark against the cityscape beyond. Bullet holes.

The chilling reality struck me like a lightning bolt. Someone had fired a gun at this room. My fingers reached out to touch the ruptures in the glass, confirming my fear. The indents were sharper on the inside, indicating the bullets had come from outside in. I felt a shiver down my spine, a visceral reaction to these tangible remnants of violence.

It was clear then that I was not just a tourist in a far-off land. I was a foreigner in a place of profound political unrest. The bullet holes, the warnings about carrying books on the Dalai Lama, the tragic history of self-immolations—all were stark reminders of the tension simmering beneath the surface.

With a sinking heart, I drew the curtains shut, attempting to shield myself from the disquieting reality outside. My sanctuary felt tainted, its lavishness now a stark contrast to the tumultuous history etched on its windows.

There was no romance in this revelation, no spiritual awakening, only the cold, hard touch of reality. As the adrenaline subsided, a wave of exhaustion washed over me. I took a sleeping pill, lay down on the bed, and let sleep pull me under, while outside, the pulse of Tibet continued to beat, as complex and mysterious as ever.

The next morning, I confided in my guide about the bullet holes and the lingering fear they'd left me with. She offered me a long, knowing look but said nothing in return, her silence speaking volumes.

Despite the unsettling start, I had a destination, one that had drawn me to Tibet in the first place: the Potala Palace. Dubbed the "Palace in the Sky", it is a majestic structure standing proudly against the stark landscape, its red and white walls contrasting vividly with the blue sky.

It is a testament to Tibetan architecture and a symbol of the nation's rich cultural history, perched atop the Marpori hill, seemingly reaching out to the heavens. Its grandeur is undeniable with intricate carvings adorning its walls, while the inside houses countless artefacts, scriptures, and statues. It's a palpable symbol of Tibetan Buddhism and a breathtaking tribute to the spiritual devotion of the people who practise it.

The journey up to the palace was another matter. With the combination of thin air and an elevation that left me breathless, I found myself stopping halfway, gasping for breath and watching as people of all ages clambered past. I remember wondering how the elderly or disabled would ever manage to make such a climb.

My guide offered a simple answer. Elders, she explained, were often carried up to the monastery by the younger generation, an act of devotion and respect. But the more I observed, the more I became aware of the youthful faces of the monks. Their cherubic faces lacked the wisdom lines I associated with Tibetan monks.

In hushed tones, my guide confided in me that these were not true monks, but stand-ins hired by the Chinese government. The real monks, she said, had been forced out of Lhasa and were now scattered throughout the region.

This was another blow to the romanticized image I had held of Tibet. The Potala Palace, the spiritual home of the Dalai Lama, had become a stage for a false performance.

The Dalai Lama himself was exiled in 1959, amidst a failed uprising against Chinese rule. He had to flee Tibet, leaving behind his beloved Potala Palace, his people, and his homeland. For the decades that followed, he has been leading the Tibetan government-in-exile from Dharamshala, India, continuing his spiritual and political work, advocating for the rights of the Tibetan people and the preservation of Tibetan culture.

Being in the Potala Palace, knowing that the Dalai Lama himself was unable to step foot in it, was a haunting reminder of this history. The grandeur of the palace was tinged with the sadness of its history and the ongoing struggle of the Tibetan people.

In the afternoon, our usual driver had to step away to attend to some family matter, leaving just my guide and me to explore the bustling local market. We wove our way through the labyrinth of stalls, revelling in the colours, sounds, and smells of Tibetan culture that was so beautifully displayed there.

When it was time to return to the hotel, we hailed a taxi. The driver seemed like any other local, polite but mostly quiet, keeping his eyes on the road. But halfway through the journey, he turned to my guide, apprehension written on his face.

"Who is she?" he asked in Mandarin, nodding towards me.

The guide reassured him, "She's just a tourist."

"But then why is she being followed by the nonuniform police?" the driver pressed, his voice barely above a whisper.

My guide's eyes flickered to the rearview mirror. She hushed the driver and fell silent, a stern look on her face. I noticed her gaze occasionally darting back to the car following us. The atmosphere in the cab suddenly felt charged, and an icy shiver of realization crept up my spine.

Suddenly, I was seeing the scenes from the past few days in a new light: the cigarette butt in my room, the guide's silence about the bullet holes, and now a suspicious car trailing us.

All the while, I had been keeping a secret of my own. Although I'd been speaking English throughout the trip, I actually understood Mandarin. A skill I'd thought would be a simple convenience had now become a critical tool. I was now part of a conversation I wasn't supposed to hear, privy to a side of this journey I wasn't meant to see.

The remaining ride was spent in tense silence, the earlier warmth of the day having been replaced by a chilly fear. Was I really being followed? And if so, why? A thousand questions raced through my mind, each one making the situation feel more surreal.

In the privacy of my hotel room, I found myself glancing at the bullet holes again, a constant reminder of the stark reality that was starting to unfold. I was a foreigner in a land marked by turmoil, a place where even tourists might not escape the watchful eyes of those who wielded power. It was a chilling prospect, a suspenseful undercurrent to an already complex journey.

The next morning, we found ourselves back in the grounds of the Jokhang Temple, the spiritual heart of the city, adjacent to the imposing Potala Palace. Amidst the temple's stone terraces and gilded roofs, a mundane and, for me, shocking event unfolded.

An elderly woman—a grandmother, perhaps—pulled down the pants of a young boy of about three, directing him to relieve himself right there in the middle of the bustling square. As if the act itself wasn't surprising enough, once it was done, she simply left the mess there, carrying the child away as if it were the most natural thing to do in the world.

I was left there, gaping and incredulous, as people simply moved around the offending pile unfazed. The guide noticed my stunned expression and proceeded to explain a cultural phenomenon that was beyond my understanding.

Many Chinese couples from rural areas leave their homes, she explained, seeking better pay and opportunities in the bustling cities. In their pursuit of a better life, they often leave their children behind in the care of grandparents until they reach school age, typically around six years old.

This reality left me with a heavy heart. These children spend their formative years without their parents, instead being guided and nurtured by their grandparents. Their mothers and fathers become distant figures who visit once a year during the Spring Festival, previously known as the Chinese New Year.

This pattern of parenting has complex social implications. These children, while showered with the doting love of their grandparents, miss out on the unique bond that forms between parent and child. Their world view and understanding of relationships can be markedly different from those of children who grow up with their parents.

The incident at the square was just a drop in the ocean, a hint of the deeper issue, a tiny reflection of the far-reaching effects of economic migration on familial bonds. The child's being encouraged to defecate in public was not just an act of seeming disregard for public cleanliness; it was an echo of a disconnect between the traditional rural upbringing with grandparents and the rapidly modernizing cities where the children's parents were.

Standing there in the square, amidst the grandeur of the Jokhang Temple and the mundane scene that had just unfolded, I felt an unfamiliar pang. It was a potent mix of wonder, confusion, and sympathy, a cocktail that only intensified when I dived deep into the intricate sea of a culture so profoundly different from my own.

From the heart of Lhasa, we ventured outwards, journeying to a monastery located two hours away. Sera Monastery, a serene refuge, revealed itself to be an intriguing symphony of sound and movement, something that I had never encountered anywhere else.

The first thing that struck me was the volume—a cacophony that at first seemed chaotic. Laughter, shouting, and the sharp, definitive claps of hands echoed from the stone walls of the complex, lending the place a lively, carnival-like ambiance.

This wasn't the quiet, contemplative image of a monastery I had in my mind. Here, Buddhist learning happened through spirited debate, each monk an active participant in a loud and passionate dance of thought. The boisterous intellectual engagements spilled out into the open as they took place in the monastery's courtyards, under the open sky.

Each debate was a spectacle. A monk would propose a point, his words forceful and direct. In response, his partner would refute or support the argument, punctuating each point with a forceful clap of his hands. It was as if the clapping intensified their words, serving as a kinetic echo of the verbal argument.

These debates weren't just intellectual exchanges; they were physical performances, punctuated with theatrical gestures that underlined the points being made. There was a choreographed elegance to the monks' hand movements, from the expressive arch of the fingers to the dramatic slice of a hand through the air.

As an observer, I was swept up in the rhythm of their discourse. Each movement, each word, each clap, was a piece of a larger, vibrant mosaic of dialogue and discovery. Hundreds of maroon-robed monks congregated in the courtyard, their voices weaving an incredible auditory tapestry that resounded with their dedication and fervour.

The spectacle was a beautiful paradox—monks deep in intellectual thought, yet full of vigour and animation, and a monastery resounding with spirited noise, yet profoundly immersed in the pursuit of knowledge and wisdom. An embodiment of contrasts, the Sera Monastery was a testament to the harmony that can exist between apparent contradictions. I stood, captivated and moved, amidst the swirling dance of debate with the clapping hands and resonating voices. Here, in a monastery high up in the mountains of Tibet, I had stumbled upon a spectacle as grand and riveting as the landscape itself.

Mount Everest

As we navigated away from the serenity of Lhasa and journeyed deeper into the heart of Tibet, the landscape began to change. The urban hum was gradually replaced by the whispering of the wind against rugged mountains and over vast, open plains. Our destination was the Mount Everest base camp, the proverbial doorway to the "Roof of the World".

As we neared the base camp, we were informed that tourists were not allowed to venture beyond a certain point. But, as it turned out, we didn't need to go any farther. There it was, in all its towering majesty—Mount Everest—or as the locals reverently call it, Chomolungma, the "Goddess Mother of the World".

Here I was at the base of the world's tallest peak, a place many consider to be the very doorstep of the heavens. The Everest base camp, much to my surprise, bore no mark of human encampment, no hard evidence of the countless hopeful souls who had made it their temporary home on their quest to conquer the mountain. Instead, the terrain was decorated with a vibrantly colourful prayer flags, their lines crisscrossing against the stark, wild landscape. It was a breathtaking sight. The flags, each a brilliant hue of blue, white, red, green, and yellow, danced merrily in the wind, fluttering in subtle harmony with the whispering of the wind.

I watched, entranced, as the flags formed a wavering kaleidoscope against the pristine backdrop of snow and sky, their motion painting stories of aspirations and dreams, of human courage and determination. Each gust of wind, carrying with it the fervent prayers inscribed on the flags, seemed to murmur a tale of human endeavour amidst the imposing majesty of Everest.

And here I was, having arrived in the comfort of a vehicle, not on foot. I hadn't endured the gruelling ten-day trek from the Nepal side that many brave souls embark upon. I felt a pang of guilt, a strange kind of shame, for having taken the shortcut. For all the marvel and beauty around me, I hadn't really earned it. Or so it seemed.

Yet, deep down, I also felt relief and secret gratitude that I hadn't had to endure the exhausting trek. I laughed quietly to myself, admitting that, in truth, I may not have survived the daunting hike. I was a guest in this rugged wilderness, a privileged spectator of a world few get to see. And in that moment, I made peace with my journey, savouring the splendour before me. I allowed the fluttering flags and the stark, grand beauty of Everest to simply be enough.

The sky, often a moody palette of greys around Everest, was crystal clear that day—not a cloud in sight. It was as if the universe had parted the curtains of the heavens to offer us an unobstructed view of the world's tallest peak. The mountain, standing in its solemn grandeur against the startling blue of the sky, took my breath away. I was mesmerized by the ethereal beauty of the snowcapped peak glowing in the golden light of the sun. It was a sight so stunning, so overwhelmingly majestic, that it dwarfed every other grand spectacle I had ever witnessed.

My guide, a seasoned veteran of these parts, turned to me with a gleam in her eye. "In my fifteen years," she confided, "this is the first time I've seen Chomolungma without her cloak of clouds." The awe in her voice matched the marvel in her eyes, her reverence a palpable force. Then she added, "In our culture, it's said that only those with pure hearts can witness the Goddess Mother in a clear sky."

I, of course, was sceptical of such superstition. And yet, there I was, standing under the clearest of blue skies, gazing at the unadulterated Everest in all its grandeur. Despite my scepticism, a little thrill of delight ran through me. For a fleeting moment, I let myself believe in the magic of that moment, standing in the clear view of the mountain, feeling insignificant and yet completely connected to the grandeur of the world.

The drive along the lofty mountain road unfolded like a splendid panorama, punctuated with visions of a mirror-like lake that reflected the imposing snowcapped peaks, the lake's still surface much like the serene calmness of the high altitude. Yak butter tea in hand, I stared out the car window, watching a world seemingly untouched by human hands unfurling in the misty distance. It was as if we were traversing the roof of the world, skirting the edges of the heavens, the vast expanse of the landscape stretching endlessly before us.

Our nourishment came in small packets, consumed in makeshift shacks dotting the highway. The roadside itself was dotted with weathered dwellings, offering hot tea and bowls of steaming noodle soup, an invitation to pause and partake of these humble bits of sustenance. Bathrooms, however, were a luxury that these high-altitude refuges couldn't afford.

I faced the daunting prospect of relieving myself in a hole in the ground, a simple, unceremonious slit in the earth that served as a makeshift toilet. Suddenly, I found myself laughing, remembering the time I'd had to dig my own hole in the sandy wastes of the Kalahari Desert during a tour in Namibia. The starkness and the bare minimum of necessities brought me closer to the rawness of nature.

The journey continued on a road unusually large and expansive. Looking at the two grand lanes spreading out in either direction, I found myself puzzled at the sight of this vast, seemingly excessive infrastructure in a land where the human population was so sparse. Was it designed to accommodate military tanks, a strategic artery in the event of a military confrontation?

Shaking off the grim thoughts, I chose instead to see the road as a project completed with foresight, an optimistic overture to economic progress, a pathway blazing a trail for the expansion of a region still held captive by its own remote beauty. It seemed fitting that in this beautiful, rugged terrain, even the road was a testament to ambitious dreams and hopeful aspirations. It was a road less travelled, but perhaps not for much longer.

Amidst the evening shadows in the Chinese border town, my guide appeared at my hotel room with an envelope bulging with one hundred renminbi notes. With the caution of someone sharing a deep secret, she revealed a deeply personal predicament—her brother was studying and living in exile in Kathmandu, having been stranded because of circumstances and being sustained by familial ties. The price of his return to China would be the loss of freedom, a price too steep for a young man just embarking on his journey in life.

The envelope that my guide thrust into my hands was more than just money, it was a lifeline, a connection between a sister in Tibet China and a brother in Nepal, a relationship maintained across borders and amidst difficult circumstances. No, it was not just money, but a testament to love and sacrifice, a desperate plea for help, and a show of trust.

I could not shake off the gravity of what she was asking me to do, the responsibility it entailed. The risk wasn't just that I might lose the money, but also that I might lose the trust this woman had placed in me. And my charge was about carrying a burden, not of cash, but of familial love and responsibility, across international borders.

As I hesitated, my guide insisted I take the envelope to her brother, trusting me in a way few people had before. I was the vessel she had chosen to deliver her love and support to her brother. She had seen something in me, a trustworthiness that was as clear to her as the unobstructed view of Mount Everest we had just witnessed.

As the evening wore on, I held the envelope, feeling the weight of the money and the trust it symbolized. The gravity of the task that lay before me was not lost on me, but it was tinged with a sense of honour in that I found it a privilege to play a small part in maintaining the undying bond between siblings living miles apart. In that moment, despite my trepidation, I felt connected—to this woman, to her brother, and to the web of human stories that crisscrossed the borders and landscapes we had traversed. It was a connection as profound and piercing as the clear, unobstructed view of the mighty Everest that still lingered in my memory.

There are fascinating and profound mysteries that dance in the shadows of spiritual traditions, and my time in Tibet offered me a front-row seat to the drama and intrigue of one such mystery: the enigma of the Dalai Lama's lineage, playing out on the world stage in a way that defies simple explanation.

You see, the Dalai Lama, as I had always understood it, was one from a lineage of reincarnated spiritual leaders who possess(ed) a thread of the divine consciousness guiding the Tibetan people with wisdom and grace. This thread currently finds itself embodied in the person of Tenzin Gyatso, known as the Fourteenth Dalai Lama, living in exile in Dharamsala, India, many miles and borders away from the heartland of his people.

Yet, here in Tibet, the story I encountered was different, twisted, as if viewed through warped glass. Here, the "Dalai Lama" was a man appointed by the Chinese government, a puppet leader with no spiritual authority beyond a politically convenient title. An interloper Dalai Lama, if you will.

And even more intriguing was the tale of the true "future" Dalai Lama, the boy identified as the legitimate reincarnation by Tenzin Gyatso himself, said to be living under house arrest, in circumstances far removed from the ascetic lifestyle typically associated with a spiritual leader. Allegedly, this boy Dalai Lama is ensconced in the pleasures of the world, even to the point of fathering children.

All these paradoxical realities spun around in my head like a disorienting mandala, asking more questions than I had answers for. I thought of the Tibetans who were torn between these various versions of reality, their spiritual compass disrupted. The terrain of faith, I realized, was as dramatic and treacherous as the craggy landscapes we had traversed, shaped and distorted by political upheaval, by time, and by the profound human need for a guiding light or a true north.

Despite my nonreligious leanings, I couldn't help but be deeply moved by this tale of disrupted spirituality and the longing for an authentic spiritual guide. It was a human story as old as the mountains themselves, one of power, faith, truth, and the lengths to which we will go to find—or control—our guiding stars.

Arriving in Kathmandu was like slipping into a vividly colourful dream, one where temples and palaces made of intricate woodwork rose from narrow streets and the air was dense with the smell of incense, spices, and humanity in all its many hues. The vibrancy and sensory overload of the city were in stark contrast to the serene and expansive landscapes of Tibet. But this was a different leg of my journey, and I embraced it with the same curiosity and openness that had guided me thus far.

I made contact with my tour guide's brother, a young man with the easy charm of the Nepalese and with obvious gratitude for the lifeline his sister had extended through me. The act of handing over the money was oddly ceremonial. The exchange took place over a cup of sweet Nepali tea. Our words sparse, our eyes avoiding betraying knowledge of the weight of the moment.

Once the deed was done, I spent my remaining time wandering through the bustling labyrinth of Kathmandu, its temples and markets, its alleyways full of artisans. My new local guide, a sixty-something sage with a teacher's heart and a philosopher's mind, spun for me a tale not found in any travel brochures or history books, but one that thrummed with the very heartbeat of Nepal.

As we meandered through the alleys, which were alive with the scent of incense and the vivid hues of hanging tapestries, my local Nepali guide spoke of Nepal's intricate ballet with its colossal neighbour China. Their relationship, he explained, wasn't one with a shared political doctrine but rather had arisen out of economic necessity. Billions, he said, had poured into Nepal's coffers from China, which was overflowing riches, earmarked for promised grand infrastructure projects meant to modernize this timeless nation.

Yet as we wandered deeper into Kathmandu, my eyes, trained to spot disparity, sought in vain for the fruits of this bountiful investment. Where were the sleek highways, the bridges stitching together communities, or the schools rising like beacons of hope for the bright-eyed youth? The city, with its raw beauty, seemed to whisper forgotten promises and speak of invisible transformations.

My puzzlement nestled itself within me; I felt a quiet ache for understanding. Was the money a ghost, its presence proclaimed but its touch never felt? Or perhaps it was a subtle current, a slow seeping force that worked beneath the surface, too gently for the impatient and their expectations?

There was an elusive poetry to it all—the aged guide with his well of knowledge, the city clinging to the hem of progress, and the invisible threads of economic alliance. It reminded me of the complexities of our global ties, of the fact that nations lean on each other in ways that often blur the line between altruism and necessity, and that progress sometimes whispers its arrival like a secret discerned only by those who know where to listen.

Amidst the cacophony of life that sings through the valleys of Nepal, my guide led me to a sacred refuge. It was a temple, ancient and wise, crowned with a stupa that reached towards the heavens as if to commune directly with the divine. This hallowed ground, he told me, bore the weight of countless hopes and prayers whispered fervently by those who journeyed from far-flung corners of this mystical land. They came seeking solace, answers, miracles—anything. The air around us thrummed with the palpable heartbeat of their collective longing.

As we stood there, the breeze delicately twirling prayer flags into a symphony of silent hope, he turned to me, his eyes an invitation to join the chorus of souls who had laid their wishes at the feet of the unseen. But I hesitated. My heart swelled with a profound sense of gratitude for the tapestry of experiences, both bitter and sweet, that life had lovingly woven for me. What more could I ask for when I was already walking through the world drenched in life's abundant richness?

Yet, he insisted gently, like the first light of dawn coaxing the night away. And so, I acquiesced, not for lack of contentment, but to honour the tradition and to engage in the sacred dialogue between human and the divine that had been whispered across the canvas of this temple for centuries.

I closed my eyes, my heart drumming a quiet rhythm in the cathedral of my chest. If I were to ask, it wouldn't be a whisper for myself, but a clarion call for the collective. And so, I wished for world peace, a wish as expansive as the sky, as boundless as the oceans—a hope that peace might cascade into the turbulent corners of the world, soft as silk and potent as a mother's love.

As the words tumbled into the ether, I wondered if the gods and goddesses ensconced in the celestial realms above would hold my wish in the same tender regard they had all the others. Would they understand that this was more than just a phrase uttered reflexively, that it was a deep, aching yearning for harmony that hummed in the marrow of my bones?

In that moment, amidst the incense and the age-old stone, I was merely a single thread in the infinite tapestry of humankind. With a heart brimming with the wishes both spoken and silent, I cast my hope into the universe, trusting in the ancient magic that swirled around us that these prayers, too, might find their wings.

Then, as swiftly as I had landed in this whirlwind of a city, it was time for me to leave. With a last backwards glance at the majestic temples fading into the dusk, I boarded a flight bound for the familiar cosmopolitan charm of Shanghai. This journey, one of introspection, transformation, and wonder, was coming to a close, but I knew that the echoes of these experiences would continue to resonate within me, perhaps for a lifetime.

3.3 Bridging Worlds

Back in Shanghai, as dawn gently unfurled its radiant blanket across the sky, I marked the prelude to a day that was to define the contours of my new role as international dean of the coveted *Financial Times*–ranked MBA programme, a day, that in retrospect, served as a microcosmic representation of what was to become my life for the next decade.

I sat pondering in my Shanghai office, recalling my Parisian morning that had begun with a meeting with my Chinese co-dean of the master's programme. My new Chinese co-dean was a man who, like a perfectly aged wine, carried the complexities and subtleties of his experience with grace. A fervent believer in his convictions, he held the French responsible for the problems we were currently facing. With a furrowed brow and a steely determination in his eyes, he made his position known.

The sun stood high and proud in the sky as I sat down with the outgoing French dean, whose shoes I was about to fill. A man of great intellect, he painted a different picture, pointing towards the Chinese as the crux of the programme's problems. Between the Chinese co-dean's conviction and the outgoing French dean's perspective, I found myself in a dance of diplomacy, teetering between two worlds.

The contrast between the narratives painted by the two deans was stark, as if they had each sketched a different landscape and called the two by the same name. It felt as though we were discussing different universes altogether—different programmes, different stakeholders, different students. Everything seemed to move in opposing orbits. I found myself standing at the precipice of this vast divide, gazing across the chasm of differences.

This was a programme that shimmered with potential, a gem that was touted as being luminous within the field of academia. Yet, it was being tugged in two distinct directions by the gravitational forces of contrasting beliefs. I couldn't help but wonder, *How can such a programme endure such polarities? How can it continue to shine amidst this dichotomy?*

These questions weighed on my mind as I grappled with the enormity of the challenge that lay before me. This was precisely what the French director had asked of me—to bridge the differences between these two distinct cultures, to be the fulcrum that would balance the scale.

So, I began to ask myself, *What can I bring to this daunting endeavour? What unique value can I add to harmonize these disparate voices?* As I contemplated these questions, I realized the answer lay in the very challenge itself.

As an international dean, I was uniquely positioned to be a cultural translator, a bridge-builder. My role was not to side with one culture over another, but to create a dialogue, a shared language that could weave these diverging narratives into a unified story.

I needed to bring understanding where there was misunderstanding, empathy where there was discord, and collaboration where there was contention. It was about championing the strengths of each culture and leveraging them to build a stronger, more resilient programme.

The road ahead was not going to be easy to travel. It would require patience, diplomacy, and a deep commitment to fostering a culture of mutual respect and understanding. But as I looked at the challenge that lay before me, I felt a sense of excitement and a sense of purpose. After all, wasn't this the very essence of being an international dean?

I found myself filled with a renewed sense of determination. I knew that the journey ahead would be challenging, but I also knew that I was ready to embrace it. Because at the heart of this challenge lay an opportunity to bring about change, create harmony from discord, and illuminate the path forward for this luminous programme.

As the afternoon sun gave way to a Parisian evening glow, I was in conversation with the research director, an American. A beacon of wisdom, the research director encouraged me to be neutral in my role. But more than that, he emphasized the importance of finishing my PhD dissertation. In his words, I had found a clarity and purpose that were to become the bedrock of my leadership journey.

As the day meandered towards evening, I found myself in the company of the charismatic dean of the business school, an acclaimed academic turned minister in his mother country before he joined an international non-profit organisation. As we shared a bottle of Evian, the Eiffel Tower twinkling in the background, he sought to instil in me a sense of reassurance and conviction.

His eyes showed certainty as he told me that I was the right person to breathe life back into the strained Franco-Chinese partnership. The way he spoke made me feel as if I was not merely stepping into a role, but embarking on a sacred journey, one that had the power to bring a glimmer of hope back to this alliance.

I listened, my mind teeming with thoughts, my heart touched by his faith in me. The weight of my new responsibility was tangible yet strangely exhilarating. The challenges were evident, but so were the opportunities. I was not to be only an international dean; I was to be a torchbearer, a beacon of hope for the two very different cultures.

That cold Parisian day, I realized that it was not just a day. It was a prologue to my decade-long journey, a glimpse into the world I was about to inhabit, one of divergent views and diplomatic dances, of academic pursuits and leadership challenges, of inspiring individuals and enriching encounters. And as I leaned into this journey of promise, I felt a sense of anticipation; a readiness to embrace the demands of this new role; and an excitement about the symphony of experiences that was about to begin.

Navigating academic rigours in two cultures is a herculean task, one that brought an unexpected depth to my experience here. But the political landscape? Oh dear, that was an entirely different beast altogether.

I recall the words of the director of this prestigious engineering school I was attached to, a formidable character who held his own as a NASA-affiliated genius, a man who knew how to juggle the weight of the world in one hand, smiling while doing so. As he led me through the bustling hallways of his esteemed institution, he leaned in, his voice barely more than a whisper as he pointed towards a woman shuffling through papers in her office.

"She's a Chinese spy, implanted here by the Communist Party," he confided, his gaze never leaving the woman. His revelation sent a ripple of shock through me.

"Why is she still here then?" I asked, the words tumbling out before I could stop them. The question hung in the air between us, unanswered for a moment as the director gave me a smirk that was both chilling and charming in equal measure.

"It's better the devil you know than the devil you don't," he finally replied, his eyes twinkling with a secret amusement that was as contagious as it was disconcerting.

"But wouldn't she know that you know?" I pressed on, my mind spinning from the complexity of the situation. He merely smiled again, a knowing, wise smile that held a world of mystery within its creases.

"We keep feeding her useless information to pass back to the CCP," he confessed, his voice expressing an undertone of slyness and victory. At that moment, I realized the chess game that was being played on a grand scale, with the CCP having severely underestimated other nations and their sophistication and intelligence.

From that day on, my life in the French academic world was far from what I had expected it to be. It was a world filled with intellectual rigour and political intrigue, where I had to walk a fine line between what is seen and what remains hidden. It was part of the tapestry of my journey, and like every good tapestry, it had its unexpected threads, which I was only just beginning to unravel.

The Scholar's Solitude

Every night in Shanghai, after immersing myself in the whirl of activity that made up my day, I retreated to the tranquillity of my hotel room, armed with a mind buzzing with new perspectives and insights. Here, in my self-fashioned scholar's solitude, I burrowed deep into writing my PhD dissertation, often working till the wee hours of the morning.

My research drew its lifeblood from my interactions with an eclectic array of people, from eager students and insightful scholars to resourceful entrepreneurs and high-ranking officials. Their narratives, coupled with my experiences and observations, gave my research authenticity and depth, causing it to pulse with life.

My MBA and EMBA students were a rich sampling of the determined, the ambitious, and the influential. Entrepreneurs, managers, senior officials—whatever their professions, they each carried with them unique perspectives and world views. In their eyes, I was not just a teacher but a *nu-shen* (女神)—a goddess. They placed me on a pedestal, treating me with a reverence that was both humbling and, sometimes, a little uncomfortable.

Dinners were a regular affair, often lavishly hosted by my students. There would be white wine and red wine, decadent food, and warm camaraderie. I would usually nurse a single glass through the evening, preferring to stay clear-headed while others indulged. These dinners brought enjoyment, but they also served a deeper purpose, providing my students with a window onto the world outside the restrictive purview of the Great Firewall of China. These were the young minds eager to learn about what lay beyond their borders, many resorting to virtual private networks (VPNs) to access the information that was readily available elsewhere.

The academic life in China was fraught with its own set of challenges. Censorship was a constant companion, often limiting the scope and depth of my faculty's and my own teaching. The contents of certain business magazines were off-limits, and use cases had to be carefully selected to avoid falling afoul of the censor and his or her red pen. The life of a scholar, while enriching and rewarding, was also a walk through a labyrinth of restrictions and a constant dance on the thin ice of censorship. Yet, in this dance, on this journey, I found a purpose, a passion, and a challenge that kept me pushing forward and striving for more.

What It Means to Be Accredited

Amidst the academic scene in China, I found myself in a peculiar position. My programme was internationally accredited and we, as a team, were committed to maintaining the quality and integrity of our work. We honoured the international standards required for our accreditation status, treating them not just as guidelines but also as a moral compass, guiding our decisions, shaping our approach, and determining our actions.

Still, as I navigated this landscape, I found myself confronted with practices that challenged my understanding of academic integrity. There were other programmes with other academic teams who approached the accreditation process in a way that was starkly different from ours. Their approach seemed less of an ongoing commitment and more of a frantic scramble in the months leading up to the accreditation visits.

These teams seemed to work backwards, drawing on months, even years, of notes and material to create minutes and documents retroactively. Student work was hastily compiled, not as a progressive reflection of the students' academic journey but as a rushed assemblage to direct attention instead to the impressively bound binders. This flurry of activity, all crammed into a short period leading up to the accreditation visits, made me question the process.

But it didn't stop there. Accreditors, the supposed guardians of quality and standards, were treated less as evaluators and more as esteemed guests. They were showered with gifts, flattered with praise, and treated like royalty. Their role seemed to become blurry, shifting from objective assessors to privileged dignitaries.

The stark contrast between our painstaking efforts to uphold the integrity of our work and the questionable practices I observed elsewhere left me in a state of disquiet. I found myself grappling with questions about the very nature of academic integrity and the implications of these practices on the credibility of the work we were all involved in.

There was a dissonance that rang out, a discord that permeated the halls of academia, challenging me, testing me, and forcing me to question, not just the practices around me, but also the essence of my role within this institution.

Research in China

One typical Shanghai afternoon, humid and bustling, I approached one of the marketing professors with a task. I wanted her to compile research on the MBA market in Shanghai—a task right up her alley, considering her expertise. I remember the moment very well: I had expected an eager nod, a series of quick-fire questions regarding the parameters of the research, and maybe even an outline of her proposed methodology. But instead, I received a question that gave me pause.

"What results would you like?" she asked nonchalantly.

At first, I was taken aback. I hadn't anticipated this question. It was as if she were offering to tailor the research to suit my narrative. The question left me grappling with how research, the pursuit of truth, could be moulded to produce a preconceived outcome.

I took a moment to collect my thoughts. My eyes travelled around the marketing professor's office, taking in the stacks of books, the pristine whiteboard full of complex marketing models, the desktop computer—a conduit to a world of information.

"I want the truth," I finally replied, "whatever it may be."

The professor nodded, but I saw a flicker of surprise in her eyes. I left her office that day feeling an odd mix of satisfaction and unease. On one hand, I felt gratified for having stood up for the integrity of the research. On the other hand, I was troubled by the casualness of her initial offer to sway the results.

As I navigated the labyrinthine halls of my academic institution, this encounter remained etched in my mind. I had stepped into a world where the pursuit of knowledge sometimes was twisted into a dance of convenience, a world where information could be manipulated to serve an agenda, where the sacred was sometimes profaned. But I held steadfast, guided by a fundamental belief in the pursuit of truth.

After all, in the world of academia, as in life, there are no tailor-made answers—only hard-earned discoveries.

3.4 The Lure of Success

The corridors of the executive MBA programme hummed as if alive. They were home to a band of bright, talented individuals, handpicked by China's visionary Thousand Talents Plan, who had been lured back to their homeland with promises of abundant resources and opportunities. Each one was a sparkling gem, plucked from some diverse corner of the world, now united on common ground, bonded by shared roots and the noble purpose of advancing their homeland.

I was privileged to be part of their academic journey, nurturing their minds and hearts, inspiring and being inspired. Each of my EMBA students was an accomplished professional or entrepreneur, having honed his or her skills and built a rich repository of knowledge in prestigious institutions across the globe. As they returned to China, they carried in their intellects the seeds of innovation and expertise.

The savvy strategists behind China's Thousand Talents Plan had an unparalleled vision. They recognised the potential of these extraordinary individuals and knew just how to channel their skills. These students were showered with resources, whether monetary, infrastructural, or intellectual, to harness their potential so they could make a meaningful contribution to the motherland.

I saw my students flourish under this spotlight. They embraced this unique opportunity and began to make their marks. The technology front was particularly affected by their contributions. Innovation began to sprout from the seeds of their knowledge, influencing various sectors and propelling the nation towards a future marked by growth and development.

Yet, this was not merely a tale of technological advancement and national progress. This was a testament to the power of knowledge, the resilience of the human spirit, and the profound impact that vision and determination can make on an entire nation. But more than anything, it was about coming home, contributing to a society that had raised these students and nurtured them. It was about harnessing the power of their global experiences and channelling it for the growth of their homeland. It was about planting seeds of knowledge and reaping the harvest of progress.

Witnessing their journey, I was reminded that the pursuit of knowledge and the willingness to share it was a beautiful, empowering journey. And that, indeed, is the crux of being an educator: to inspire minds, transform lives, and make the world a better place, one student at a time.

The scent of prosperity wafts thick through the air of Shanghai. In this metropolis of steel and glass, aspiration is the only currency that matters. Success is a siren song, calling to everyone who dares to dream, but there is a particular melody that resonates above the rest—the echo of wealth. Not just any wealth, but wealth worthy of a spot on the Forbes 500 list. In this vibrant city, beneath the glittering skyscrapers and amidst the bustling markets, the relentless pursuit of riches is the one true North Star.

But as I moved through this society, meeting entrepreneurs and tycoons, managers and moguls, I began to realize that the song of success was not a solo melody. It was a symphony, conducted by an unseen maestro—the Communist Party. Their presence was like a shadow, falling over every corner of the public and private sectors. A party secretary or a head of personnel, people with seemingly innocuous positions, held more power than did a chairman of a publicly listed company. The invisible threads of power stretched from local governments to boardrooms, influencing decisions, guiding strategies, and exerting control.

The theme of common prosperity, although not explicitly acknowledged, was an undercurrent that flowed strongly through the making of every business move and of every financial decision. It was as if an unseen hand was gently guiding the market forces, ensuring that the wealth of the nation was channelled to empower the state. State-owned enterprises and local governments were lavished with resources, allowing them to expand not just domestically, but also globally, buying into soft power and influencing international spheres.

Money was more than currency: it was a symbol of success. But beneath the glamour and glitter, to succumb to the allure of success was to do a dance with controlling and powerful forces. Here, in the throbbing heart of China, I saw how the invisible hand of the party guided the dance, shaping society and redefining the meaning of success. The lure of success was indeed powerful. But, as I discovered, it was not free of the strings of political orchestration.

Amidst the ever-shifting sands of China's political and economic landscape, a recent transformation caught my attention. More than a mere alteration in step or rhythm, this change signals a fundamental reshaping of the dance floor itself, representing a shift that seems to echo something I've seen before, in Russia perhaps, yet it is uniquely Chinese. In the past few years, state civilian activities have found themselves with a new choreographer: the military command.

This new alignment is more than just a formal restructuring; it's a philosophical reshuffling of priorities and allegiances. The five- and ten-year plans that once guided economic strategies are now intertwined with military objectives, and the threads of these two distinct realms are being woven together in a pattern that is as bold as it is intricate.

And what of the listed companies? Ah, here is another layer of complexity. The party's hand reaches out, not as a dominating force, but as a guiding presence. Through various channels and means, the party ensures its stake in these enterprises and its voice in their decisions, being a silent partner whether they succeed or fail. There's a resemblance here to what I've seen in Russia, a Putinesque interplay between the state and the oligarchs, but this Chinese version has its own unique tempo, its own style.

As I look deeper, I find small-to-medium enterprises that seem to dance to a slightly different beat. Under the radar, they move with a bit more freedom and a touch more autonomy. Yet, even here, one senses that the eyes of the party are never far away and that the dance is never wholly unobserved.

It's a transformation that is as fascinating as it is nuanced. This blending of civilian and military, of state and commerce, creates a dance that is rich in complexity, filled with moves that are sometimes subtle, sometimes overt, but always carefully calculated.

What does it all mean? What is the melody that guides this new choreography? I find myself both enchanted and puzzled by this new phase of China's journey. It's a path that's filled with paradoxes and contradictions, one that's moving forward with determination and purpose yet that leaves behind questions that are profound and unsettling.

Perhaps that's the very essence of China's dance: it's a performance that is at once beautiful and bewildering, a melody that is both harmonious and haunting. It's a dance that invites us to watch, to learn, and to question but that always keeps us at a distance, offering glimpses of understanding but never fully revealing its secrets. It's a dance that continues to evolve, to challenge, and to intrigue, and I, for one, cannot look away.

In my journeys across China, I have often found myself walking the enigmatic streets of a country that is at once ancient and yet very modern, a country that breathes the mystique of its rich history yet simultaneously embraces the technological advances of a futuristic world. One of the most curious paradoxes that I've encountered is the dichotomy of openness and restraint that permeates Chinese society, especially when it comes to the Great Firewall.

Yes, the Great Firewall of China, a term so well known, so notorious, that it has almost become synonymous with China's governmental control. It is not just a technological barrier but also a symbol of something far greater—a manifestation of a philosophy, a belief in the need to maintain social harmony by sanitizing what is seen, read, and discussed. It is a wall that seeks to shield against the winds of unrest and the tremors of revolution.

But the control, the watchful eyes of the CCP, goes far deeper and is more nuanced than what is often portrayed in Western narratives. It penetrates the fabric of everyday life. In the towering apartment buildings and busy corporate buildings, there is often a figure representing the party. These individuals serve as overseers whose task is subtle yet profound. Their business is to know everyone else's business. Not in a way that's abrasive or overtly intrusive, but in a manner that's quiet and pervasive.

The relationship between the party and the people is like an intricate dance, where the steps are learned and rehearsed and where every twirl and spin is carefully orchestrated. And it extends beyond China's shores. For those living overseas, they too become part of this elaborate choreography. Who they are, where they live, who they marry—all these facets are noted.

Foreign companies are not immune to the prying eyes of the party either. They are welcomed into the grand ballroom of Chinese commerce, invited to participate in the economic waltz, but there's a price to pay, a ticket to be handed over. Data—the lifeblood of modern business—must be shared. The demarcation lines, the barriers erected through VPNs and other technological safeguards, are not always enough. The music of the dance continues, and all must move to its rhythm.

The dance is not without its grace, its beauty, or its logic. It's rooted in a philosophy, a belief in the balance of order and progress. Yet an outside observer can't help but feel a gentle tug of disquiet or hear the whispered questions that hang in the air: What is the cost of this harmony? What are the subtle nuances and the silent sacrifices that keep the dance in motion? The answer, perhaps, is as complex and multifaceted as China itself, which is a riddle wrapped in an enigma, continuing to fascinate, challenge, and inspire.

In a candid, almost disarming, way, my Chinese friends rationalize the complexities of their society. "You see," they often tell me, "foreigners just don't understand the mammoth task of managing 1.4 billion people." It's a pragmatic world view, honed on the grindstone of personal hardship and national tumult. I found myself marvelling at the resilience of a population that sees control as a reasonable trade-off for chaos; order for disorder; and prosperity for freedom.

For those over forty years of age, the vast Chinese landscape is painted with vivid reminders of struggle and deprivation. Sent down to the rural hinterlands, they toiled in harsh conditions, survivors of Mao's Cultural Revolution. The hardships they bore, while unimaginable to many of us, became the crucible in which their spirits were made indomitable.

No, they didn't want the "freedom" that came with empty stomachs, the "liberty" that tasted of want and need. They hungered for something more tangible, more real: prosperity. "I don't want my children to ever know what it's like to be hungry," one friend confided, his eyes holding the ghostly remembrance of a past famine. The dreams they spun for their children were woven not with threads of abstract notions of freedom, but with solid strands of material prosperity.

The words of Deng Xiaoping, the architect of modern China, reverberate strongly in their hearts: "Black cat or white cat, as long as it can catch mice, it is a good cat." Deng's pragmatic approach, favouring economic growth over ideological purity, resonated with the people. It didn't matter if the cat was socialist or capitalist, or black or white: as long as it could deliver prosperity, it was a good cat.

This, then, was the paradox of China, a nation of people who had traded a measure of freedom for prosperity, guided by a leadership that prioritized pragmatic growth over ideological dogmatism. In this delicate balancing act, I found a testament to the indomitable spirit of the Chinese people, their pragmatic approach to life, and their unshakable faith in the future.

In the midst of it all, I saw the quiet, intelligent workings of the Chinese Communist Party, a cadre of incredibly shrewd and pragmatic individuals who read the tea leaves of society with a discerning eye. They understood the massive change that the social fabric of their nation was undergoing: a burgeoning middle class, flourishing prosperity, and existence of the precious commodity that is free time.

The party, in its wisdom, saw the writing on the wall and recognised that the Chinese people, now blessed with more leisure, would yearn to explore the things they were curious about and satisfy their own wanderlust. So, the party set the wheels in motion, creating a panoply of domestic travel destinations, places as breathtaking as they are diverse. From the stunning karst peaks of Guilin to the enchanting landscapes of Jiuzhaigou, the party offered their people the gift of discovery in their own backyard.

By focusing on domestic consumption, the party not only stimulated their own economy, but also tethered the hearts of their people more tightly to the homeland. There was a cleverness in this that led to a twofold outcome: businesses that were seeking to expand internationally were subtly reined in, and their ambitions were gently redirected towards the domestic sphere. The world was vast, yes, but the party showed these business leaders that their homeland was equally as, if not more, magnificent.

But the party's wisdom did not stop at economic strategy. Knowing the power of narrative, of storytelling, and of history, they revisited the brutal memories of the Japanese occupation of the 1930s, their wounds reopening for the nation to bear witness. The less savoury aspects of United States history—enslavement of blacks, unfair treatment of the Indigenous populations—were held up as a mirror to Chinese society. The message was clear: China, with all its complexities, was the best country in the world. And the people believed it, as they saw the evidence in the prosperity around them, the opportunities they had been given, and the pride they held in their hearts for their homeland.

As I immerse myself deeper in Chinese society, I couldn't help but ponder over a paradox that was too glaring to ignore. If the Chinese people found contentment in their homeland, if they revelled in the prosperity that their government had so meticulously cultivated, then why were they sending their children away to the Western world? Why did the glittering towers of New York, the ancient halls of Oxford, the cafés of Paris, and the sunny coasts of Australia beckon to them? Why amongst them was there a relentless pursuit for English education and life in a foreign land?

Perhaps it was because these children had tasted something so intoxicating that it made the comforts of wealth pale in comparison: freedom. Freedom of expression, freedom of thought, and freedom to challenge, to question, and to dream—an elixir so potent that, once tasted, it was impossible to forget.

Or perhaps it was because the younger generation had different values, placing individual liberty above collective prosperity. Money, after all, was just a means to an end. And if that end was a life shackled by fear and censorship, then the allure of wealth lost its charm.

This brought me to another perplexing question. The Chinese are known for their sense of community, their familial ties, and their collectivist outlook. Were they willing to share their wealth in pursuit of this greater freedom? And if so, with whom, and what were they willing to share? Their resources, their dreams, their struggles? Or perhaps something more profound and intangible—their sense of identity, their culture, or their heritage?

As these questions swirled around in my mind, I realized that my understanding of China was merely a scratch on the surface. Beneath the veneer of economic prosperity there lay a labyrinth of cultural and social complexities that defied simplistic interpretations. Like a Chinese scroll painting, every layer I unrolled revealed a new perspective, a new insight, a new question. And so, my journey to understand this enigma that is China continued.

In the grand tapestry of China's cultural heritage, one thread that remains beautifully vibrant and undeniably strong is the concept of family values and community spirit. My own lineage traces back to the province of Guangzhou, where our ancestors spoke Hakka—the language of the Zhong-yuen ren（中原人）or the original Chinese from the Middle Kingdom.

Growing up, I was always fascinated by the architectural marvels of the Hakka houses—known as Tulou. They were round, like a full moon, symbolizing unity, completeness. The households were built around a central community centre of sorts, each individual dwelling a bubble clinging to a larger one, with all of them forming a harmonious whole. This unique layout for a physical structure was a reflection of the values the community held dear.

The principle of sharing was ingrained in our tradition. The families shared meals, joys, sorrows, and dreams. The community thrived on collective strength, each member contributing to the larger whole. But as I observed the winds of change sweeping across China, I couldn't help but wonder, *Are these values eroding?*

Had the relentless pursuit of wealth and status diluted the essence of these age-old traditions? Did the gleaming skyscrapers of Shanghai and Beijing cast a long shadow over these communal houses? Did the sound of clinking coins drown out the laughter of shared meals and communal gatherings?

Indeed, the quest for individual prosperity was a double-edged sword. On one hand, it brought material comfort, but on the other, it seemed to sever the ties that bound people together, replacing the warmth of shared experiences with the cold detachment of self-centred ambitions. Yet, I held on to the hope that beneath the shiny veneer of modernity, the spirit of the Hakka community, the values of togetherness, and the essence of sharing had not been lost but were merely dormant. I hoped that they would re-emerge, not as remnants of a bygone era, but as guiding principles for a society trying to balance the lure of material success with the wisdom of its cultural heritage.

I wondered, then, about the younger generations. As they look outwards, drawn by the gleaming promise of Western opportunities, are they simultaneously looking inwards, appreciating their heritage? When Chinese parents send their children abroad for education, is it simply to pursue worldly knowledge and gain exposure, or is it to allow them to search for the freedom and individuality they feel is stifled in their homeland?

These questions led me down a path of introspection. Each student I encountered, each entrepreneur I engaged with, every conversation I had, was a prism refracting my own understanding of the Chinese psyche. The love of one's homeland, the yearning for personal freedom, the lure of success and prosperity—these things were not mutually exclusive, but instead they interplayed in complex, often surprising ways.

Just as an ancient Hakka house can stand amidst the urban landscape, perhaps the essence of traditional Chinese values can coexist with modern ambitions. But the path to this coexistence isn't a straight, wide highway. It's a narrow, winding mountain trail, marked by struggles and triumphs, victories and setbacks, wisdom and folly.

The challenge is to chart this path without losing one's footing, to embrace the new without forgetting the old, to dream of success without compromising on values. As I observed the transformation of China, I realized this was not just a question for the Chinese people. It's a universal quest, a common theme running through all societies as they navigate the turbulent currents of modernity.

Whether in the high-tech metropolis of Shanghai or the quaint, traditional Hakka houses, whether savouring prosperity or battling poverty, the true measure of success, I believe, lies in our ability to remember our roots, honour our heritage, and build a future that, while acknowledging the allure of success, never loses sight of the importance of community, sharing, and togetherness. The journey might be arduous, but the destination, I am certain, is worth it.

In a realm of kaleidoscopic memories, my mind veered towards the vivid recollections of my Chinese upbringing in Malaysia. Growing up as a third-generation Chinese girl in an environment steeped in centuries-old traditions, my childhood was a complex ballet of cultural expectations and societal norms. My family, deeply rooted in Confucian principles, unfailingly reminded us of the importance of respect, duty, and family honour.

These values were not merely abstract ideals to be mused upon—they were the pillars upon which our lives were constructed, and they drew some lines we dare not cross. Our lives were scripts penned in traditional ink; a daughter was not as cherished as a son, marriages were not as much about love as they were about family honour, and divorces—well, they were the ultimate transgression, the indelible blot that tainted the family honour.

I stood out like a single swan amidst a flock of geese. I was the first in my family to marry a foreigner, stepping beyond the boundaries of tradition. But the ink of my script ran deeper; I was also the first to divorce, in defiance of the societal norms that I'd been raised to uphold.

Witnessing the cracks in the façades of "happy" families that clung to the traditional ways, I couldn't help but wonder—were these traditions binding us, or were they choking us? Were we sacrificing our individual happiness at the altar of family honour? Were we so terrified of social judgement that we preferred a life of quiet desperation over the freedom to pursue our own happiness?

As I gazed at people of the younger generation, all of them yearning for the Western values of freedom and happiness, I saw a reflection of my own struggles, my own search for something more than the gilded cage of tradition. As I gazed, I asked myself, *Is it not time we redefine honour? Is it not time we realize that the greatest honour lies in being true to ourselves, in pursuing happiness over social approval, and in cherishing the freedom to love, laugh, and live?*

Such were my musings as part of my journey of self-discovery, my quest for understanding. The answers, like elusive shadows, danced at the edges of my thoughts, waiting to be grasped. But for now, I could only wonder.

3.5 A Heart in Turmoil

You know that strange phenomenon of meeting a person and knowing almost instantaneously that they are different? That they are important, that they will carve out a space in your story that you didn't even know existed? That was how it felt when I first met Mr. G.

We were introduced in a high-rise conference room lined with imposing portraits of previous chairmen, the weight of decision and power heavy in the air. Amongst the men and women who held the economic fate of empires in their hands, Mr. G stood out—not for his power, but for his calm and his unabashed self-assurance, which stood far from arrogance yet spoke volumes about his achievements.

Over a breakfast of perfectly cooked congee and Chinese green tea, he spoke of his view of the world, an open perspective that came as a refreshing surprise to me considering the society in which he thrived. He was self-made, self-reliant, successful businessman who defined success in his own way and was immune to the social pressure of achieving some rank. He referred to such ranking as pretentious, a shallow measure of success that has little to do with the reality of one's achievements.

"Success," he told me, his eyes meeting mine across the table, "is not about comparisons or competition. It's personal. It's real. And it doesn't require a public announcement."

What struck me about him was not just his worldly outlook, but also his intention to bring the best of the international world to China, not for personal gain, but to better the lives of its people. It was not just his words, but also his actions that resonated: his quiet philanthropy, and his initiatives to improve education and healthcare; showcasing his unwavering commitment to making a difference.

As the weeks passed, our professional relationship subtly shifted. Breakfast meetings turned into late-night talks, boardroom discussions transformed into intimate conversations, and before I knew it, I was drawn into a relationship where I was walking a thin line between friendship and something deeper, something more potent.

I found myself facing a moral struggle that I had not anticipated. He was married, successful, and magnetic, a force I was not equipped to resist, yet I knew I had to resist it for the sake of my integrity and his. The temptation was immense, the connection palpable, but I knew that the choices I made next would define, not just our relationship, but also who I was as a person. The lure of success and of intimacy was pulling me towards uncharted territory, and it was a journey I had to navigate with great caution and self-awareness.

There's a unique brand of pain that comes with desiring something—or someone—and choosing not to reach for it. It's a hollow ache that echoes within you, a dull roar that's always present but never all-consuming. That was the pain I learned to live with as we embarked on the careful dance of distance.

Our mutual attraction was as potent as the moral obligations that held us at arm's length. We limited our meetings to only those that were necessary, professional meetings and the occasional board meeting in Shanghai and Paris. Our growing intimacy morphed into a complex tango of affectionate friendship and respectful distance. This became our rhythm, a delicate balance we maintained for over a decade.

And yet, our bond endured. It was as if we had forged a connection that, despite its unconventional contours, was too profound to be easily severed. We communicated with stolen glances across crowded rooms, in brief exchanges over tea during board meetings, in curt emails discussing matters of business. Each interaction was charged with the tension of unsaid words, with the weight of emotions we were too honourable—or perhaps too cowardly—to express.

One could argue that a relationship, if it is to survive, needs either time or intensity. But ours seemed to thrive on its own rhythm, undeterred by the sparse contact, undiminished by the years. It was like a dance—two steps forward, one step back, always in motion, but never quite reaching the finish line.

Everything changed, though, during an unexpected meeting outside China. Fate, it seemed, has a flair for drama. The chance encounter, devoid of our usual formalities and professional boundaries, threw our careful choreography into disarray. Suddenly, the dance that we had so painstakingly mastered was replaced with a new, unfamiliar rhythm, leaving us both reeling.

Can two people from two distinct cultures, but who both identify with Chinese culture, and who grew up in such different environments—controlled country vs. free country—possibly be happy together?

Contemplating this question, I found myself navigating a vast expanse of thoughts and emotions, much like an explorer seeking a path through unknown territory. Could two individuals sculpted by different societies and bound by the same cultural heritage, but divided by the realities of their existence, find common ground, find a rhythm, find happiness together?

In many ways, we were products of our respective environments, one of these being a world where control was the norm, where the collective prevailed over individual desires, and where personal freedoms were seen through the lens of societal well-being, and the other being a flourishing open society where personal liberties were paramount, where individuality was not just respected but also celebrated, and where the question of happiness was intrinsically linked to a person's individual journey and not just the welfare of the community.

Even with these seemingly stark contrasts, there was a common thread that connected me and Mr. G —our Chinese heritage. It was like an unseen river that flowed through our lives, shaping our identities, our values, and our beliefs. We spoke the same language, we revered the same ancestors, and we found comfort in the same customs and rituals. We were both anchored in the same historical narrative, a saga of resilience and evolution that is a part of the collective consciousness.

I realized that our cultural heritage was not a monolith but a mosaic, made up of different shades, patterns, and textures. The beauty of our heritage lay not just in its uniformity but also in its diversity. It was a complex tapestry woven with threads of different experiences, different realities, and different interpretations of the same principles.

So, could we be happy together despite our different upbringings, different social systems, and different life experiences? I believed so. Happiness, I've found, is not contingent upon sharing the same realities or the same experiences. It stems from showing understanding, acceptance, and mutual respect. It is rooted in the ability to embrace differences, to learn from them, and to grow through them.

Our diverse experiences enriched us, offered us unique perspectives, and provided us with a broader understanding of our shared heritage. Our distinct journeys could potentially create a profound and resonant harmony, like two notes of music that are different but come together to produce a melody that is more beautiful than the sum of its parts.

This was my hope, my belief. As I navigated this new terrain of thought and emotion, I held on to this understanding as if it were a beacon guiding me through the uncertainties, the questions, and my introspection. Because beneath it all, Mr. G and I were two halves of the same whole, unique in our journeys yet united in our essence.

3.6 In the Heart of the Dragon

As I walked through the labyrinth of my thoughts, teetering between the enchanting allure of the East and the bracing liberty of the West, I felt the simmering paradox within me. I was a scholar in the heart of the Dragon, trying to make sense of a culture that both inspired and challenged me a culture that had been part of my ancestral fabric but that now felt like an intriguing enigma.

I pondered the personal decisions I had made—decisions that not only met with social disdain but also clashed with the age-old values I'd been raised with. I had willingly flouted tradition and let my heart lead me. As I stood in the aftermath of my choices, I felt a strange tranquillity wash over me. I had no regrets, only lessons learned. My decisions, for better or for worse, had etched the path that led me to this point—standing in the heart of the Dragon, mesmerized by its captivating rhythm and imbued with a sense of purpose and belonging.

But there were academic decisions to be made too. The academic life in China, as intellectually stimulating as it was, had its own challenges. I grappled with the constraints of censorship, with the manipulation of data, and with living on the fringes of intellectual freedom. I was committed to authenticity, but I was ensnared in a system that often prioritized appearance over substance.

My soul yearned for resolution and for the freedom to teach and learn unhampered. I knew I had to make a decision—continue in the paradoxical embrace of this world, or retreat to the West, to familiar ground.

As I pondered over my choices, I realized that my struggles were not mere roadblocks. They were guideposts, reminding me of my mission—to be a bridge between cultures, to impart knowledge, to inspire. I chose to stay, to rise above the challenges and fulfil my academic calling.

In making this decision, I found my resolution. I found strength in my struggle, courage in my conflicts. I recognised that my journey, with its meandering paths and steep climbs, was not just about understanding the heart of the Dragon—it was about understanding my own heart. In this beautiful dance of exploration and discovery, I had found my rhythm, my place in the heart of the Dragon. I had found my home.

3.7 The Dance of Liberation

In this land of contradictions, where skyscrapers cast shadows over centuries-old temples and where ancient wisdom commingles with the pulsing drumbeat of modernity, I had a startling revelation. The China I had come to know, rooted in deep-seated Confucian ideals and propelled by the relentless force of progress, was rewriting its social code in ways that both startled and fascinated me.

The rise of communism in China, for all its challenges, truly marked a transformative era for the women of the Middle Kingdom. For more than a millennium, the ancient teachings of Confucius had cast a long shadow over their lives, placing them as second-class citizens in their own homes. Traditionally, they were denied the gift of education, save for those born in the cradle of wealth. The rest were bound to the hearths of their households, their roles signified by a Chinese character that depicts a woman with a broom.

But the winds of change blew strongly with the communist revolution, ushering in an age of equality unseen in the annals of Chinese history, effectively lifting the status of women from marginalization to mainstream. It was as if a new era had dawned, one where women were no longer shackled by the customs of yore. This change, like a key to a lock, opened the door to a myriad of opportunities for women. It was perhaps one of the most consequential strides made under the red flag of communism.

Still, old habits die hard. Despite the gains made over the decades, remnants of the old traditions persist, especially amongst the older generations. However, the winds of change continue to blow, gradually eroding traditional norms. The younger generations, those under thirty, bear less of these traditional burdens, signifying the relentless march towards a future where men and women will stand as equals.

One of my students, a woman of fierce ambition and relentless spirit, confided in me about her secret life. She was a modern-day Madame Bovary, seeking solace in the arms of different men in each city she worked. Her confession was both startling and surprisingly liberating. This was not the China I had come to know, the China whose moral compass seemed permanently aligned with the ancient teachings of Confucius. No, here was a woman who had taken the reins of her life and was rewriting her own narrative.

"I have the means," she told me, her eyes sparkling with a defiant energy. "And if men can do it, why can't we women?" This bold assertion, this audacious claim of equality on the battlefield of desire, struck me. This wasn't just about sexual liberation, it was about challenging gender norms, about a woman's seizing control of her own destiny, and about claiming her place in a rapidly changing society.

I thought about the moral fabric of this society, woven with threads of Confucian teachings. I pondered on the tension between the conservative values deeply entrenched in the culture and the relentless drive towards progress. This dance of liberation was not confined to the shadows, but was being choreographed in the glaring light of China's burgeoning metropolises.

There was an almost French-like acceptance of extramarital affairs, something that would have been kept hush-hush in the more traditional China. In this brave new world, money had become the great equalizer, bestowing upon its bearers the power to challenge norms, to defy expectations, and to redefine the contours of their lives.

Could it be, I wondered, that the rapid economic progress had in some way unshackled society from the constraints of the past and that, in its quest for prosperity, China was also unknowingly fostering an environment of social liberation and creating a platform where age-old norms could be challenged and perhaps even discarded? This wasn't just a shift in social norms, but a seismic cultural upheaval.

Yet, as I reflected on this, I also wondered if this was a loss of tradition or the dawn of a new era. Was it possible that China was losing its cultural identity, or was it merely reshaping it, moulding it to fit the contours of a rapidly evolving world?

There is a potent allure in the old ways, a comfort in the familiar rhythm of tradition. Yet, there is also an undeniable vitality in change, a sense of freedom in redefining norms and forging new paths. Maybe modern China, with its pulsing blend of the old and the new, was onto something. Maybe the dance of liberation was the next step in the evolution of a culture. As I pondered these thoughts, I couldn't help but marvel at the complexities, the nuances, and the startling contrasts that make up the captivating dance that is China.

Even with the liberating openness I observed in modern Chinese society, my mind could not help but wander back to my own marriage—a dark labyrinth of despair and longing where I felt caged and unheard for fourteen long years. You see, my marriage was not the typical tale of two souls eternally in love. It was, rather, a story of a slow but ceaseless drifting apart, a waning of connection that left me and my husband yearning for a sense of intimacy and understanding.

There is an inhumane quality to sexual deprivation, a certain hollowness that eats at your core, slowly siphoning away your sense of self. Try as we might, my husband and I could not bridge this void, and despite countless therapies and desperate attempts at revival, our bond remained tattered. Impending divorce began to cast its shadow over our life together, its imminent presence a spectre of shame amidst the traditional Chinese family landscape.

The words my late father once told me echoed in my ears: "I'd rather see you unhappily married than happily divorced." This traditional dictum, reflecting the social preference for an illusion of marital bliss over the reality of individual happiness, weighed heavily on me. Honouring my father's dying wish, I attempted a reconciliation. Yet, despite my sincerest efforts, I found myself at the precipice of despair once again, feeling my sanity slipping through my fingers like fine sand.

But there was a new catalyst this time around—my daughter. A mirror reflecting my own past, she embodied my fears, hopes, and dreams. I saw in her the life I had led—bound by social norms, riddled with fear, compliant to the point of self-harm. And it struck me that I could not, would not, let her tread the same path. I wanted her to inherit my strengths, not my weaknesses.

I came to realize that divorce wasn't a symbol of failure but a sign of self-awareness, courage, and growth. It was the sign of an acceptance that two people who once shared an ineffable bond had grown apart, their paths diverging like two rivers branching off from a common source. The acknowledgement of this truth was neither an act of betrayal nor a marker of shame; it was a step towards individual liberation.

Thus began my dance of liberation, a dance that would lead me out of the dark labyrinth of despair and into the light of self-discovery and new-found freedom. As I twirled in this dance, each step brought me closer to the woman I aspired to be, unshackled from the chains of social norms and embracing the profound peace that comes with being true to myself.

3.8 Dinner Tables and Winding Rivers

In China, the business dinner is a ritual as sacred and deeply rooted as the preparation of tea. It is a place where partnerships are born, contracts are signed, and relationships are strengthened. But it is also a sphere where excesses are often indulged in, where copious amounts of strong liquor flow freely, and where the lines of personal boundaries often blur into a hazy oblivion.

Mao-tai, the fiery spirit that's almost synonymous with Chinese banquet culture, is prominent at these gatherings. Formidably potent, it is a drink that demands respect and a willingness to surrender to its uncompromising power. More recently, the landscape of the social rites surrounding banquet culture has been graced by the presence of Bordeaux and Burgundy wines, a testament to China's increasing global influence and its love affair with Western luxuries.

In this environment where alcohol loosens tongues and lowers inhibitions, extramarital affairs often become part of the fabric. A brief shared glance across a crowded room, a whispered conversation under the veil of night, a seemingly harmless walk in the dimly lit hallways of the hotel—all this, stirred by the potent cocktail of alcohol and power, often evolves into clandestine relationships that play out in the shadows of these gatherings.

As I navigated this intricate dance during my twelve years in China, I was often asked—with a twinkle in the eye or a knowing smile—how I managed to avoid falling into the swirling vortex of extramarital affairs. The truth is simpler than the exotic imaginations of my curious inquisitors that often ran wild.

You see, I was an unmarried woman and a teacher, and not just a teacher, but a dean in fact. This unique confluence of circumstances allowed me to traverse this landscape with an aura of authority and respect. My academic status served as a shield, deflecting the advances of even the most influential men, billionaires and senior ministry officials alike. Their deference to my role and the respect that it commanded created a barrier that preserved my professional integrity and personal dignity.

Of course, I would be lying if I were to claim that this journey was absent of challenges. There were instances when the lines seemed to blur, when the shadows of temptation threatened to invade my peace. But each time, I found the strength within myself to return to the path of integrity and hold my ground with grace and dignity.

And so, I walked this delicate tightrope, balancing the requirements of my professional life with my personal values. As I look back on this journey, I realize that my ability to navigate this labyrinth is not merely a testament to my strength, but also a reflection of the underlying respect for education and educators that is woven into the fabric of Chinese society. In this dance of power, alcohol, and temptation, I held my own and emerged unscathed, my integrity intact.

3.9 Tracing the Fragments of China

A weekend away from China: a sudden change in landscape—a new territory, but a palpable familiarity. As I stepped onto the vibrant soil of Taiwan, I was embraced by the heritage that hums through its streets, its people, and its art.

The grandeur of the National Palace Museum in Taipei took my breath away. I walked in quiet awe through halls, which whispered ancient tales, and past walls adorned with handwritten poems in delicate Chinese script, the ink faded but the spirit resolute. The sight of jade, carved into forms as impressive as a giant fish, and ceramics hailing from the Song dynasty held me spellbound, their raw beauty a testament to the talent and craftsmanship of their creators. Every piece was a portal into the past, offering glimpses into the heart of a civilization that was ancient when Rome was young, a civilization I was tied to by birth, by ancestry, and by the intangible bonds of culture.

As I navigated the bustling local markets, absorbing the vibrant food scene, the city unfolded its many layers. From the soaring heights of Taipei 101, a beacon of modern engineering, to the humble *taiyaki* stalls nestled in its shadows, the city is a perfect illustration of the dance between tradition and progress, a microcosm of the broader Chinese narrative.

My conversations with locals, from scholarly guides to wise taxi drivers, revealed something surprising: they held tight to Chinese values—loyalty, respect for elders, an ingrained sense of community—more fervently than any of their mainland counterparts I had encountered. Their language was rich with the nuances of traditional Chinese; their homes were adorned with symbols of Chinese philosophy; and their lives were steeped in the customs and rituals passed down through generations.

A question bubbled to the surface of my thoughts. What truly defines us as Chinese? Is it the landmass we call China, with its political boundaries and geopolitical interests? Or is it something deeper, more resilient? Is it the shared cultural tapestry woven with threads of Taoist and Confucian values, ancestral reverence, linguistic heritage, and communal spirit?

The world, as I've come to see it, is akin to a rich, vibrant tapestry. Every thread has its own colour and texture, representing individual cultures, values, and experiences. As we weave these threads together, we create a masterpiece that reflects the diversity of our shared human existence.

While in Taiwan, I became aware of a contrasting yet profound sense of being Chinese. Here, the people, rooted in their rich cultural history, carried their traditions with pride and reverence. They existed under a different flag but shared the same language, food, and festivals, along with a legacy that spoke volumes of their collective memory and identity. These threads of shared cultural heritage seemed no less Chinese than those in the mainland.

So, what indeed defines us as Chinese? Is it merely a geographical location, or is it a deep-seated cultural identity that transcends borders? Could it be a shared historical legacy or, perhaps, a collective memory that resonates with similar melodies? The more I mulled over these questions, the more blurry the lines of definition became.

What I did realize, however, was that the beauty of being Chinese, much like having any cultural identity, lay not in rigid definitions, but in the fluidity of one's interpretation. It's a blend of shared roots, individual interpretations, collective values, and personal experiences.

Moreover, being Chinese, or belonging to any nationality, is but one thread in the vibrant tapestry of identity. The essence of who we are cannot be contained within the boundaries of a single identity. We are more than our nationalities. We are dreamers, seekers, lovers, explorers, artists, scholars, and so much more.

The rich fabric of our lives is woven with threads of various experiences, relationships, and learnings. And it's in the gentle art of weaving these threads together that we can create a life filled with colour, texture, and meaning.

Our ability to embrace this complexity, to accept our multiple identities and to respect others' interpretations, is what enables us to thrive in a diverse world. It's what bridges the gap between individuals and nations, paving the way for understanding, empathy, and peace.

In the end, perhaps it's not about finding definitive answers but about cherishing the questions, embracing the uncertainties, and celebrating the diversity that makes our world a vibrant tapestry. Every thread matters, every colour adds beauty, and every weave strengthens the whole.

3.10 The River of Ancestry

Sometimes, our roots have an inexplicable way of calling to us and reminding us of who we truly are beneath the veneer of our carefully constructed identities. My roots lie in a tiny village in Malaysia nestled amidst lush greenery with the music of life echoing in the whispers of the wind and the humming of the river.

I was born in a place far removed from the sterile white halls of a hospital. The river, tinted yellow by the silt churned up from its depths, was present during my first moments of life. My mother often remarks how it is nothing short of a miracle that I survived those early days, given the state of things. I suppose the river and I began a dance of resilience from that moment onwards.

My grandfather was the sole Chinese merchant of the village, his life made up of hard work and simple pleasures. In the quiet moments between the hustle of commerce, he would find himself sitting by the river bend, his gaze lost in the undulating dance of the waters, his mind traversing the vast ocean to the life he had left behind in China.

The diaspora Chinese, the first generation of immigrants like my grandfather, were shaped by the dual forces of hardship and hope. They worked tirelessly, their sweat and perseverance the foundation stones for the lives of future generations. Yet, they were often met with discrimination, their dreams and hopes confined behind the invisible walls of prejudice and bias.

Traditional Chinese values, the bedrock of their identity, provided solace amidst the storms of life. However, the Cultural Revolution sweeping their homeland eradicated many of these traditions, replacing those traditions with an austere vision of modernity. This erasure was both brutal and nuanced, eradicating harmful practices, but also stripping away the richness of cultural heritage.

Does this make me less Chinese? I've often wondered. *Do the threads of tradition that no longer exist in my homeland but persist in my culture and upbringing dilute the essence of my Chinese identity?*

I've come to understand that being Chinese, much like the river that witnessed my birth, is not a stagnant pool but a dynamic, ever-evolving flow. It's a tapestry woven from the threads of tradition and modernity, struggle and triumph, the past and the present. My Chinese identity is a river flowing with the wisdom of my ancestors and the insights of my experiences, forever changing, forever constant.

Being Chinese is not about conforming to a set of customs or traditions. It's about embracing the mosaic of experiences that shapes us. It's about honouring the legacy of our ancestors even as we carve our own paths. It's about understanding that our identity is not diminished by change, but rather enriched by it.

So, am I less Chinese because some traditions have faded into the annals of history? No, I believe I am more: more aware, more accepting, and more adaptable to the winds of change that life inevitably brings. After all, we are not just the sum of our traditions, but also the essence of our experiences.

3.11 The Diaspora Dialogue

In the mosaic of human history, the tales of the Chinese and Jewish diasporas are particularly compelling. These are stories of peoples who have been uprooted from their homelands yet who maintain a vibrant connection with their ancestral culture, a bond that transcends borders—much like a sturdy tree that even when transplanted does not forget the earth of its origins.

The Jewish people, for instance, are a fascinating example of a Diaspora who have managed to maintain a unique identity, independent of their association with the state of Israel. A Jew born and raised in Brooklyn is as much Jewish as a Jew living in Tel Aviv. Their Jewishness doesn't exist in their nationality but rather in the history, culture, religion, and traditions they adhere to. The state of Israel is a political entity, whereas Jewishness is an ethno-religious identity that has its roots in the heritage of the Jewish people.

In a similar vein, Chinese diaspora communities around the world have preserved their cultural identity distinct from the People's Republic of China. An ethnic Chinese person in Malaysia, like me, or in San Francisco, Lima, or Johannesburg, retains a deeply personal connection to the Chinese culture, irrespective of the political landscape in China. These Chinese diaspora communities are called *hua-yi* (华裔), as in descendants of Chinese heritage, rather than "Chinese" (中国人).

Being Chinese is to embrace Taoist and Confucian philosophies, respect for elders, the importance of education, the nuances of language, the rituals of festivals, the artistry of calligraphy, the centrality of family, and the mouthwatering diversity of cuisine. It's a kinship that is nurtured by a shared heritage and a collective memory that spans millennia.

What I see is that nationality, the political aspect, is transient, ever changing, like a river carving out new paths. But our cultural identity, our "Chineseness" or "Jewishness", is the riverbed, worn and shaped by the waters over time, but steadfast and resilient. These identities remain etched deep within us, undisturbed by the political tides that may sweep over the surface.

So, just as one can be Jewish but not Israeli, one can be Chinese without having an allegiance to the People's Republic of China. The differentiation is strong and the understanding essential as we navigate the complex terrain of cultural identity in an increasingly interconnected world. It reminds us that we are not merely citizens of nations, but members of a global family, each of us carrying a unique yet interconnected piece of the human story.

It was during my travels that I found myself in Jerusalem, the sacred city that serves as the convergence point of many faiths, a city where the stories of humankind intertwine, blending together in a tapestry of collective memory. I ventured towards the Wailing Wall, the Western Wall, the remains of the ancient temple and a symbol of faith that stands tall, silent, and majestic in the heart of the city. Without paying heed to the separate entrances marked for men and women, I accidentally took the path designated for males. A guard, spotting me, shouted, "*Stop!*" directing me towards the "right" path, the female entrance.

The encounter sent ripples through my thoughts. I found myself dwelling on the stark contrast between the egalitarian principles fostered by Chinese communism and the gender segregation dictated by religious institutions. Chinese communism, in its ardent pursuit of equality, had deliberately distanced itself from religion, seeking to foster a society where men and women would stand shoulder to shoulder, undivided by the prejudices of the past. However, even today in numerous religious spaces across the world, men and women are often asked to sit separately as if an invisible barrier is needed to maintain the distinction.

This disparity, I pondered, is not about labelling one system as right and the other as wrong, but is a testament to the diverse ways in which human societies have evolved. Each system, each tradition, carries within it the imprints of its own history, reflecting the unique paths that different cultures have trod over centuries. While communism aimed to dismantle social hierarchies, traditional religions often upheld them, not necessarily out of a desire to suppress, but perhaps as a way of preserving a social order that those in charge believed was divinely ordained.

However, it also made me wonder about the potential power of transformative change. Just as Chinese communism managed to elevate women's status by breaking away from the old order, religious institutions could inspect their age-old practices and make any needed changes. While respecting the sanctity of tradition, are they not able to redefine their norms in a way that reflects the evolving understanding of gender equality? Could they not create spaces where both men and women can connect with the divine as equals without any demarcations?

As I continued my journey, this experience served as a poignant reminder of the intersections and divergences of culture, politics, and religion. It underscored how each social structure, each system of belief, is but a thread in the larger fabric of human existence. Just as the river of nationality flows over the riverbed of our cultural identity, so do these systems interplay, shaping our world views, our actions, and our understanding of ourselves and others.

3.12 A Confluence of Cultures

My journey into Judaism was like stumbling upon an unexpected wellspring in the middle of a vast desert. My marriage to an Australian Orthodox Jew was an unforeseen detour, a fork in the road that led me into an entirely new landscape. From this union blossomed two radiant children, testaments to our shared love, our shared history, and our shared culture.

Being married into a Jewish family was much like walking into a grand library and having a universe of knowledge and stories open up to me. But more than that, it was about entering a new familial orbit with an extension of warm and supportive Jewish relatives and friends. Even when the marriage ended, the ties did not: they remained as vibrant and sturdy as ever, proof that love can continue to flourish in the most unexpected ways.

There were stumbling blocks, of course. The Orthodox rabbi in Sydney, being the guardian of traditions, expressed his reservations about my conversion. After all, my husband was a "Cohen", a priestly title carrying historical weight that forbade intermarriage. But the walls that seemed insurmountable were mere impediments that opened up to us a place of acceptance and inclusion.

Stephen Wise Temple in Los Angeles offered sanctuary. The people there welcomed me with open arms, providing me with a safe space to study, to learn, and to grow. For a year, I delved deep into the teachings, navigating the rich heritage and deep-rooted traditions of Judaism. The journey of self-discovery led me to stand before the congregation upon my conversion, my heart brimming with a joy that I had never known. Standing under the chuppah for our Jewish wedding, I felt the winds of change gently caressing my face as I embarked on a journey that was as profound as it was transformative.

Marrying into the Jewish faith was not a renunciation of my Chinese heritage but rather a symbiotic integration, much like two rivers meeting to form a confluence. It added another dimension to my identity, an additional layer to the palimpsest of my cultural consciousness. I became a bridge between two rich and diverse cultures, my life a celebration of this beautiful duality.

The journey was not always easy, nor was it straightforward. But every twist and turn, every challenge and victory, brought me closer to understanding the complex tapestry of human culture. It allowed me to appreciate the beauty in diversity, to find unity in difference, and to truly comprehend what it means to be a citizen of the world. In the process, it revealed to me the multifaceted nature of identity—how it is neither static nor singular, but rather a fluid and layered tapestry that is continually woven over the course of our lives.

3.13 In the Web of Silent Whispers

The landscape of international politics is often riddled with meshwork made up of invisible threads, a web that links the corners of the world in ways more intricate than we can imagine. In this delicate balance, the lines between vigilance and paranoia can sometimes blur, a fact that seems to ring true for both China and the United States. I've often pondered over the mirrored fears of these two nations and their obsession with keeping an eye on each other, which at times seems like twins trying to outwit each other in an endless game of chess.

Now, it is no secret that Chinese spies have infiltrated academic institutions around the globe, subtly contributing to the Chinese ambition, which reaches far beyond the South China Sea. It's a high-stakes game of stealth with unseen players moving across a worldwide board.

My last trip to China was a vivid testament to this fact. My stay in Beijing, where I was housed in a double-story two-bedroom suite at a five-star hotel, was opulent, and there seemed to be a shadow hovering behind the glittering veneer. This was a state hotel, operated under the aegis of the Foreign Ministry, an important fact as I would later discover.

One night, while the moon was gazing down upon the silent city, I woke up. A strange restlessness nudged me downstairs to fetch my phone. As I navigated the silent suite, an unusual odour caught my attention. It was the sharp, pungent scent of smoke. It was faint, but distinctly present, wafting out from the second bedroom.

I stood at the doorway, my heart skipping a beat. My curiosity wanted to push me to investigate further, but a wave of caution held me back. I retreated without venturing into the second bathroom, a decision that in hindsight seemed instinctual, almost prescient.

When I returned to my belongings, something felt off. There was a sense of intrusion, a spectral fingerprint indicating that someone had been here. My passports, my phone, and my laptops had been tampered with. The evidence was subtle, a mere shifting of angles, but it was enough to send a chill down my spine and shake me out of my sense of security.

This experience left me with more questions than answers, serving as an unsettling reminder of the invisible dynamics at play on the world's political stage. And yet, it was also a poignant testament to the resilience of human spirit, the courage to seek truth and knowledge even in the face of unseen threats. Because isn't that what we do? We keep moving forward, we keep seeking, even when the road gets tough, even when the path is shrouded in shadows. Because the quest for understanding, the thirst for knowledge, is greater than any fear. And it is this pursuit, this unwavering determination, that truly defines us.

In a world churning with divisive rhetoric and simplifications, it's easy to be swept into the prevailing narrative, one that often pits the United States against China and Russia, sketching the latter pair as tech-stealing villains in a global drama. Yet, it's crucial to pull back the curtain of political oratory and take a look at the nuanced realities that often remain shrouded.

Take, for instance, the account of a dear friend of mine, a data scientist whose work spans the vast technological terrain. According to his first-hand accounts, the chasm between US and Chinese technological advances is not a shallow trench but an abyss as deep as the night sky. So, when politicians sound the alarm bells over alleged Chinese theft of technology, are they not failing to account for the intricacy of the technological ecosystem, where innovation, not imitation, is the thread that binds us all?

Furthermore, the United States remains unsettlingly silent about Israel's advances in spyware and surveillance technology, a quiet that stands in stark contrast to the uproar surrounding China's technological feats. If we are to engage in a conversation about technology and ethics, shouldn't we strive for a dialogue that is inclusive, nuanced, and above all, honest?

You see, in this discordant symphony of world politics, the most jarring note is one that prohibits harmonization, showing an unwillingness to converge and create a collective melody. The world watches as the two most powerful nations lock horns, fighting for technological supremacy while ignoring the potential for collaborative advancement. How can we ever aspire to create a unified global narrative when the storylines we choose to follow are so divergent?

So, here I am wondering, what if the world's most powerful nations were to view technology not as a battlefield, but as a fertile ground for collective human advancement? What if, instead of erecting walls, we built bridges, united in our understanding that the future belongs to those who can see beyond the narrow confines of nationalism? How might that change the narrative and, more importantly, the outcome?

This isn't naive idealism; it's a call to action. To navigate the labyrinthine complexities of our time, we must arm ourselves with curiosity and gain the courage to question the stories we're told and the boundaries we're given. After all, aren't we all, regardless of nationality or political affiliation, chasing the same dream—a world where technology serves as an instrument of collective liberation, rather than becoming another chain that binds us?

3.14 The Red Thread Connecting East and West

In the swirling vortex of history, there are strange parallels that connect different civilizations in a beautiful dance of shared ideas and influences. The genesis of communism in China is one such fascinating event that spiralled out from the streets of Paris, wound through the harsh tundra of the Union of Soviet Socialist Republics, and nestled deep in the heart of the Middle Kingdom.

Communism's entrance into China was like a river flowing east, originating from the intellectual currents of the French Revolution with a large drop of Marxism, which heralded a deep respect for egalitarianism and the idea that every citizen had a part to play in the nation's journey. This democratic-socialist spirit found fertile ground in the USSR, which in turn became the tutor of China at the dawn of the latter's communist era. The values of communism, therefore, are not uniquely Eastern or Western but a collective inheritance of philosophical ideals from different corners of the world.

France's early recognition of Communist China was not merely a diplomatic act but an affirmation of shared ideologies, a nod to the invisible threads that bind these two great civilizations. French socialism and Chinese communism might seem different on the surface, but they are both rooted in a profound desire for equality, a belief in the power of the collective, and a commitment to the welfare of the ordinary citizen.

The authority of the French president, similar to that of the Chinese president, is not merely an artefact of power but a manifestation of the country's political ethos. Both systems vest in their leaders an exceptional amount of authority, a sign that these nations believe in strong centralized leadership as a means to steer the ship of state. The US president, by contrast, operates in a more divided system with checks and balances curtailing unilateral power.

But it's not just in the political structure where similarities lie. There's a shared commitment to culture, to intellectual pursuits, and to the beauty of language. In France, the philosophers, poets, and playwrights are national treasures. In China, too, the scholar is exalted and the artist revered. There's an appreciation of the finer things in life, a belief that beauty and wisdom are not frivolities, but essential components of a good life.

Yet, these cultural parallels do not make these two nations identical twins. They are more like two rivers flowing from the same source but carving out their own distinct paths, shaped by the unique landscapes they cross. French socialism, steeped in the rich history of European enlightenment and democracy, is a blend of individual rights and collective responsibility. Chinese communism, moulded by China's ancient traditions and the collective memory of the Chinese people, places a higher premium on social harmony and the collective good.

As I pondered over these fascinating interconnections, I was struck by the reality that our world is more connected than we give it credit for. Ideas and influences flow across borders, shaping nations and cultures in profound ways. In this grand dance of civilizations, we are all participants, borrowing, adapting, and evolving together. This realization was not just an intellectual epiphany, but also a profoundly heartening one. It reminded me that even in our differences, we share a common heritage of ideas and a common journey in our quest for a better world.

3.15 Threads of Harmony

In musing on the potential harmony between two people from vastly different backgrounds, I found my thoughts expanding, reaching towards something larger and grander. Can two nations differing as much as the sun and the moon not merely coexist, but also thrive together in harmony? After all, nations are but collections of people, shared experiences, and collective aspirations.

International relationships are far more complex than personal ones, yet at their core, the two bear striking similarities. Understanding, acceptance, and mutual respect remain vital components. The common threads that have the potential to stitch together a rich tapestry of global harmony are embedded within these simple principles.

One such thread is the acknowledgement of our shared humanity. Beneath the diverse social, political, and economic systems that govern us, we are all human beings sharing a common home—our planet. Each nation has its strengths, its unique wisdom, and its invaluable experiences that could contribute towards the well-being of all earth's inhabitants.

A controlled system might offer lessons in stability, unity, and collective progress, whereas a free system testifies to the power of individual liberty, creativity, and democratic decision-making. Rather than viewing these systems as conflicting, we can seek to understand their underlying values and appreciate the lessons they teach.

Another thread is the pursuit of mutual prosperity. In our increasingly interconnected world, the prosperity of one nation inevitably influences the well-being of others. We have the potential to create a global system where each nation contributes to and benefits from the collective progress, creating a virtuous cycle of mutual upliftment.

The third thread is our shared responsibility towards our planet. Environmental preservation and combating climate change are common goals that transcend national borders and ideological differences. These shared objectives could serve as a powerful unifying force, prompting nations to work together towards a sustainable future.

The final thread is perhaps the most important one—empathy. The ability to empathize, to put oneself in another's shoes, can foster understanding and build bridges between the most disparate of cultures and systems. Nations, like individuals, are shaped by their histories, their struggles, and their aspirations. Recognising this can engender respect for different paths and appreciation for the diversity that each nation brings to the global table.

The world we imagine—one where nations, diverse in their cultures and systems, coexist and thrive together—is not beyond our reach. It requires a paradigm shift, a broadening of perspectives, a willingness to learn from each other, and above all, the courage to weave these threads into the fabric of our global society. The result would be a masterpiece, a world that is more understanding, more cooperative, and ultimately, more harmonious.

3.16 In Pursuit of Common Ground

There is a subtlety, a certain finesse, to seeking common ground. We must learn to see beyond the façade of difference and tap into the wellspring of shared human experience that unites us. We might be born in different corners of the globe, nurtured by distinct cultures, or influenced by contrasting political ideologies, but beneath these layers of difference lies a deep, enduring sameness.

In our hearts, we all seek happiness, peace, and fulfilment. We yearn for connection and understanding. We hope for better days and brighter futures for ourselves and our children. These shared aspirations serve as a compass guiding us towards a landscape of mutual understanding.

Can a man from a controlled system find harmony with a woman raised in the land of liberty? A fascinating thought, yes, but also an inspiring possibility. It's in the exploration of this question that we uncover the essence of human adaptability, the strength of shared values, and the resilience of love.

In the face of seemingly insurmountable odds, individuals from starkly different backgrounds have found ways to bridge the divide, to communicate, to understand, and to love. The same spirit, I believe, can inspire nations and encourage us to view differences, not as roadblocks, but as opportunities for learning, growth, and mutual enrichment.

Our respective strengths—the collective purpose and unity of a controlled society, the individual freedom and innovation of a free one—can complement each other, creating a synergy of balanced progress.

We must remember that we are not only citizens of a country, but also inhabitants of the world.

The potential for the harmonious coexistence of nations hinges on our willingness to embrace diversity, to accept different perspectives, and to learn from one another. It requires a conscious shift from competition to collaboration, from exclusion to inclusion, and from discord to understanding.

Living and working in the midst of two worlds has allowed me to witness first-hand the profound potential of these threads of unity. With every conversation, every shared meal, every student enlightened, and every spark of understanding kindled, I am reminded that despite our differences, we share a common narrative of aspiration, resilience, and humanity.

At the end of the day, our shared goals of peace, prosperity, and happiness can inspire us to transcend our differences and focus on what truly matters. And maybe, just maybe, in seeking these common threads, we'll discover that we're not so different after all.

3.17 Happiness Is ... Sharing What You Know

In China's rapidly changing society, I found a mirror of my own journey, much like the beloved businessman I met who, with his down-to-earth charisma and vision, endeavoured to make the world a little bit smaller and a little bit more connected. He brought the outside world to China, introducing innovations in healthcare and inspiring new ideas for tourism, yet in his heart, he held a sacred space for Chinese traditions. He shared not just knowledge, but also his spirit of exploration and enterprise, making his imprint on the dynamic narrative of China's progress.

It struck me that he and I we were on similar paths, each in our own way, sharing what we knew with the world around us. His was a mission fuelled by entrepreneurial energy; mine, ignited by an academic flame. Yet, the essence remained the same. It was the joy of sharing knowledge, the thrill of catalysing change, and experiencing the fulfilment of connecting the threads of understanding across borders and across cultures.

As I walked into the classrooms where I taught, which were brimming with eager minds and expectant faces, I saw an opportunity and a purpose. I was here to share what I knew, to bridge the gulf of understanding, to be a beacon my students' journey towards knowledge. Each lecture was not only a dissemination of information, but also a tapestry of stories, experiences, and insights. It was about lighting a spark of curiosity, nudging my students towards adopting a global perspective while honouring their Chinese roots.

Amidst the quiet of late-night research, or in passionate discourse when delivering a lecture, or in the proud moment when a student would have epiphany, I found my happiness. It wasn't merely in the accolades or the intellectual achievements; it was in the act of sharing itself.

The joy of seeing minds awaken to new concepts, the thrill of witnessing the blossoming of a fresh perspective, the satisfaction of nurturing intellectual growth—these became the milestones of my journey. I was an academic in China, but my heart belonged to the world, and it was my mission to help my students see beyond their immediate horizons. It was my mission to share what I knew. In this act of sharing, I realized, lay the path to true happiness. The path was not in the solitary pursuit of knowledge, but in the generous sharing of it. For in the end, we are all interconnected, threads in the same tapestry of life. Our stories, our knowledge, and our experiences are gifts to be shared as there are bridges to be built and ladders to be climbed. And in this shared journey, we find our joy, our purpose, and our home.

In this strange and wonderful dance we call life, our steps are orchestrated by an innate curiosity, a compelling urge to understand the cosmos that spins around us. It's a quest for truth, a hunger to peel back the layers of existence and uncover the hidden meanings that lie just beneath the surface. And it is this very journey, this ceaseless exploration, that leads us towards the wellspring of true happiness.

Throughout my life, I've found myself on this very path, meandering through landscapes of discovery, navigating the winding corridors of wisdom. I've sought truth in the dusty corners of academia, in the silent depths of introspection, and in the bustling heart of diverse cultures. My pursuit has spanned continents and cultures, and ideologies and identities, weaving a tapestry of understanding that is as rich as it is vast.

One of the pivotal points in this journey has been my exploration of different perspectives. I've come to realize that truth, like a diamond, has a multitude of facets, each offering a unique view and a fresh interpretation. It is through these different perspectives that we gain a comprehensive understanding of the world, of life, and of ourselves.

Take, for instance, my time in China. I experienced the complexity of a society that balances traditional values with modern aspirations, a culture that is rich in history yet eager to embrace the future. I had the privilege to witness first-hand the silent battles waged in boardrooms and classrooms, the enduring spirit of a people marching steadfastly towards progress, and the profound beauty of ancient traditions nurtured and preserved amidst the clamour of modernity.

On the other side of the world, my life in the West introduced me to the power of individualism, the audacity of innovation, and the intoxicating allure of freedom. I learned about resilience in the face of adversity, about the pursuit of dreams fuelled by an unyielding belief in oneself, and about the value of questioning, challenging, and pushing boundaries.

But my journey didn't stop there. As I plunged deeper into this quest, I found another compelling avenue for seeking truth: sharing knowledge. The act of imparting wisdom, of lighting up another's path with the spark of understanding, brought me a joy that was profound, and a fulfilment that was deeply gratifying.

I realized that sharing knowledge is not just an act of generosity, but also a form of communion, a bridge that connects minds and hearts. It creates a space where ideas can be exchanged, perspectives can be broadened, and connections can be deepened. It's an invitation to step into another's shoes, to view the world through his or her eyes, to understand his or her hopes, fears, dreams, and struggles. It's an opportunity to sow seeds of empathy, compassion, and unity.

This quest for truth, this journey towards understanding, is my pathway to happiness. It fills me with a sense of purpose, a sense of connection, and a sense of belonging. It reminds me that we are all a part of the grand tapestry of existence, woven together by threads of wisdom, experience, and love. As I continue to journey down this path, I carry with me a sense of joy, a sense of fulfilment, and a sense of purpose that is deeper and more profound than anything I've ever known: Happiness is real when shared.

Chapter 4

REFLECTION IN SINGAPORE

4.1 Rekindled Flames and Closed Doors

It was in Singapore, beneath the towering elegance of Marina Bay Sands, where Mr. G and I met again. This was a place that boasted an artificial beauty and was the site of authentic heartbreak for me.

The lunch we shared was simple and unassuming, but the connection was as immediate and palpable as it had ever been. It was as if years hadn't passed since we last looked into each other's eyes, as if we were picking up a conversation left unfinished only moments ago. Each glance we shared, each laugh, and every incidental brush of our hands across the table was charged with a yearning that neither of us had expected or knew quite how to handle.

We met again, and then again, unable to resist the pull of something that felt so right and yet that was profoundly wrong. Each time we said goodbye, there was the unspoken hope, a desperate wish really, that it wouldn't be the last time. But deep down, we knew we were playing with a fire that could only burn us both.

And then it happened: the moment of clarity, the realization that we were balancing on the edge of something dangerous. It came from him, the voice of reason. He told me, his voice shaking, that he couldn't face his wife if he saw me again. The words were a sword cutting through the fantasy we'd been indulging in.

In the middle of the night, the emptiness and longing too much to bear, I called him. My voice trembled as I told him he had done the right thing for his family. I could hear the relief and the agony in his silence. My heart sank. I was unfulfilled and yet consumed by shame that I had fallen in love with a married man for more than a decade.

Why him? There were thousands of men who pursued me. I was no stranger to being the centre of attention. Beauty, charm, intellect—these had never failed me. But why was I so fixated on the one who was unavailable, unattainable?

The door had closed, and yet the flames were still there, flickering in the dark, a haunting reminder of what might have been. It was a lesson learned in the harshest way, and it was also a longing that would remain etched in my soul, a fire that neither time nor distance could fully extinguish. But it was a door that needed to be closed, a chapter that had to end so that the rest of my life could begin.

As I walked away from Marina Bay Sands, the shimmering waters seemed to whisper a farewell, and the skyscrapers stood tall, like silent sentinels to a love that was never meant to be. The world moved on, and I realized that so must I, carrying with me a scar that was both a wound and a reminder that sometimes the heart wants what it cannot, and should not, have.

It was he who first suggested Singapore, a suggestion that tickled my ear, luring me like the siren's song. "Singapore may be the right place for you," he'd said, his voice a mixture of conviction and longing. Those words had danced in my mind, a melody that was at once enchanting and haunting.

So I went, driven by the twin engines of curiosity and desire. But being in that city and knowing that he was near yet untouchable was a torment unlike any I had ever known. I felt his presence in the rush of the wind, in the murmur of the crowds, and in the very pulse of a city that seemed to throb with the beat of my own aching heart.

He and I didn't see each other again since the last time we'd parted. The words were left unspoken, but the silence spoke volumes. The city that had once promised so much became a landscape of what could have been, a panorama of longing painted in hues of absence.

It was too much to bear.

I found myself restless, driven by an urge to escape the city's relentless energy and its unyielding reminders. Every other weekend, I travelled to nearby islands—Lombok, Indonesia; Phu Quoc, Vietnam; Penang, Malaysia—where I could be close to the ocean to find clarity and centre myself.

By the shores of the South China Sea, I would sit and meditate, letting the rhythm of the waves soothe the tumult in my soul. The vast expanse of water, so different from the familiar Pacific Ocean, seemed to echo my own sense of displacement and my yearning for connection.

Each wave that lapped at my feet whispered secrets of surrender and acceptance. The salty air filled my lungs with a bittersweet taste of longing and release. The sand beneath my fingers grounded me, a tactile reminder that life was here and now, tangible and real, not trapped in the memories of what once was or the dreams of what might have been.

In those moments, I learned to breathe again. I learned to find joy in the little things—the warmth of the sun on my face, the laughter of children playing by the shore, a meal shared with strangers who soon became friends.

And slowly, with the gentle persistence of the tide, I found my way back to myself. The city, with all its allure and agony, faded into the background. The love that had brought me there transformed into something else, something deeper and more profound: a love for myself, a compassion for the woman I had become, and gratitude for the journey that had brought me to this place.

It was a lesson hard-won, a journey that took me to the edges of desire and despair. But in those quiet moments by the sea, I found a peace that had eluded me amidst the city's chaos, a peace that whispered, "You are enough just as you are."

In that acceptance, I found the strength to move on and to embrace the life that was waiting for me, in Singapore and beyond, with an open heart and a soul ready to soar.

A Weekend at Somewhere Resort, Lombok

Janine and I reacquainted serendipitously at a philanthropy forum in Singapore. Since then, she had been my bedrock. Being a hotel connoisseur, I entrusted her with all travel arrangements. One weekend, Janine and I arrived in Lombok, Indonesia, a place still untouched by the manic rush of tourism, a paradise that retains its natural grace and charm. Lombok felt like stepping back in time—a glimpse of Bali as it must have been thirty years ago. *Serenity, simplicity, authenticity*—these were the words that danced on my tongue as we made our way to the newly opened Somewhere Resort.

Nestled between the hills and the whispering waves of the sea, Somewhere Resort welcomed us with open arms. Our rooms were adorned with traditional Indonesian art. The scent of frangipani filled the air, and the sounds of nature were a gentle symphony accompanying our every step.

At Tanjung Aan, we found our spot on the beach, a secluded haven where the sands were soft and golden and the water was so pristine that we could see our feet, clear and unobstructed at four feet deep. The world seemed to pause, holding its breath in reverence of the beauty before us.

As we settled on our sun loungers, local peddlers approached, a gaggle of women with bright smiles and eyes gleaming with determination. They were armed with pineapples and sarongs, and they would not leave until we'd made a purchase.

A young girl, no older than twelve, was particularly determined to make a sale. Her eyes, alive with youthful ambition, met mine, and something in her spirit resonated with me. I found myself engaging with her, practising my Bahasa, the local language, and exchanging laughs and stories.

Janine, meanwhile, contentedly put on her shades, reclined in her chair, and let the sounds of our conversation wash over her. The sun, the sea, the laughter—it was all part of a tapestry that wove us into the fabric of Lombok.

That evening, as the sun dipped below the horizon and painted the sky with hues of gold and pink, Janine and I shared a bottle of wine. The conversation turned personal, intimate. For the first time in twelve years, I revealed my love secrets to her. My heart, heavy with the weight of unspoken truths, found relief in her empathetic gaze.

Her words were a balm; her understanding, a gift. She listened without judgement, offering wisdom and compassion. Our friendship, always strong, deepened in those precious moments because of the vulnerability and trust that can only be found in the sanctity of true connection.

Lombok became more than a destination; it was a place of revelation, healing, and growth. The young girl's determination, the women's resilience, the unspoiled beauty of the land—they were all reflections of my internal journey.

As we left Somewhere Resort with sand still clinging to our feet and the taste of salt on our lips, I knew that Lombok had given me something profound. This was a reminder that life's most beautiful treasures are often found in the simplest places, in the most unassuming encounters, and in the hearts of those we love. In those quiet spaces where the world feels pure and untainted, we find the courage to bare our souls and embrace the beautiful complexity of being human.

It was on the sun-kissed shores of Lombok that Janine and I met a woman who struck me with the force of her independence and joy for life. She was Dutch, was married to an Australian, and was living happily in Adelaide without children. There was a sparkle in her eye indicative of a zest for life that was both inspiring and invigorating.

We struck up a conversation, our feet buried in the sand, the waves providing a gentle accompaniment to our words. Her story unfolded easily like a well-worn book, its pages filled with love, adventure, and wisdom.

Her husband, she explained with a smile, couldn't make it to their anniversary trip. Rather than cancel or postpone, she had chosen to come to Lombok by herself for seven days. There was no regret in her voice, no longing in her eyes. Instead, there was an expression indicative of a mutual respect between her and her spouse that allowed her the freedom to explore and enjoy life on her own terms.

Her mindset struck me, especially when contrasted with the more traditional views often found amongst Asian women, where dependence on husbands and a concern for losing face can shape choices and create boundaries.

In this individual, I saw a European woman fierce and independent with a self-assuredness born from knowing her worth and embracing her individuality. She knew how to live life alone, not out of necessity, but out of choice and in confidence. Her happiness was not tethered to another but was rooted in her understanding of herself and her relationship with the world around her.

By contrast, some of my Asian female friends, bound by cultural expectations and social norms, would never dream of taking a solo trip without their husbands or girlfriends. Their sense of identity is often interwoven with their roles as wives and mothers, their value measured in their relationships rather than by their individuality. A husband's absence for a significant occasion might be seen as a failure or a loss of face, rather than an opportunity for personal growth or enjoyment.

Both perspectives, equally valid in their contexts, offered me a lens through which to examine my own beliefs and biases. I found myself drawn to the Dutch woman's sense of self, her ability to carve out space for herself in a relationship, and her refusal to be confined by expectations or traditions. Yet, I also understood the profound connection and commitment that comes from a more interdependent way of life where family and community play a central role.

As the sun dipped lower, casting a golden glow over the sea, we continued to talk, our conversation meandering through the landscapes of love, culture, womanhood, and freedom. We were, in that moment, three women from different worlds, finding common ground in our shared humanity.

In the Dutch woman, I saw a reflection of the woman I was striving to become—independent, joyful, and unapologetically myself. In me, I hoped she saw a willingness to learn, to question, and to grow.

We parted as friends, our lives briefly intertwined by the serendipitous choice of travel destinations. But her spirit, her joie de vivre, stayed with me, a reminder that there is no one right way to live or love, but rather a beautiful mosaic of choices, each reflecting the multifaceted nature of the human heart.

A Reveling Weekend at JW Marriott Resort, Phu Quoc

The fiery orb of the sun had just dipped below the horizon when I found myself sauntering down the soft sands in front of JW Marriott Resort in Phu Quoc, Vietnam, where Janine recommended we spend a long weekend away from Singapore. The cool water lapped against my feet, tenderly washing away the remnants of the day. The sound of gentle waves playing a soothing symphony, along with the soft murmuring of the night, brought a sense of tranquillity that was as pervasive as the sea itself.

Here in the heart of the unspoiled beauty of Phu Quoc, the waves danced over sands of gold, and the beach stretched out like a tapestry woven by Mother Nature herself. The landscape's tranquil beauty was a testament to how nature, untouched and unfettered, flourished in all its glory.

Amidst this idyllic scenery, a yearning rose within me, an urge that had been hibernating in the recesses of my heart, an echo of a past love. Compelled by an inexplicable instinct, I reached out to him, confessing that my eyes hadn't danced to the sight of any other man in more than a year.

His response was swift, a sharp sword that severed the strings of attachment: "Let it go now. An ending preserves beautiful memories." The words cascaded over me, stirring up a whirlpool of emotions. An era of my life, one tied so closely to him, was being swept away in the tides of time. I felt my heart plunge into a deep abyss, the echoes of his words resonating within me.

For two hours, I let the sea cradle me, the cool waves lapping over my body as if trying to soothe my aching heart. The immensity of the ocean reflected my turmoil, and my feelings were a tumultuous tide—relief and regret, loss and acceptance, churning within me. I felt a sense of release, recognising an end to a chapter that had spanned time and space.

Emerging from the water, I felt reborn, cleansed of past regrets and ripe with the promise of new beginnings. I turned to Janine, her silent presence a pillar of strength through the emotional tide, and confided my resolution. It was time to move on, to venture into the future without the weight of a past love. It was time to step into my new life with courage, to let go of what was, and to welcome what is and what could be.

Love, I realized, is not about possession but appreciation, not about ties that bind but connections that liberate. With that revelation, I was ready to let the winds of life carry me forward on my journey, towards the person I was yet to become.

A New Chapter: Resigning and Reimagining

Life has a way of unfurling itself and revealing new paths at the most unexpected moments. For me, such a moment came when I faced for the first time the bittersweet reality of an empty nest. My children, my heart and soul, were stepping boldly into their own lives, and I found myself standing at the threshold of a new beginning.

My son, heading to his first year of college, was a bundle of excitement and nerves, his eyes sparkling with anticipation. On move-in day, we navigated the maze of dorm life together, assembling his bed and organizing his belongings with a mixture of joy and melancholy. He hugged and kissed me goodbye, his voice tinged with a confidence I hadn't heard before. "Go have fun, Mum!" he said, as if granting me permission to explore, to dream, and to rediscover myself beyond the role of motherhood.

In New York, the bustling energy of Manhattan served as a backdrop to my visit with my daughter. Working in this vibrant city, she had found her footing, her place in the world. Over dinner, with the city lights painting the night in hues of gold and silver, she asked me a question that stopped me in my tracks: "Is there anything you regret doing or not doing in your life?"

I pondered her words, my mind retracing the steps of my journey, the choices I'd made, the roads I'd taken and not taken. Finally, with a sense of peace and conviction, I replied, "I would not change a thing!"

Her smile was both an affirmation and my reward. When I asked her if there was anything she wished I would have done differently, her response was a balm to my soul: "Not a thing, Mum! Everything is perfect the way it is."

From that moment onwards, I knew that a new chapter was calling me, beckoning me to step into a fulfilling and meaningful journey without my children. It was time to resign from my academic life, to untether myself from the familiar, and to plunge into the uncharted.

With my children's blessings and the wisdom of years, I found the courage to embrace the unknown. My heart swelled with gratitude for all that had been and all that awaited. I was no longer just a mother, a professor, or a partner; I was a woman standing at the precipice of reinvention, fuelled by love, guided by faith, and armed with the knowledge that life's greatest adventures begin with a single step.

So, I took that step, not with fear or trepidation, but with joy and expectation. I danced into the unknown, trusting that the universe had a plan and a purpose that was uniquely mine.

In the echoes of my children's words, in the memory of their hugs, and in the promise of tomorrow, I found my compass, my true north. I was ready—ready to explore, to create, to love, and to live. I was ready to write a new story, one that was authentically, unapologetically mine. The future was wide open, a blank canvas waiting for the colours of my soul. And I knew with every fibre of my being that it was going to turn out beautifully.

Wandering and Finding

If freedom has a taste, then it's the flavour of the unknown or the untried. It's the savour of myriad possibilities laid out before you like an uncharted territory, waiting for you to explore. It's exhilarating, intoxicating, and occasionally daunting. For the first time in many years, my life was no longer tethered to school schedules, sports days, or parent-teacher meetings. Instead, it was tied to the rhythm of my own heart, to the whims and fancies of my curious spirit.

I decided to use this new-found freedom to travel and quench my thirst for unfamiliar cultures, new faces, and unique experiences. I journeyed with my mother across Thailand, Malaysia, Australia, and Singapore. I spent lazy days on the sandy beaches of Indonesia, delved into the rich history of Vietnam, and marvelled at the technological marvels of Japan. These trips, whether for leisure or business, filled my soul with a sense of joy and wonder that I hadn't known in a long time.

There were moments of epiphany too. During one of my customary trips to Singapore, while heading to my favourite sanctuary in the city, the five-star hotel, I found myself counting the countries I had visited in the past ten months. The number surprised me. I had crisscrossed nations, oceans, and continents and had entered Singapore six times. Six times! An unexpected realization dawned on me: the universe had been gently nudging me towards this city-state, and I had been unknowingly heeding its call.

Singapore, with its dynamic blend of tradition and modernity, its pulsating energy, and its confluence of cultures, had been silently drawing me in. Every visit felt like a homecoming, something comfortingly familiar amidst my nomadic lifestyle. And so, guided by the whispers of my subconscious, I made a decision that felt as natural as breathing: I would call Singapore home.

This island city, a jewel in the crown of Southeast Asia, would be my new anchor, my place of rest amidst the constant motion. Not an anchor that restrains, but one that grounds, serving as a haven of calm amidst the stormy seas of exploration and discovery.

Embracing Singapore as my home felt like accepting a long-awaited invitation, like slipping into a cherished, comfortable robe. It was an affirmation of my freedom, my journey, my evolving story. Singapore was not just a place on the map; it also became a reflection of my wandering spirit and a symbol of my transformation.

My wanderings had led me home. And I was ready, with an open heart and a curious mind, to embrace this new chapter, this new adventure in my life. The next phase was about to begin, and I could hardly wait to dive into the beautiful chaos that was Singapore.

4.2 Embracing a Tropical Symphony—Singapore

Singapore, a city-state flourishing amidst lush greenery and tall skyscrapers, welcomed me with open arms, a perfect blend of the urban and the organic. The island, often referred to as the "Garden City", unravelled its secrets to me one leaf at a time. This haven in the tropics presented a myriad of shades, both of the sky and of the landscape, a veritable canvas painted by the divine artist herself.

In the radiant embrace of Singapore, there's a hushed undertone, a whisper that speaks of a government's delicate touch in ensuring the happiness of its citizens. Strolling through its shimmering streets and looming skyscrapers, I found that the economic vigour was palpable. But so too was the heart-warming collection of privileges the city-state extends to its denizens.

One afternoon, as I sat under the canopy of a local cafe, I watched as elderly citizens exchanged bright blue coupons for steaming bowls of laksa or plates of Hainanese chicken rice. These weren't mere food vouchers, they were a gentle reminder, an emblematic representation, of the state's care, a gesture to mitigate the city's sometimes staggering cost of living.

Transportation in Singapore, an orchestra of systematic routes and rhythmic movements, is yet another feather in the city's cap. With its nominal fares, it's as if the city gently nudges you to explore its every nook and cranny, making sure that economic constraints don't tether people.

In the midst of this urban environment, there are oases—gardens that seem to be plucked straight out of Eden, cultivated with a precision and love that is rare. These lush expanses, along with the city's museums, are open to the public, either gratis or for a minimal fee. It's in these spaces that I have often felt the pulse of Singapore, a rhythm that beats with history, nature, and artistry.

But the pièce de résistance? The monthly gift of music that the city bestows upon its people. "Beautiful Sunday", they call it, and oh how aptly named! On these days, the soul of the city seems to hum, buzz, and sing with the tunes of symphonies. The performances, illustrating the city's embrace of culture and arts, take place in the most unconventional of venues, the Durian, a concert hall that from the outside mimics the spiky appearance of the notorious fruit but that inside is nothing short of a sanctuary for melody and rhythm.

With the foregoing gestures, both grand and understated, Singapore doesn't merely provide for its citizens: it romances them, serenades them, and envelops them in a tender embrace, reminding them that amidst the hustle, there's always room for beauty and benevolence.

I found my soul resonating with the soul of Singapore, this small but robust island that pulsates with energy yet maintains a harmony with nature. The Singapore Botanic Gardens became a place of solace for me, a sprawling sanctuary where orchids kiss the air with their perfume and where ancient trees whisper stories of time's embrace. Here, I walked amongst a mosaic of flora, each plant singing a song of existence as the garden seemed to breathe with life.

My daily meditations, once surrounded by the blue sky and the Pacific Ocean of California, were now accompanied by Singapore's different shades of blue and a panorama of greenery. The change in landscape was not merely physical; it also reflected a shift in my consciousness. I was growing, adapting, and blossoming just like the tropical plants that surrounded me.

My fitness regime took on a new rhythm as well. The gym at the five-star hotel became a new temple for my body. Here, under the watchful guidance of a friendly and hunky private instructor, I rediscovered the joy of challenging myself, pushing boundaries, and celebrating every victory, big or small. My instructor became more than just a trainer: he was a companion on my journey towards a healthier self.

Swimming in the hotel's lap pool was another delightful ritual. The pool, quiet and devoid of the rambunctious energy of children, provided a space to glide, float, and lose myself in the soothing embrace of water. The dance of ripples and the feeling of weightlessness became a meditation in itself, a symphony played by my body and soul.

Singapore also introduced me to a community of new friends. Through connections at the US Embassy, I became part of monthly walking tours into the heart of Singaporean culture. We explored hidden alleys, tasted local flavours, and shared laughter and stories. These friends became my companions in discovering Singapore's character and my own evolving identity. The walking trips would inevitably end at a local food court, a testament to Singaporeans' love for reasonably priced decent food.

In this tropical garden city, I found more than just a home: I found a reflection of myself. The greenery and the vibrant life of Singapore resonated with the new chapters of my life that I was penning down. It was a dance of synchronicity, a harmony of existence that transcended mere geography and rooted itself deep within my soul.

In Singapore, I was no longer a visitor; I was part of the island's tropical symphony, a note in its endless melody. Here in this city where nature and humanity perform a ceaseless dance, I found a rhythm to match the beating of my heart.

A Home Away from Home—the American Club, Singapore

The decision to settle in Singapore brought with it a longing to connect with something familiar, something that resonated with my American roots. That connection manifested in the form of the American Club in Singapore, a haven for expatriates and a place that became for me not merely a club, but a home away from home.

The American Club in Singapore is more than a mere establishment; it's a microcosm of comfort, familiarity, and luxury designed with a deep understanding of what an American expatriate might seek in a foreign land. Located in the heart of the city, the club epitomizes the quintessence of American hospitality mixed with the charm of Singaporean efficiency.

Upon entering, you're greeted by a range of amenities tailored to make you feel right at home. There's the Second Floor restaurant, an elegant yet cosy space that became my preferred venue for business lunches and dinners. With a menu that tantalizes the taste buds and an ambiance that fosters both formal and informal conversation, it's a place where business blends seamlessly with pleasure.

The Thinking Space on the third floor became my sanctuary for work. Equipped with a well-stocked library, conference rooms, and meeting areas, it's designed to cater for every professional need. Whether engrossed in a book or engaged in a video conference, visitors here find that the environment encourages productivity and creativity. Here, I found a space that allowed me to be both contemplative and connected.

But it's not just the physical spaces that make the American Club special; it's the people. The staff, with their attentive and personalized service, know me by my name. They anticipate my needs, greet me with warm smiles, and create an atmosphere that's truly homey. Their commitment to making every member feel special adds a layer of warmth to the already inviting environment.

Perhaps one of the most striking features of the American Club in Singapore is the sense of security it offers. I was told that if war were ever to break out in Singapore, there would be two places where the USA government would seek to evacuate its citizens: the US Embassy and the American Club. This is a testament to the club's stature and the trust it commands.

The membership fee structure is another reflection of the club's alignment with its US and Canadian patrons. The fees for citizens of these two nations are just one-third of what they are for non-Americans, a gesture that speaks of inclusiveness and connection.

Joining the American Club as a lifetime member was more than a commitment to a lifestyle; it was an affirmation of my identity. In the midst of

Singapore's bustling diversity, the club offered a slice of familiarity without isolating me from the local culture. It became a melting pot, a confluence of the East and West, where I could revel in the best of both worlds.

In this unique space, I found camaraderie, comfort, and a connection to my roots, all wrapped up in the elegance and efficiency for which Singapore is renowned. The American Club became my American oasis in the heart of Asia, a cherished space where I could be myself and yet be a part of the ever-unfolding Singaporean story.

A Modern Paradox—Singapore's Dance between Tradition and Progress

Singapore, a place that has captured the world's imagination through the way it is portrayed in the movie *Crazy Rich Asians*, defies conventional understanding. It's a city-state that is as fascinating as it is complex, striking a careful balance between tradition and modernity, East and West, and conservatism and progressiveness.

Politically, Singapore has enjoyed a remarkable stability since 1965 with one party at the helm. This might evoke comparisons to China's single-party rule, yet Singapore is anything but communist. It's a unique hybrid where the government actively looks out for its citizens, offering perks and initiatives to enhance their standard of living, all within a market-driven economy that resonates more with the USA's capitalist principles.

The population is fewer than six million, and half of these are foreigners, adding to the cultural mosaic that makes Singapore both vibrant and intricate. The city's cosmopolitan charm is met with an underlying conservatism that often surprises visitors.

But it is Singapore's international stance that places it in an intriguing predicament. Positioned as a significant hub in Southeast Asia, it boasts strong economic and cultural ties with both the USA and China. The recent tensions between these superpowers have thrust Singapore into a delicate balancing act. The government's proclamation that Singapore is a great friend to both China and the USA isn't mere diplomacy; it's a tightrope walk that the country must approach with grace and tact.

And yet beneath the polished façade, the incumbent government has been beset with political scandals, investigations into ministers' abuse of power, and even revelations of extramarital affairs amongst members of parliament. These scandals, which might seem trivial to some Western nations, have deeply affected Singaporean society, stirring discomfort and debate.

These controversies serve to illuminate an underlying tension in Singaporean society. Despite its glittering skyscrapers, world-class infrastructure, and reputation as a hub of innovation and finance, Singapore's heart beats to a conservative rhythm. Modernity is embraced, but traditional values are held dear, and the private lives of public figures are expected to conform to these values.

Singapore is a place where contradictions live side by side. It's a nation that revels in its success and wealth but clings to traditions and societal norms. It's a place that boldly steps into the future but keeps one foot firmly planted in its cultural roots, and it's a country that welcomes the world with open arms but insists on maintaining its unique identity.

As I settle into life here, I find myself fascinated by this dance between the old and the new, the progressive and the traditional, the local and the global. Singapore is not merely a place; it's an ongoing story, a lesson in harmony, a testament to what can be achieved when diversity, innovation, and tradition find ways to coexist. Singapore is an example of the richness of human experience and serves as a reminder that complexity can be beautiful.

Behind the Academic Veil—Discovering Singapore's Hidden Facets

In the field of academia, I have encountered countless souls, each carrying his or her own cache of knowledge and experience. Amongst these was Yvonne, the embodiment of dedication and passion. With more than a quarter century of commitment to the university, she had recently taken up the cause of championing both the circular economy and sustainability. There was a fervour in her voice and fire in her eyes every time she spoke about her new mission. Her passion was infectious.

Singapore, with its gleaming skyscrapers and meticulous urban planning, often feels like a place apart from the rest of the world. Yet beneath its modern façade is an academic realm that Yvonne introduced me to that seems distant from the city's global image. Over some durian—delectable and pungent—at a local market, we delved deep into conversations about Singapore's academic achievements.

"Singapore might be tiny," I began, savouring the creamy flesh of the durian, "but its academic prowess is undeniably colossal. Given my involvement in academic rankings, I've always wondered how this little island so consistently punches above its weight class. It can't just be about publications or student learning outcomes."

She paused for a moment, a twinkle in her eye, then said, "Well, it might surprise you to know that our university has an entire team of fifteen people dedicated to managing our ranking." I was taken aback. This was a testament to the depth of strategy underpinning the city-state's ambition.

As our conversation meandered, Yvonne touched upon another sensitive topic: the undeniable dominance of males in Singaporean academia. "While our faculty has almost an equal gender split," she mused, "leadership roles are overwhelmingly male-dominated. The reasons? They're as elusive as they are complex."

The revelation came unexpectedly to me. This was a conundrum in a nation known for its progressive strides.

Yvonne then shared another startling truth: despite the grand dialogue concerning sustainability, it remained a largely peripheral concern within academic corridors. "Much of the focus on sustainability," she confessed, "is often mere window dressing, an attempt to appease government and corporate interests."

This was a revelation. Greenwashing, a term I had often associated with corporations and their PR practices, was infiltrating the hallowed halls of academia. It was a reminder that no institution is immune to the pull of optics over genuine intent.

Yvonne's insights were invaluable, opening my eyes to the intricacies of an academic world in Singapore I scarcely knew. She remains, for me, a beacon of dedication and integrity amidst the challenging landscapes she navigates. Her journey is a testament to the resilience and determination of those who choose to forge their own paths, even when the terrain is fraught with complexities and contradictions.

The Flight of Minds—Singapore's Youth Dilemma

In the midst of the glittering success and the balance between tradition and modernity, Singapore faces an internal struggle that threatens to shake its very foundation: brain drain amongst its young generations.

There is an undeniable allure to the wider world, and it beckons Singapore's youth, casting a seductive spell that entices them to live and work outside their homeland. English-speaking countries such as the USA and Australia, and those on the Europe continent, have become fertile grounds for these young minds, drawing them in with vast opportunities, cultural richness, and a promise of greater freedom.

It's not just the allure of foreign lands that tempts the youth but also the respect and recognition for their high level of education. Singaporean youth, schooled in a rigorous system that has been consistently ranked amongst the highest in the world, find themselves welcomed with open arms. Singaporean students' math ability, on a par with Finland and top western European countries, is but one example of the nation's educational prowess.

But what does this mean for Singapore itself?

Those who remain are often driven to pursue stability, enticed by the corporate world, and employed by multinationals. Becoming a salaried individual in this thriving hub of commerce can be appealing, yet it has a hidden cost: the stifling of local entrepreneurship.

The flight of bright young minds abroad and the seduction of stable jobs within large companies is a phenomenon that creates a void where innovation and local enterprise might otherwise thrive. Entrepreneurship suffers, not necessarily from a lack of talent, but from a redirection of that talent, either overseas or into the well-established pathways of corporate life.

This trend reflects a deeper conflict within Singaporean society. The same education system that garners international acclaim also fosters a certain conformity and risk aversion. The very qualities that make Singaporean youth attractive to foreign employers can also stifle their entrepreneurial spirit at home.

It's a complex issue, one that is not easily resolved. Singapore, in its pursuit of excellence and global standing, has created a paradox where its greatest strength is also a potential weakness.

I ponder this as I walk through the bustling streets of Singapore, witnessing the incredible energy, efficiency, and orderliness that characterizes this city-state. It's a place that seems to have everything, yet it finds itself facing a unique challenge that threatens its vibrancy and future growth.

How does a nation keep its young, talented minds engaged and invested in building a future at home when the world is calling to them with promises of adventure, freedom, and recognition? It's a question without easy answers, a challenge that will require creativity, courage, and perhaps a reimagining of what success looks like for the youth of Singapore.

As I settle into my new home, I find myself invested in this story, curious to see how this city, so adept at balancing contrasts and complexities, will navigate through this difficult situation. The future of Singapore may very well depend on Singapore's finding a way to not only educate its youth but also inspire them to build, create, and innovate within their own beautiful, unique land.

There is hope. The vibrancy of Singapore's youthful energy remains an intoxicating pulse. These are individuals with brilliant minds refined in the crucible of rigorous academia and cosmopolitan culture, poised on the precipice of a future both uncertain and rife with possibility. The city-state's eminent universities are incubating these potential leaders of tomorrow, carving out spaces for innovation and fostering an entrepreneurial spirit. One such initiative that I've had the privilege to witness and participate in is the Enterprise Group of a renowned Singaporean university.

The Enterprise Group, which is an ecosystem, is an ambitious endeavour that sprang into existence more than a decade ago that is devoted to nurturing the entrepreneurial dreams of the university's student body—a striking testament to the university's commitment to groom, not just employees, but also employers of the future. I have been fortunate enough to be roped into their orbit, participating as a judge in their competitions, a mentor to their bright-eyed students, and a facilitator of workshops for students from across Southeast Asia.

Engaging with these young minds is a singular experience, one that leaves me both inspired and pensive. On one hand, the intellectual vigour, the voracious curiosity, and the intrinsic motivation these students exhibit is nothing short of awe-inspiring. Their ventures not only align with, but often anticipate future mandates of, the Singapore government, be it in technology, sustainability, or food.

However, Singapore continues to grapple with a contradiction—the flight of minds—even as it works tirelessly to foster a home-grown culture of innovation and entrepreneurship. The question remains, how can the city-state balance its ambition of becoming a global hub of innovation while retaining the talent to make this ambition a reality? As I look at these bright faces brimming with ideas and dreams, I find myself hoping they find their answers, as this would enable them to contribute to their homeland's progress while fulfilling their personal aspirations.

For now, I continue to share, mentor, and learn. I continue to marvel at these young minds that dare to dream big and work hard to transform these dreams into reality. Their spirit, their determination, and their vision serve as a reminder that despite its dilemmas, Singapore's youthful energy remains a beacon of hope and potential, also serving as a testament to the power of education, innovation, and ambition and a promise of an exciting, vibrant future.

At an innovation competition, I found myself gathered with a group of young women in a warm circle, a cocoon of young aspirations and dreams, a place of safe exchange. Five female students, each with a fire in their eyes that bore witness to their ambition and intelligence, were looking at me as if they were reading a book that would guide their way. There was mutual respect and interest in the air, each one of these young women eager to learn, engage, and be inspired.

Amongst them was Sara, a final-year business student who is currently interning at McKinsey. She was the team lead, and her poise and air of confidence made it evident. Her presentation had been impressive, so clear and articulate that it captured the essence of the discussion. The way she spoke with such conviction and understanding made me realize that this was not just a team lead presenting a well-prepared report: this was a future leader ready to carve her niche in the corporate world.

"Sara," I said, looking at her across the circle, "your presentation was fantastic. It was informative, well structured, and thoroughly engaging. Can you tell me more about your creative process?"

She looked at me, her eyes shining with the recognition, and began sharing her journey. She spoke about how she always started by understanding the root of the problem, then lead her team through brainstorming sessions, and then worked together with them to refine their ideas. As she spoke, her words were not merely a recounting of her process but an embodiment of her leadership style—collaborative, strategic, and thoughtful.

As the conversation flowed, the other students chimed in, sharing their experiences and perspectives. The room was abuzz with youthful energy, each woman contributing her unique insights to the discussion.

The bond that we shared in that room, along with the mutual respect and the eagerness to learn from each other, reinforced my belief in the importance of such conversations. Our discussions were not just a way for these young women to learn about the professional world, but were also a chance for them to see themselves as integral parts of that world. It was about empowering them, reminding them that they are capable of making their own decisions, that they are not just participants in the game but potential game-changers themselves.

"Sara," I began, sensing a deep restlessness beneath her poised exterior, "there's a spark in you that is bright and promising, but there's also a nervousness whose origins that I can't quite place. Is there something on your mind?"

Sara hesitated, looking at me with wide eyes that gave off a flicker of vulnerability. She nodded slightly as if agreeing with my unspoken question.

"It's just … I've always wanted to make a difference, you know?" she began. "I feel like there's a bigger world out there that I have yet to explore. But I also have this fear." She paused. "What if I'm not good enough?"

I looked at her, acknowledging the fear that many of us feel when we're on the cusp of stepping into uncharted territory. I could see in her a reflection of myself.

"Sara," I said, gently, "the nervousness you feel is normal. In fact, it's a good sign. It means you're stepping out of your comfort zone, challenging yourself, and that's where the real growth happens."

"But what if I fail?" she interjected.

"Well, failure," I said, "is a part of the process. It's not a dead end, but a detour. A learning curve. It helps you identify what you don't want, so you can focus on what you do want."

She nodded, seeming to absorb my words.

"Besides," I continued, "in my experience, making a difference doesn't mean you have to do grand things. Often, it's about doing small things with great love and sincerity. It's about using your skills and passion to touch lives wherever you may be."

Her eyes seemed to brighten at this, as if a weight had been lifted.

"I've travelled far and wide, Sara," I said, "and if there's one thing I can assure you of, it's that the world needs more women like you—bright, empathetic, and ready to make a difference."

And just like that, I saw a shift in Sara. Her nervousness seemed to settle, replaced by a new-found determination. The world was waiting for her, I thought. And I had no doubt she would make her mark.

Our conversation flowed naturally towards the topic of gender in STEM. The disparities had been clear to me even before Sara broached the subject, a problem reflected worldwide but particularly pronounced in certain parts of Asia.

"Surely you've noticed," Sara started, her fingers twirling a lock of her hair nervously, "that there aren't many women in STEM programmes here?"

"Indeed." I nodded, letting the silence hang in the air for a moment to convey my knowledge that the issue is a weighty one. "It's a problem not just in Singapore, but also in many other places around the world. And we need to question the reasons behind it."

She looked at me thoughtfully, perhaps surprised by my agreement. "I think it's because people still believe that STEM areas are reserved for men. Women are discouraged from an early age from exploring them, and it's hard to change that."

"And that's where we need to start," I suggested. "Change doesn't happen overnight, but it begins with conversation, with challenging those old stereotypes, with making it clear that any field is open to anyone, regardless of gender."

But breaking these social norms isn't easy. It's like standing in front of a massive dam and knowing you need to create an opening for the water to flow through, but only having a tiny chisel in your hand. Yet, even that tiny chisel can make a mark by beginning to chip away at the massive structure. It's all about starting somewhere.

"We need to ensure girls are exposed to STEM from a young age, to plant the seed of curiosity and confidence in their minds," I continued. "Encourage them to question, to explore, to create. Then we need to reinforce that through education, through mentors and role models who show them that it is possible to succeed in these areas."

"I also believe it's important to have more women in leadership roles in these fields to serve as role models and pave the way for others," I added. "Like what you're doing right now, Sara. By challenging the status quo, you're proving that women are not just capable but are also excelling in these fields."

Sara looked at me, a spark of resolve lighting up her eyes. I felt a surge of pride—for her, for us, for all the women who dare to dream and strive. It's these tiny chisels, these ripples of change, that will one day bring the dam down.

There's something both humbling and energizing about being regarded as a source of inspiration. With each mentoring session, I am approached by young women, their eyes brimming with dreams and ambitions, each of them seeing a reflection of their future paths in my journey. They see an Asian woman, well-educated and worldly, unafraid to carve her own path in a realm still largely dominated by men.

I am often surrounded by these young women at the end of each session, each of them eager to have a photo taken with me. I can't help but be reminded of my time in China when female entrepreneurs would line up for the same reason, their expressions a mix of admiration and aspiration. These moments, while flattering, serve as a profound reminder of my responsibility and my role in this ecosystem that extends beyond being a mentor or judge or teacher. I am a beacon, a tangible manifestation of these women's dreams and potential.

To these young women, I embody defiance of the stereotype, which they likely read a declaration that they too can stand tall in the corridors of power and they too can assert their brilliance in domains traditionally dominated by men. But my message to them goes beyond just breaking glass ceilings. It is about redefining their identities, judging themselves not by the social norms that have long determined the roles of women, but by their own standards.

I urge them to push boundaries, not just the ones set by society, but also those they have drawn for themselves. I encourage them to seek not just success but fulfilment, and not to let their careers eclipse their personal lives, but to strive for a balance that enables happiness and growth in all aspects. I remind them that their femininity is not a weakness to be hidden but a strength to be celebrated and that their voices are not just valuable but also necessary in shaping the future.

Being a role model to these young women is an honour, a role I didn't actively seek but one that I have come to embrace. To be able to play a part in shaping these brilliant minds, help them navigate their paths, and witness their transformations into the leaders of tomorrow is a privilege I am grateful for. Their fire and potential reassure me that the future of business, indeed the future of the world, is in capable and determined hands.

As I continue to engage with these young women, my hope is that my journey serves, not as a path to follow, but as a reminder that they can and should carve their own paths. And as they redefine who they are and their roles in the business world, they will inevitably redefine the business world itself. For it is they who hold the power to shape not just their own futures, but the future of the world.

The Sun and the City: Singapore's Dance with Sustainability

Singapore—this modern marvel of a city-state is a place where innovation and efficiency meet in a perfect tango. As I navigate through the pristine streets, past glass façades reflecting an almost utopian image of the future, I can't help but marvel at the commitment here to sustainability and circular economy. Recycling bins as commonplace as streetlights, green building initiatives, and campaigns for zero waste—it's all very impressive.

But then I find myself circling back to a question that I just can't shake: Where are all the electric cars?

For a nation that seems to have its finger on the pulse of the future, the absence of electric vehicles is striking. I delve into this issue a bit and discover that Singapore buys electricity primarily from Malaysia and Indonesia, rendering it a scarce and precious resource. Ah, so that's the rub! I can't help but think, though, of the irony of it all. This little island is practically bathing in sunshine all year round—could the sun itself not be the answer to this electricity problem?

Now, I know space is at a premium in Singapore. Real estate here is as precious as a Cartier diamond. But surely, in this hub of ingenuity, there must be ways to harness the energy of the ever-abundant sun. The scarcity of space might hinder traditional solar farms, but what about vertical solar panels or rooftop installations?

As I ponder these questions, sipping my sustainable, locally sourced herbal tea, I find myself hoping that by the time *Happiness Is ...* is published, Singapore will have figured out how to tap into the most obvious and abundant resource it has: sunlight. The metaphorical richness of it all isn't lost on me: a nation that has so meticulously engineered its own rise now stands at the threshold of a new challenge, much like an evolving soul searching for the next leap of growth.

I find comfort in the thought that Singapore, like any enterprising entity—be it a person or a country—will find its way. And when it does, it'll do so in a manner that is elegantly efficient. It'll look as though the solution had been there all along, just waiting to be discovered under the brilliance of the tropical sun.

Subterranean Dreams and Sunlit Realities: A Conversation with Frederick

As I found myself wandering along the lush pathways of Singapore Botanic Gardens, my mind still swirling with questions about the nation's curiously tentative stance towards solar energy, I happened upon Frederick, an earnest young Singaporean wrestling with the complexities of his own identity and his homeland's aspirations.

We sat on a bench, shaded by the mature trees that seemed like wise old souls listening to our conversation. It was as if we had entered a leafy sanctuary, far removed from the buzz of the city's indefatigable progress.

"I've been thinking about the absence of electric cars here," I began, "and the untapped potential of solar energy. Any theories?"

Frederick leaned back, crossing his arms thoughtfully. "You know, it's not that we're unaware. But Singapore is always playing the long game. The government is deeply pragmatic, you could even say visionary. There's a plan for a completely underground city. Did you know that?"

"An underground city?" I blinked in astonishment.

"Yes." He nodded, his eyes intense but far away as if visualizing this subterranean world. "It's part of preparing for an unpredictable future—global warming, rising sea levels, and perhaps even a war. Singapore doesn't have the luxury of space, but it does have the depth below. We're digging down while other countries are reaching for the stars."

My mind reeled at the idea. An entire city underground was as poetic as it was mind-bendingly practical. It was Jules Verne meets urban planning, the stuff of both science fiction and stark realism.

"So, you think the hesitancy in implementing electric cars and solar energy has to do with this underground vision?"

"In a way, yes," Frederick continued. "You see, an underground city would require an enormous amount of electricity, more than we currently produce or can even store. If we become too dependent on electric cars now and have to suddenly divert electricity to sustain life below, it could create chaos."

"And solar energy?" I pressed.

"Sunlight, obviously, doesn't reach underground." He chuckled. "Solar power, as promising as it is, may not be the solution for an underground city. The government is probably eyeing other forms of sustainable energy that can be harnessed below the surface." *Hydrogen fuel cell and nuclear power then?* I wondered.

I sat there both amazed and slightly unsettled, my imagination running wild with images of a bustling underground metropolis, like a hive hidden from the world. It was as though I had peeked into a secret chamber of Singapore's aspirations, and this aspiration was as practical as it was fantastical.

"Wow, Frederick. That's a whole new lens through which to see this incredible little island."

He smiled, perhaps grateful that someone was willing to entertain his ideas without immediate judgement. "In a city that never ceases to look forward," he said, "sometimes the most enlightening perspectives are found by looking down."

As we sat in silence, absorbing the profundity of the moment, I thought, *Here in this paradox of a country, even the untapped potential of the sun is overshadowed by dreams that burrow deep into the earth.* In that thought, I sensed the grand narrative of Singapore—an ever-evolving story where the ending, no doubt, will be as surprising as it is logical.

The Pulse of Prosperity—Singapore's Investment Landscape

In the complex equation of Singapore's socioeconomic dynamics, there's another factor that plays a vital role in the nation's prosperity: the magnetism of foreign direct investment (FDI). It's like a pulse, steady and strong, that pumps financial lifeblood into the city-state.

Unfortunately, this influx of investment isn't always as transformative as one might hope. The capital flowing in from China's affluent individuals, eager to escape the "common prosperity" theme being trumpeted by the Chinese Communist Party, doesn't necessarily contribute to value-added industries within Singapore. Instead, these funds are often deployed for investments outside Singapore's borders.

Singapore acts as a conduit that draws in wealth and then redirects it. The benefits for Singapore are perhaps subtle, found in the gainful employment of its permanent residents and citizens. It's a legal requirement when these affluent Chinese investors establish family offices in Singapore to ensure that some of the wealth finds its way into the local economy.

Yet, Singapore's government isn't content with being a mere financial hub for the world's wealthy. A lack of space for manufacturing factories has steered the focus towards the future, namely, encouraging technology and innovation in Web3, AI, and sustainability.

Singapore is positioned as a convenient crossroads for global dialogue and collaboration. Whether it's a business meeting, a conference, or a large event, almost everything is just a short twenty-minute drive away from all major hotels. It's a city designed for connections, for bringing together minds and ideas from every corner of the earth.

But this requires a delicate balance. While FDI fuels economic growth and creates opportunities, the nature of the investment matters. A reliance on capital from those seeking to park their wealth can create a sense of transience, a fluidity that lacks roots. The challenge for Singapore is to channel this investment in ways that align with its broader vision for a sustainable, innovative future.

I reflect on this as I walk through the financial district, the towering skyscrapers reflecting the ambition and energy of this vibrant city-state. I can feel the pulse of prosperity and the constant hum of transactions, deals, and innovations that shape Singapore's place in the world.

Yet, I also sense a yearning for something deeper, a desire to create, not just wealth, but value. This is a desire that resonates with me, as in this part of my journey, I've been seeking meaning and fulfilment in a place that, despite its modernity and efficiency, still holds onto its soul.

Singapore's future may well depend on its ability to navigate this place fraught with dangers, to harness the power of investment, not just for economic growth, but also for a vision of progress that is inclusive, creative, and rooted in values that transcend mere financial gain.

This is the quest of Singapore, and it's a journey that I, too, am now a part of—a journey towards a future that is not only prosperous but also wise, mindful, and deeply connected to what truly matters. It's a vision that excites me, and I can't help but feel that in this city-state, amidst the gleaming towers and bustling markets, something extraordinary is taking shape that speaks, not just to the mind, but also to the heart, something that could be a model for the world.

The pulse of prosperity in Singapore is palpable. Everywhere I've looked, I've seen signs of growth, ambition, and relentless drive: skyscrapers reaching for the heavens, glittering with the promise of wealth; meeting rooms filled with eager entrepreneurs pitching their dreams; investors, serious and calculating, ready to fuel those dreams with capital. There is a frenetic energy, a sense that anything is possible.

And yet, as I have delved deeper into this landscape, I have begun to notice the undercurrents that run beneath the gleaming surface. There is a tension, a complexity, that defies easy categorization.

The process of raising funds, for example, was a revelation in itself. I found myself meeting with business development professionals who seemed more suited to a runway than to a boardroom. They were young and beautiful, some of them talented, but their appearance seemed to be the primary thing that had qualified them. This was a phenomenon I hadn't encountered in my previous roles, and it left me unsettled.

I began to understand that there was a game being played here, one that had its own rules and rituals—a game that demanded certain concessions and certain compromises that I was not willing to make. This realization was both troubling and enlightening. It forced me to confront the unspoken truths of this world, including the subtle power dynamics that governed relationships and the tacit agreements that were made, often at the expense of integrity. But it also led me to a deeper understanding of what it means to navigate this landscape on my own terms. My journey than became a journey of self-discovery, a test of my values, my beliefs, and my sense of self. I had to learn to stand firm, to trust my instincts, and to know when to walk away.

Through this process, I came to see that the pulse of prosperity is not just about money, or success, or status. For me, it is about finding a way to engage with the world that is authentic, ethical, and true to who I am.

In the midst of the glittering towers and bustling markets of Singapore, in the complex web of investments, deals, and relationships, I found a path that is uniquely mine, a path that honours, not just the demands of the market, but also the demands of my soul.

I knew that the road ahead would be filled with challenges, seeing as the world of venture capital is a place of high stakes, intense competition, and often ruthless pragmatism. But I also knew that I had found my place in it, not by conforming to its norms, but by redefining the norms in a way that aligned with my integrity.

The pulse of prosperity in Singapore is not just a beat that drives the economy; it is a rhythm that resonates with the very essence of life. It is a reminder that success is not just about accumulation but also about alignment, not just about wealth but also about wisdom, and not just about gaining but also about growing.

In this thriving city-state, I had found, not just a new career, but a new way of being, a way that honoured the complexity and contradictions of this world and that allowed me to thrive, not in spite of my values, but because of them.

The Paradox of Prosperity: Singapore's Quiet Struggle

Within Singapore's prosperity, its architectural marvels, and its soaring financial indices, lies a complex narrative, one that the nation grapples with even as it continues to dazzle the world. Singapore, for all its rigour and discipline, has become an unintended sanctuary for those who gains are ill-gotten.

Walking down the opulent lanes of Nassim Road, where Good Class Bungalows sprawl like miniature kingdoms, or strolling past the high-end condominium buildings that populate the luxurious enclaves of Sentosa Cove, you may not realize that these impressive façades often house stories far murkier than their polished exteriors suggest. Behind some of these gates and beyond those closed doors lie funds and assets of dubious origins—vehicles for money laundering primarily from mainland China and the Middle East.

The Singaporean government, always in a constant state of vigilance, has not turned a blind eye to this influx of shadowy wealth. There is a rigorous campaign under way to seize these unfairly acquired assets, from gleaming Lamborghinis to lavish pieces of jewellery and designer handbags. Yet, it's a double-edged sword: as the country gains renown as a global financial hub, it becomes increasingly difficult to fully filter out the fast money that inflates its economy artificially, including the property market.

For a nation often touted as one of the least corrupt and most efficient in the world, this quiet struggle raises ethical and existential questions for Singapore. Can Singapore preserve its integrity while still being the magnet for global capital it aspires to be? What are the trade-offs for rapid growth and ethical governance, and can these two things coexist harmoniously?

Just as individual citizens, like my academic friend Yvonne, grapple with reconciling their personal aspirations with social norms and expectations, the nation itself is doing the same thing. For Singapore, the quest for financial supremacy comes with its own set of moral and ethical conundrums. These are lessons and questions that require as much introspection as action, which fact invites us all to ponder the price of progress and the ethics of ambition.

From Wall Street to Maldivian Islands

The sheer magnitude of Anton's influence in the world of finance is nothing short of awe-inspiring, from his early days at Goldman Sachs to his now legendary status as the man with the Midas touch. I found that every encounter with him was a lesson in ambition and audacity.

I met him in a cafe off Orchard Road in Singapore. He was clad in a crisp linen suit and was sipping on an espresso, his gaze fixated on a laptop screen that flashed numbers and charts I couldn't even begin to comprehend. As we spoke, it became clear to me that the world he inhabited was both enigmatic and exhilarating.

He shared tales that seemed almost too cinematic to be real. There was the story of the Russian oligarch who, on a leisurely sail through the turquoise waters of the Maldives, caught sight of an island so mesmerizing that he felt compelled to own it. Just two meetings and the deal was done. An entire island exchanged hands, the deal sealed with a handshake and a hefty bank transfer.

But what truly fascinated me was Anton's connection with the Malaysian sultans. As guardians of age-old Malay heritage, they hold vast tracts of land, gifted to their ancestors and passed down through generations. They turned to Anton, seeking ways to make these ancestral lands yield more than just crops: they also wanted it to yield profits. They weren't just looking for money; they were looking to solidify their legacy for the generations to come.

Anton's ability to bridge the modern and the ancient, to understand both the algorithms of today and the traditions of yesteryear, is what sets him apart. He's not just a broker; he's a storyteller, weaving narratives of fortunes made, lost, and remade. In his tales, history meets the future, and the two dance in a ballet of business acumen and cultural respect.

When I prodded Anton about his investment philosophy, he leaned back, looking past the skyscrapers that framed our cafe view, deep in thought. "It's a blend," he began, "of respecting the old and embracing the new."

To Anton, finance is not just about spreadsheets and balance sheets; it is about narratives. He told me that he saw every stock, every commodity, and every investment opportunity as a story waiting to be told. But while he had an old soul's appreciation for the long view, he also had a technologist's hunger for the latest tools. Enter artificial intelligence (AI).

Anton had always been a math prodigy, but AI had supercharged his capabilities. With AI, he could sift through a mountain of data, identify patterns that no human could spot, and make predictions that were uncannily accurate. It wasn't just about crunching numbers faster; it was about understanding the world in a way that previously had been impossible.

I asked him about the newest kid on the block: cryptocurrency. He chuckled, taking a moment before answering. "Cryptocurrency," he mused, "is like a wild stallion—beautiful and powerful, but unpredictable." He told me that he respected cryptocurrency's potential to disrupt traditional financial systems and said that he admired the technology behind it. But he also warned of its volatility. "It's not for the faint of heart," he said, a wry smile playing on his lips. "But then again, what in finance truly is?"

Anton believes that while the underlying technology of blockchain has immense potential, the world of crypto is still in its infancy. It needed to mature, he said, and find its footing. Until then, he would tread carefully, watching from the sidelines, ready to jump in when the narrative became clearer.

He leaned in towards me, his eyes gleaming with that familiar intensity. "Remember, it's not just about embracing the future. It's about understanding it." As I looked at Anton, this enigma who straddles the worlds of ancient legacies and cutting-edge technologies, I realized that he didn't just understand the future; he was helping to shape it.

The Tightrope Walk: Navigating the Political Ballet of Singapore

Singapore is a nation that exists at the crossroads of multiple worlds. Here, the East meets the West, ancient customs merge with cutting-edge technology, and political alliances resemble a graceful dance more than a resolute march. In this tiny but potent island nation, the adage "walking on a tightrope" takes on a literal, living form.

There's an air of subtle but deliberate diplomacy that pervades every political statement emanating from the corridors of power in Singapore. "The United States of America is our great friend. China is our great friend," declares the Prime Minister, crafting a sentence so carefully balanced that it could serve as a textbook example of political finesse. To the casual observer, it might appear that Singapore is simply playing it safe. But to those who have lived here, like me, it's clear that this precarious balancing act is a matter of survival, an intricate strategy in the global board game where Singapore aspires not merely to exist but to excel.

I find a curious kind of resonance between my position and Singapore's position. I am an American, nourished by the principles of liberty and the freedom to pursue one's personal path. But I am also a third-generation Chinese, imbibed with Confucian values of family and social harmony. This cultural mosaic that defines me finds its geopolitical parallel in Singapore—a nation in a perpetual balancing act, tethered between the colossal powers of the United States and China yet ceaselessly striving to maintain its own distinct identity.

In a world where passports are more than just travel documents, but are emblems of national power, Singapore boasts the strongest one. It is a manifestation of the country's ongoing efforts to etch its significance on the global landscape, albeit in "any small way it can", as the locals often tell me. As a person who embodies a hybridisation of cultures, I feel a sense of belonging here. I understand the compulsion to be globally significant while remaining uniquely oneself. And just as I strive to contribute my patchwork self to the rich tapestry of US and Chinese heritage, so does Singapore strive to contribute its meticulously crafted self to the world—it is a country, much like an individual, always in the process of becoming.

Singapore's endeavour to be at once globally influential and also uniquely its own serves as a vivid reflection of the universal human struggle to belong while standing out. As I traverse this island state, seeing my own inner contradictions mirrored in its complex political and social landscapes, I realize that the quest for equilibrium is a journey that neither nations nor individuals can escape. It is in the fine balance of these contradicting worlds that we find our most authentic selves.

Secrets of Hotels

Hotels. They are a universe unto themselves, teeming with stories and secrets hidden within the grandeur of their chandeliers, the whispering sounds of their linen, and the silence of their midnight hallways. A hotel room is more than just a temporary address. For some, it becomes an intimate confidante, a safe haven, a home away from home. I have, in my globetrotting escapades, found refuge in the hushed sanctity of hotels, living a nomadic life between crisp sheets and with room service and, in the process, stumbling upon an unexpected revelation.

The heart and soul of a hotel is not in its grand architecture, its gourmet restaurants, or its plush amenities, but in its unsung heroes: the housekeeping staff. These humble warriors work in the shadows, quietly slipping in and out of rooms, tidying up guests' messes and ensuring their comfort, all the while maintaining an invisible presence. They may seem to be mere custodians of cleanliness, but they are so much more. They are the silent observers of our lives, the uncredited actors in our travel stories, the secret keepers of our hidden truths. They move like phantoms through the labyrinthine corridors, performing a ballet of service and discretion.

Theirs is an occupation of extreme intimacy and anonymity. They are privy to our personal spaces, our daily routines, and our hidden habits. They know what time we sleep, what we like to eat, which side of the bed we prefer, even the books we read. It's an understanding born out of routine and proximity, a bond that forms, unbeknownst to the guests, in the quiet moments of tidying up and cleaning.

In a sense, hotel housekeepers are the best spies in the world—not by design, but by circumstance. Their role grants them access to our most private moments and our most personal spaces, and they often go unnoticed and unacknowledged. But even in this silent observation, there is respect, a careful preservation of the guest's dignity and privacy.

That such people are able to live amidst such a beautiful paradox is a testament to the human capacity for respect and understanding. It causing us to realize that even in the seemingly ordinary act of cleaning, there is a story, a silent connection, an unseen bond. It's a tale of unseen caretakers, the silent custodians of our transient lives. And it's a reminder that sometimes, the most profound stories are the ones that unravel quietly, in the hushed corners of a hotel room, tended to by the gentle, unseen hands of the housekeeping staff.

In the geographical areas of my constant travelling, I've become familiar with the recurring faces of the people who are employed by the hotels I frequent. They've become a constant in my transitory existence, a comforting certainty in the blur of time zones and customs forms. One particular group amongst them especially piques my curiosity: the male cleaners.

As I watched the men housekeepers, I saw that a sort of pattern began to unfold, a coincidence too uncanny to ignore. Many of them seemed to give off an air of being highly disciplined, an understated demeanour that hinted at something more than just the routine of changing sheets and replacing mini shampoos. Their precise movements were reminiscent of military precision, and they had the stoic expressions to match.

After months of silent observation, curiosity finally got the better of me. I began striking up conversations with some of these male house-keepers, exchanging pleasantries and sharing snippets of our respective worlds. With the gradual build-up of trust, they became exceptionally familiar with me. They seemed to know which rooms I had occupied before and the nationality inked on my passport, and at times it even seemed that my casual WhatsApp chats were no secret to them.

Was I reading too much into what was going on? Or was my privacy being subtly violated? I was walking a thin line between paranoia and intuition, left to juggle my thoughts on that tightrope. The world out-side had become a stage of high-strung tension with the echoes of war resounding from Europe and the Middle East, and simmering unrest threatening to boil over in Asia. In this volatile landscape, the prospect of being monitored didn't seem so far-fetched.

But I am no Bond girl, no Bourne, and no spy. My work, as capti-vating as it can be, is innocent in nature. It carries no secrets that would justify my being placed under surveillance. Yet, the suspicion lingered, sown by the unassuming staff in crisp uniforms that had become an intriguing puzzle in my global wanderings.

These events have taught me how to dance between caution and acceptance. To live in the world today is to accept that our lives are more visible than ever before. Even so, I've chosen not to live in fear. Instead, I embrace the peculiarities that accompany my globetrotting lifestyle, finding intrigue and lessons in the most unanticipated corners of my travels. As for my diligent hotel friends, I continue to greet them with a smile, a nod, and sometimes a dash of enigmatic intrigue of my own.

4.3 The Elusive Partnership

A Chance Encounter

Singapore, a dazzling city-state where modernity cohabitates with tra-dition, a global hub for finance, a crucible of cultures. It was in this vibrant milieu, at a Web3 seminar, that I met him, a young Chinese entrepreneur, William. There was a striking gap in our ages—he was twenty years my junior. With a formidable intellect, radiant with potential, and driven by ambition, he was a standout amidst the crowd. His gaze, filled with curiosity and the vibrancy of youth, met mine, and we got into a conversation that led to an uncanny connection.

And then, abruptly, a crisis. It was the second day of the seminar when William contracted Covid-19. At midnight, his call for help rang like an alarm, severing the stillness of the hotel night. Without a second thought, I threw off my pyjamas, got dressed in my clothes, and rushed into the unknown, propelled by a sense of duty towards a new friend. Together with the president of the seminar and his assistant, we formed an impromptu convoy, travelling in two cars to the hospital. From that night onwards, what with the hospital visits, the shared concerns, and the show of solidarity in a foreign land, William and I became close. And he knew that I was an American.

In a surprising turn, after a brief visit to Chiang Mai, Thailand, William decided to split from his Singapore business partner, pitching me a fresh crypto and blockchain business plan. It was as if he had meticulously studied me, discerning my skills and experience, and crafted a plan that perfectly complemented those things. What impressed me further was his willingness to bare his failures. Not many entrepreneurs would reveal their vulnerabilities while courting a new partner, but he did. He spoke about his previous business failures with an authenticity that was both disarming and appealing. This was a man who had been featured on *Forbes* magazine's list of thirty most successful entrepreneurs under thirty and was already onto his third company—and he was willing to admit his missteps.

His dream, he confessed, was to move his entire family to the USA. The glimmer of the American Dream reflected in his eyes, with stories of opportunities and possibilities that he had nurtured in his heart. It was a deeply personal ambition, rooted in his aspiration for a better life for his family. I found myself moved by it. And so, in the heart of Singapore, our paths intertwined—two dreamers forging a new entrepreneurial partnership, stepping into a future tinged with the excitement of the unknown and the promise of a shared dream.

There we were in Singapore, poised on the precipice of a shared dream. Wiliam's family—his wife and their two children—were still tethered to their past, waiting for their passports to be issued. While they waited, he and I became comrades-in-arms, launching our nascent partnership from the American Club. We sat shoulder to shoulder fuelled by a singular purpose, each of us bringing our unique gifts to the table.

Our first order of business was monumental: an application to Andreessen Horowitz, the revered A16z venture capital firm in Silicon Valley, for seed funding. We poured ourselves into the project, every day a marathon of brainstorming, drafting, and refining. It was an exercise in unyielding optimism and dedication, and a testament to our shared belief in our venture.

There was something exhilarating about those days, an intensity that seemed to imbue the air around us. We worked tirelessly, driven by a shared vision and the adrenaline rush that comes with betting on one's dreams. The proposal took shape thanks to our concerted effort, each word meticulously chosen, each argument painstakingly built. Alongside this, we also started crafting our video, intent on presenting our case in the most compelling way possible.

The crypto and Web3 worlds were uncharted territory for me, but William's expertise provided a trustworthy compass. His insights became my guiding light, illuminating a world that seemed enigmatic at first but that gradually unveiled its mysteries. But this world wasn't just abstract jargon and complex algorithms, it was an evolving reality, a brave new world in which my children would live. That made my quest for understanding personal, and it was a quest I pursued with tenacity and fervour.

Yes, I was a beginner in this world, but I embraced it with open arms and attended to it with a receptive mind. I asked questions, sought clarification, read extensively, and engaged in vigorous discussions with William. I was eager, not just to understand this novel realm, but also to become an active participant in it, a contributor, a player. It was a challenging yet invigorating period, a time of relentless learning and growth.

As we embarked on this journey together, navigating the complexities of a new world, our partnership solidified. The American Club became our command centre, our sanctuary, our shared classroom, and the site of our burgeoning camaraderie. With every passing day, the dream inched closer to reality, and I was there, shoulder to shoulder with William, eager and excited, ready to embrace the future that lay ahead.

The US Sojourn

My friendship with Williams grew with each passing day, stretching and strengthening, akin to an ivy vine reaching for the sky. This shared journey from Singapore to California, and then to Miami, seemed almost symbolic of our bond, as if we were moving together, propelled by the same gust of dreams. His whole family followed suit, stepping onto US soil a few days after me, their eyes filled with anticipation and a hint of trepidation.

They found sanctuary in my oceanfront home, a sanctuary I offered to them rent-free. It was a gesture of goodwill, an olive branch extended to a fellow dreamer and his family. My Tesla became their chariot, available at their disposal, once again, offered with an open heart without any rent. My housekeeper and property manager welcomed them with open arms, their support unyielding and unwavering.

William would greet me with breakfast every day, a warm meal prepared with care. We would spend our days working, the rhythmic soundtrack of the ocean in the background serving as a soothing accompaniment to our shared endeavours. It was a unique rhythm of coexistence, an unconventional symbiosis.

However, not all was seamless along our shared journey. His wife, from the onset, seemed to harbour some form of discontent towards me. I was not sure of its origin, whether it was a misunderstanding, a conflict of values, or simply a reflection of her inner struggles. Regardless, I chose the path of endurance. I bore her displeasure silently, voicing no resentment.

In an attempt to keep the peace, I made a decision that tugged at my heartstrings. I chose to leave the comfort of my own home in California. I packed my bags and travelled to Australia and Singapore. The goal was to allow William and his wife space and time to acclimate to their new surroundings without any discomfort. Meanwhile, I found solace in exploration and solitude, indulging in activities that nourished my spirit and focusing on the things that sparked joy in me.

The journey of friendship and partnership is often nuanced, marred by moments of conflict and resolution and misgivings and understandings, and marked by give-and-take. Yet, throughout this journey, my commitment to the dream that William and I shared remained solid. I moved forward, propelled by faith in our shared vision and reassured by the power of resilience.

It was during those sunbathed California mornings that William and I, perched by the vast oceanfront, would dive into the realms of cryptocurrency and blockchain. Stanford's Cryptocurrency and Blockchain online course was our shared textbook; the great expanse of the digital frontier, our classroom. William, with his nimble mind, was my tutor, guiding me through the winding paths of digital finance and patiently explaining its complexities.

Even when I travelled to Melbourne, to the comfort of my mother's home, William and I continued our intellectual dance. The hemispheres that separated us could not deter our collective curiosity, nor could the silence of the miles interrupt our common chorus.

In the world of our business partnership, we each had our unique parts to play. While William was the maestro of the technical melody, overseeing the code-filled symphony of our product, I was the conductor of our venture's external rhythm, setting the tempo for our go-to-market strategy. I reached out to an attorney friend, who suggested a patent to protect our innovative product. However, William, ever the cautious tactician, suggested patience. Our product was not quite ready to see the interior of any patent office; it needed more nurturing in the incubator of our shared effort.

Our days, however, were not solely filled with business and blockchain. Life, as it often does, punctuated our narrative with its unique touch. William welcomed his third child, a baby girl, into his family. With her arrival, he began a project to balance his life. His days started out with the sweet domestic task of cooking breakfast for his family and taking the kids to Montessori, interspersed with baby care. Amidst this whirl of activity, he found pockets of quiet to study, and as the days melted into evening, he attended to our growing team of employees.

I returned to California to share in the joy of the baby's arrival, keeping a respectful distance from the family to avoid contributing to the chaos that postpartum stress often brings. But soon, I felt the call of Singapore once more. Like a boomerang, I found myself journeying back, leaving the tranquillity of California for the bustling vibrant world that is Singapore.

In this fluid dance of friendship, business, and distance, William and I found ourselves growing, changing, and adapting. Our experiences were diverse and our paths often divergent, yet we were bound together on a shared journey stretching across oceans, across time zones, and beyond life milestones.

William's proposal was like a cool breeze on a hot day. He suggested that initially we could utilize the resources of his Chinese company to cover our staffing expenses. Only once our product was profitable would we need to consider bearing the staffs' salaries ourselves.

This revelation brought a wave of relief, a lightness that infused our business plan with an added layer of buoyancy. I felt a warmth spreading through me, which was a gentle acknowledgement of his generosity and his genuine dedication to our shared endeavour.

The expenses to maintain our business infrastructure; the rentals; and operational costs in California and Singapore would be my responsibility. With the burden of staffing costs off my shoulders for the moment, I found this commitment less daunting.

As I reflected on our professional partnership, I couldn't help but marvel at its unique harmonious nature. We were compatible, not only in our demeanours and attitudes, but also in the way our individual competencies complemented the other's.

It felt as though our partnership was not merely an alliance born out of shared ambitions, but one that had been carefully sculpted by the hands of destiny itself. We were different, yet our differences gave rise to mutual respect and understanding, which strengthened the bond we shared. Despite the miles between us and despite the cultural and age differences, we had found a harmonious rhythm together. We were indeed a partnership made in heaven, an example of the power of congeniality and complementary skill sets.

Reunion in Singapore

When news of William's "approval in principle" for his US L1 visa came through, it was a sigh of relief as strong as the initial intake of air after having held one's breath for too long. His family, gearing up for yet another journey, swooped in to Singapore to process their employment passes—a safety net in the event that the US Embassy in Beijing declined their application.

The fluorescent lights of Changi airport, renowned for its transcendent beauty, twinkled like low-hanging stars as I stood in the arrival hall. The scent of freshly brewed coffee wafted through the air from a nearby cafe, but my anticipation was flavoured with something sweeter—the imminent arrival of William and his family.

When they finally emerged from the airport arrival gate, it was like watching a scene in a heart-warming film unfold. William, ever the doting father, was carrying their youngest in a pouch while his wife held the hands of their exuberant four-year-old and six-year-old. The sight of them, weary from travel yet with faces illuminated by the soft light of familial love, tugged at the sinews of my heart.

I approached, my arms laden with the simplest of gifts—snacks and water, mundane yet essential, especially for the little ones. William's children, with their boundless energy, spotted me before I could even call out. They rushed over, their tiny feet pounding on the polished airport floor, their voices raised in gleeful cries of "Ah Yee!"

The affectionate title, a term of endearment that means "auntie" in

Chinese, enveloped me in a warmth that words cannot fully capture. Their little arms, brimming with innocent affection, wrapped around me, nearly toppling me over. In that moment, the world receded and it was just us, united by bonds not of blood, but of deep-seated respect and affection—my chosen family.

As we collected their bags, I caught up with William and his wife, our conversation seamlessly picking up from where we had left off months ago. The children, buoyed by their youthful curiosity, regaled me with tales of their adventures and little squabbles, punctuating the mundane with the miraculous.

Our drive from the airport was underscored by the children's wide-eyed wonder at Singapore's night-lit skyline. I explained that this gleaming city was to be the bedrock of our next big venture—an extension of our business dreams. William shared in my excitement, his eyes alight with entrepreneurial fire, yet grounded by the comforting weight of familial responsibility.

We discussed the necessity of his upcoming trip to Beijing to sort out his L1 visa. It was a step towards something greater, a future woven from the threads of professional aspirations and personal ties. As we traversed the city, the children's laughter harmonizing with the hum of the night, I realized something profound—home isn't just a place, not a static location marked by a pin on a map. Home is where your heart finds peace, where your dreams find partners, and where family—both the one you're born into and the one you create—waits with open arms and ready smiles. In the midst of the bustling streets of Singapore, inside a car filled with lively chatter and postflight exhaustion, I found it—my home, my family, my heart, and my future, all intertwined in the city's nocturnal symphony.

In the early morning light, William texted me to meet at the American Club. His words hung in the tropical air, a poignant affirmation of our journey together: "Living at your home in California was the happiest six months of my life," he confessed, reminiscing about his time living at my beachfront property. A twinge of warmth surged through me: the satisfaction of knowing that I had contributed to this happiness.

Yet, in the days that followed, a silence stretched between us. Despite being in the same city and under the same hotel roof, William was an elusive figure for two weeks. His presence dissolved into Singapore's bustling rhythm, our encounters dwindling to none.

In the background, I sensed the spectre of his wife's jealousy, a discomforting presence that began to etch fissures into our friendship. To keep the peace and to provide them space, I decided to take a step back. I departed for the serene shores of Lombok, Indonesia, leaving them my hotel room in Singapore. I offered them solitude without charge, a sanctuary amidst the urban jungle where they could find solace, gather their thoughts, and perhaps rekindle the joy that living by the ocean had brought them.

The eve of William's departure from Singapore was heavy with anticipation and cloaked in an odd sense of foreboding. His request to meet at a hotel in the financial district, far removed from my usual terrain, seemed unusual, but I brushed off the feeling as nerves settling in. As we navigated through our conversation, his demeanour fluctuated like a faulty switch.

As I broached the subject of setting up a separate company for our product, William's reaction took me by surprise. His face paled, and the ice he was crunching in his mouth seemed to lodge in his throat. Swiftly, he excused himself and disappeared into the bathroom, only to return a good quarter of an hour later looking composed yet noticeably strained. Something was off, but I attributed it to the looming uncertainty of his upcoming travels and the imminent L1 visa processing in Beijing.

His departure the following day was a hurried affair, whisking his older children off to Beijing and leaving his wife and newborn behind in Singapore to await the two-month-old baby's Chinese visa on her brand new US passport.

Despite my hectic schedule, I found time to visit William's wife at her hotel in the financial district. I wanted to ensure she was managing, what with being alone in a foreign city with a baby to care for. Over a quiet lunch, she dropped a startling revelation: "In China, no one offers a job to women over thirty-five." Her words hung in the air, a loaded statement, hinting at the impossibility of her surviving independently. Her fear was palpable, a stark contrast to the vibrant Singapore skyline we were looking at. My heart ached for her as she was stuck in a bind that was not of her making, wrestling with the disquieting reality of her circumstance.

The Unravelling of the Partnership

As we crossed the ten-month mark of our partnership, the trajectory of our venture began to waver. William's presence turned into an absence as he vanished in China, his silence echoing louder than words for two long months while waiting for his L1 visa. The uncertainty of what he had disclosed in his visa application, given the strained US-China relationship, gnawed at my peace.

Promises were made in the realms of Web3 and AI, but they remained as they were—mere promises. We pivoted not once, not twice, but three times, yet success eluded us. The mirage of achievement that once shimmered in the distance had all but vanished.

Communication was like grasping at straws in the dark. On the rare occasions when I did manage to reach him, I was met with lies that were as transparent as glass. Even in the cold, impersonal space of a video call, I could see the evasion in his eyes, as if he were a stranger who had borrowed William's face.

The man I once trusted was slipping through my fingers like sand being carried away by a relentless tide. Betrayal, it seems, doesn't always come with a thunderous revelation. Sometimes, it creeps in slowly, leaving behind a trail of broken promises and unmet expectations. The hurt welled up inside me, a silent scream echoing within, louder than any words I could give voice to.

I still carry the weight of that singular video call, recalling the ghostly presence of William on the screen and his lies and evasions, all a haunting reminder of the friendship we once shared. In a search for clarity, I turned to an old confidante, Mr. G, a man whose entrepreneurial successes in the world of Chinese business had afforded him an understanding of the game that was all too real.

He listened to my recollections—the unfulfilled promises, the betrayal—his expressions revealing nothing until the end. His verdict was simple and, in its own way, chilling: "Ninety-nine per cent of people in Web3 are fraudsters," he admitted, his voice shorn of any emotion, his eyes hardened by the battles he had fought in the entrepreneurial arena. He, a Chinese entrepreneur himself, navigated this treacherous world with a wariness that was nearly palpable.

His words hit me with the force of a gale. It was not the revelation in itself that startled me, as deceit is no stranger to the world of a businesswoman. No, it was the magnitude of the betrayal and the realization of my own naivety that hit me the hardest. This was a harsh wake-up call. It felt as though I had plunged into icy waters, the stark truth chilling me to the bone.

Revelations and Reservations

The revelation of William's return to the United States on an L1 visa gave rise to an array of new discoveries, each more startling than the last. The puzzle pieces of our broken friendship and business partnership fell into place, a jigsaw painted with hues of deceit and disappointment.

We met at my beachfront property in California, at the heart of a world that breathed innovation and ambition. As I helped him with his family's belongings, which he packed haphazardly in his car, I stumbled upon an unsettling truth: he had no automobile insurance—not a shred of precaution for his young family navigating an unpredictable world. The negligence felt intentional, a foreshadowing of the unearthing to come.

Then came the revelation that shattered my trust in him completely. He had, unbeknownst to me, registered OpenAI API licenses under the name of his Chinese company, not our joint US Limited Liability Company, the moment he had landed the United States eight months ago. Our plans for patenting our product, the dreams we had fostered, were all rendered null by his deceit. The lies I had swallowed now surfaced with a bitter aftertaste, a concoction of my naivety and his treachery.

His unwillingness to contribute financially to our ventures in the United States and Singapore now made sense. The joint Chase bank account we had opened remained untouched by him. I had thought it strange when he showed no interest in even taking the Chase debit card, leaving it on my coffee table at my Singapore hotel. The privilege of the Chase Private Bank status I had graciously extended was met with nothing but unappreciative nonchalance.

The final blow came when I realized the employees we had hired were not working on our product. Instead, they were toiling away on his company's enterprise suite in China. Our supposed joint venture was nothing more than a smokescreen for his benefit.

Feeling the pain of betrayal and the sting of deception, I also had the weight of disillusionment hanging heavily over me. It was not just the end of a business partnership, but the crumbling of a friendship built on trust and mutual respect.

As I returned to my beloved California, I braced myself to assess the damage wrought to my personal life. The ripples of William's actions had washed over more than just our business. They had also stained my home with a sadness and indignation that was hard to shake off.

My property manager approached me grim-faced with tales of near disaster. He had found my Tesla abandoned at the airport, left carelessly by William in the wake of his and his family's hasty exit. The reason given to me was a simple logistical challenge: the Uber they had booked had no seat for their baby, and William discarded my Tesla like an inconvenient piece of luggage. On yet another occasion, it was nearly impounded by the California Highway Patrol, saved only by the diligent efforts of my manager.

The shock I felt upon hearing these words was quickly replaced by a deep sense of betrayal. My Tesla, which I had offered up in the spirit of goodwill and friendship, treated like a disregarded tool! My property manager recounted the arduous hours spent trying to restore my Tesla to its original condition—six hours of gruelling work each time, a painstaking job to erase the marks of disrespect shown to a vehicle that represented so much more than a mere mode of transportation.

But that was only the tip of the iceberg. My assistant came to me with tales that turned my stomach. My beachfront houses, my sanctuaries away from the world, had been ruthlessly trashed. William and his family's reckless disregard for my properties was evident in the sordid state of disarray they had left them in.

I was left with the bitter aftertaste of my kindness and generosity having been repaid with disrespect. I was also left with the painful realization that the sanctuary I had so freely shared had been treated as a mere commodity to be used and then discarded.

I am no stranger to the ebb and flow of life, to the mixture of pain and pleasure that it offers. But there are moments when the raw disappointment becomes a leaden weight in my heart. Feeling the pressure from my Chinese friends in Beijing, William had assured me he would pay for the rental, a gesture that seemed like a weak attempt at restitution for all that had transpired. It was more than just the rental; there were my out-of-pocket business expenses, the costs of engaging external agencies, and the immeasurable opportunity cost I bore for forgoing other ventures for the past ten months.

When I relayed this to him, he responded, not with understanding or remorse, but with further evasion. He drove away in his car to Silicon Valley, leaving behind a terse text message informing me he wouldn't be able to pay the rental he had initially offered to cover until months later.

In that moment, I felt the full sting of deception. I was dealing not just with a business partner who had turned sour, but with a person who seemed to be fleeing from more than just our failed venture.

Then came another blow: William wouldn't reveal his new address in Silicon Valley. His life, like his intentions, was becoming an enigma. His evasive manoeuvres were starting to resemble the actions of someone on the run, hiding from something or someone. It was a chilling thought, his actions taking on a darker hue: perhaps he was fleeing from possible legal trouble.

With each revelation, I found myself questioning not only the man I had chosen to work with, but also my judgement. How had I been so blindsided? The disappointment was not just about lost investments and damaged property. It was about a lost connection, a friendship that I had thought was built on trust and mutual respect. This was the heavier loss, the one that stung the most.

In the course of this unsettling saga, my mind swirled with a flurry of questions. The broken trust and the betrayal had birthed in me a new vigilance. My concern was not merely about the material losses or the emotional toll of having my kindness repaid with deceit. Rather, it expanded into a realm I hadn't initially considered.

I began to wonder what the US immigration office knew about William. What had he submitted to obtain his L1 visa? Had he been as deceitful with them as he had been with me? A chilling prospect began to take shape in my mind. If he had been so comfortable deceiving me—someone he worked closely with for nearly a year—could he have been just as cavalier with the immigration authorities?

More importantly, what was my role in this? I found myself grappling with my legal and civic obligations. It was one thing to be duped in a business partnership, but quite another to be party, however unknowingly, to potential legal transgressions.

As I pondered over the implications of these questions, my mind filled with uncertainty, I began to realize the depth of the predicament I was in. This was not just about lost investments, damaged property, or even a broken friendship. It was about my integrity, about taking the right action even if it was difficult.

I found myself drawn towards seeking legal advice to understand the ramifications of what had transpired. If William had indeed lied to immigration, then there were potential legal issues on the table. As someone who has always believed in the sanctity of law and justice, I felt it was my duty to ensure I was on the right side of the law in this matter.

Just as I had to learn to navigate the strange world of Web3 and cryptocurrency, I was now compelled to understand the legalities of my situation. The journey had taken a difficult turn, but I was determined to rise to the occasion, to ensure that truth and justice prevailed.

In that moment, I realized that it wasn't just about the business or the friendship that had turned sour. It was also about my role as a citizen, about doing what was right, about being accountable, not just to myself, but also to the society I am part of. As difficult as the situation was, I was determined to navigate it with grace, courage, and integrity.

Reflecting on the Experience

As I navigated the murky waters of this turbulent episode of my life, I couldn't help but feel deeply deceived. It wasn't just a matter of betrayal: I felt I had been used and abused. William had not only gained access to my home and my resources, but also had tried to leverage my network, even after leaving my home. The art of manipulation, it seemed, was not foreign to him.

Ironically, I had often told my non-Chinese friends about the ruthlessness and cunning that sometimes characterizes Chinese entrepreneurs. I had cautioned them about the unique challenges they might face when doing business with individuals who would stop at nothing to succeed. Now, it seemed, I had fallen prey to the very thing I had warned others about.

Despite the pain and the feeling of being conned, I knew deep down that William's loss was greater than mine. Yes, I had lost some money. Yes, I had been deceived. But I would recover from it. It was what he had lost that was irreplaceable.

He had lost a true friend, someone who had extended her trust, her resources, and her unconditional support. I had offered him an opportunity that he would not otherwise have had. I had opened my world to him, and he had abused it.

I could not help but wonder if this was his pattern—to seize opportunities only to burn bridges and to exploit friendships for personal gain. If so, then I couldn't help but feel a sense of pity for him. For all his cunning, all his manipulative strategies, he'd lost the one thing that money can't buy: genuine friendship.

And while he might move on to find other opportunities and even find temporary happiness, I had to wonder: would he ever truly escape his own destructive patterns, or would he simply return to his old, unhappy self once the dust settled? After all, no amount of success can truly compensate for a life devoid of authentic relationships and meaningful connections.

In this peculiar journey of life and friendship, I found myself coming to a startling realization: I do not harbour any ill will towards William. We are all products of our environments, moulded by the experiences we've been exposed to, for better or for worse. I genuinely believe that at his core, William is no different. He is a man shaped by the sharp edges of his past, a product of a hardened reality where trust is a luxury not many can afford. His actions, as hurtful as they were, were not born out of inherent malevolence, but rather out of a deep-seated fear—a fear of trust, of vulnerability, and perhaps of genuine connection. It's as if he's trapped in an invisible cage where authenticity is a liability, not a virtue. Such a cage forces him to hide his true self and, in the process, experience a life of perpetual misery and unhappiness.

But as I reflect on the past, the betrayals and the hurt, I see that I am not defeated. Instead, I feel emboldened by my own authenticity. Despite the deceit, I choose to remain true to myself. I will continue to open my heart and lend a helping hand to those in need, for it is in this giving that I feel most loved, most alive.

While I wish the story of my friendship with William had unfolded differently, I've come to accept that learned behaviours are not easily shed. They wrap around us like second skins, often dictating our actions even when we yearn for change. It's unfortunate, but it's a reality I've come to understand.

As I move forward, I carry these lessons with me. They serve as reminders that trust, authenticity, and genuine relationships are a luxury not everyone can afford. But for those of us who can afford these things, they become the bedrock upon which we build our lives and our friendships in light of our capacity to love and be loved. Despite everything, I remain hopeful, always on the lookout for the next chance encounter, the next friendship, the next adventure life has to offer.

4.4 Behind the Gleaming Façade—a Study in Contrasts

Singapore, with its gleaming skyscrapers, ultramodern lifestyle, and reputation for wealth and success, projects a façade of perfection. But as I began to settle into my new home, I noticed subtle shades of grey colouring the picture-perfect scene. Like an intricate piece of art that reveals its true depth only upon close inspection, Singapore's society harbours complexities that might escape the eye of a casual observer.

Here, marriages often don't mirror the fairy tales they outwardly represent. Behind the smiles, luxurious homes, and picture-perfect family portraits, I discovered a longing and a restlessness. Many of the married couples I met were living lives filled with superficial contentment. They were eager to please others and needed external validation in the form of material possessions.

Marriage, in this context, sometimes serves as a façade, a neatly constructed shell hiding the real emotions and experiences within. There is an undercurrent of dissatisfaction, an unspoken yearning that seems almost taboo to acknowledge. I encountered couples living in the same house but inhabiting separate rooms, their connection limited to shared responsibilities rather than shared love.

Children, too, are caught in this cycle of outward achievement. Academic success is elevated to a status symbol, with admissions to prestigious schools such as ACS (Anglo-Chinese School), Chinese Girls' School, and Raffles Institution acting as trophies for parents. The term "tiger mom" or "tiger dad" is not just a stereotype but often a lived reality. The pressure on children to excel, to uphold the family's status and reputation, is intense.

What struck me most was the silence around sexuality and human intimacy. In a society that seems to have everything, the lack of candid conversation about sexual needs felt like a void, a deprivation that went beyond cultural conservatism. It felt inhumane, a denial of something so basic and essential to our shared human experience.

These observations made me reflect on my own journey and my own search for authenticity, love, and connection. Singapore's contrasts resonated with my own inner contradictions, and I felt a kinship with those who were striving, like me, to find a balance between social expectations and personal truth.

There is beauty in Singapore's ambition, its drive for perfection, and its relentless pursuit of success. Yet there's also a fragility, a vulnerability that lies beneath the surface. It's a city that embodies both the promise of modernity and the challenges of maintaining a connection to what is genuine and human.

My days in Singapore are filled with discovery, learning, and reflection. The city-state's contradictions are a mirror reflecting my own complexities, a reminder that no matter how far we travel or how much we achieve, our shared human needs for love, intimacy, and genuine connection remain the same.

In the midst of this bustling metropolis, I find a lesson about the universal quest for authenticity and the courage it takes to live a life that reflects one's truth. It's a lesson I carry with me as I continue to explore, grow, and embrace the richness of this incredible journey we call life.

Frederick—Commitment to Others

Frederick's bright red two-door Jaguar was more than just a car; it was a symbol, a representation of success and status, a declaration to the world that he had made it. Yet as we drove through the affluent neighbourhood filled with Good Class Bungalows (GCBs)—the vast, opulent freehold properties that are a signpost of wealth in Singapore—I sensed a certain unease in him.

"My family has been in business for generations," he explained, his voice tinged with pride and something else I couldn't quite place. "I've been groomed for success since I was a child. This car, this house, this life—it's all been handed to me."

"But?" I prompted, sensing there was more to the story.

"But," he continued, his voice faltering, "I've spent my whole life living up to others' expectations, meeting the demands of my family, my society, my culture. And somewhere along the way, I lost sight of what I wanted, of who I am."

The words hung heavy in the air, a confession of sorts, affording me a glimpse of the hidden costs of privilege and power.

We continued our drive, Frederick showing me another side of Singapore, a contrast that was both stark and poignant. We passed by the Housing & Development Board (HDB) homes, state-subsidized housing designed to offset the high cost of living for local Singaporeans. These utilitarian blocks, home to the majority of the population, stood in sharp contrast to the grandeur of the GCBs.

"It's a balance," Frederick said, his voice thoughtful. "A balance of the haves and have-nots, living right next to each other. The government tries to ensure everyone has a place to live, a chance at a good life. But the divide is still there. It's a complex system."

We drove in silence for a while, the cityscape unfolding before us, a tapestry of contradictions and complexities.

"You know," Frederick finally said, breaking the silence, "sometimes I look at these HDB homes and I wonder what life would be like if I had been born there and if I'd had the freedom to choose my path, to follow my passions, to make my own mistakes. Maybe I'd be less successful and less wealthy, but maybe I'd be more me."

His words were a revelation, offering a window view into the soul of a man who seemed to have everything and yet felt something was missing.

"What will you do?" I asked gently, knowing that the question was as much about Frederick's future as it was about the deeper yearnings of his heart.

He looked at me, his eyes filled with a mixture of uncertainty and determination. "I don't know," he said, his voice firm. "But I'm going to find out. I owe it to myself to try."

As we continued our journey through the city, I couldn't help but reflect on the paradoxes of Singapore, the juxtaposition of wealth and need, tradition and modernity, expectation and desire. I thought about Frederick, a man caught at the crossroads, daring to ask the questions that so many of us avoid.

In his struggle, in his search, I was reminded of a universal truth, namely that no matter where we come from, no matter what we have, the journey to find ourselves is one we all must undertake. It's a journey filled with uncertainty and risk, but also with the promise of authenticity, fulfilment, and perhaps—and most importantly—freedom.

I met Frederick again one evening at a bistro nestled within the bustling streets of Singapore. His sharp features were softened by the candlelight, but his eyes held a weary weight. As the evening waned, Frederick shared in hushed tones details about the silent battles he fought every day.

"You know," he said, toying with the stem of his wineglass, "in this part of the world, there's an unspoken script that men are handed, a role we're expected to play from birth."

Frederick spoke of the invisible shackles of social expectations. For many Chinese people from Southeast Asia, tradition is a double-edged sword. It provides a sense of identity and serves a compass to navigate life, but it can also be a chain holding a person back from expressing his or her true self.

He spoke of civic duty in Singapore, where national service moulds young boys into stoic men, reinforcing the age-old belief that vulnerability is akin to weakness. This is a realm where the weight of being the sole financial provider and bearing the pressure of family commitments often becomes too great, making it a herculean task to strike a balance. "In our culture," he said, sighing, "we are taught to bottle up our emotions. To cry is to show weakness. To express love passionately, openly, is deemed inappropriate."

He often wondered about the European men he saw in movies who wore their hearts on their sleeves, unafraid of judgement. He longed for the freedom to cry when the weight of the world became too much and to hold his loved ones close without the shadow of social scorn.

"I sometimes feel trapped," Frederick confessed, his voice breaking. "It's like living in a gilded cage of expectations where every move is dictated by age-old traditions and the fear of what others might think."

I looked at him, seeing the raw vulnerability in his eyes, and realized how universal the human yearning is to be seen, to be understood, and to be accepted for who one truly is. "Frederick," I whispered, "your pain is valid. And while society might not always understand, remember that it's OK to carve out your own path."

In that dimly lit bistro, amidst the hum of muted conversations and the soft strumming of a guitarist, two souls connected over shared stories of pain and hope. It is in sharing that we realize that we are not alone in our battles, and it is in understanding that we find solace.

Jennifer—a Story of Grace, Grit, and Survival

In the beautifully air-conditioned gym of a five-star hotel, amidst the rhythmic hum of treadmills and the clinking of weights, I met Jennifer. With her taut physique and the elegant strength that shone through her movements, she was the embodiment of grace and determination. She was a Peranakan, a mix of Indonesian and Chinese heritage, and her story was a stirring symphony of resilience and survival.

Jennifer was in her second marriage, wedded to a successful entrepreneur who was, beneath his veneer of success, a controlling and abusive husband. Despite his affluence and prominence, his business was in turmoil, a sinking ship that Jennifer was desperately trying to keep afloat. Yet, her radiant smile and the warmth in her eyes betrayed nothing of her struggles. It was as if she had learned to compartmentalize her life, packing away her troubles neatly, while she poured her energy into salvaging what remained of her husband's legacy.

Her first marriage had ended in betrayal and heartache. Her husband had pursued an extramarital affair while Jennifer was overseas for six months. The memory still bore a rawness that time had not managed to heal completely. But in the grand scheme of her life, it was just one chapter of her story of strength and resilience.

She had three sons and a mother who were financially dependent on her current husband. Because of them, she endured, putting up with the pain, the humiliation, and the fear. She bore it all with a grace that humbled me. Her love for her family was her beacon, guiding her through the stormy sea of her circumstances.

Jennifer's story resonated deeply with mine. Here was a woman who, like many of us, was navigating her way through life with its ups and downs. She was battling, not just external adversaries, but also her inner demons. Yet she chose to endure, to survive, to keep fighting. It was a testament to her indomitable spirit, her undying love for her family, and her unwavering determination to find a way out of the darkness.

In her strength, I found inspiration. In her courage, I found a mirror reflecting my own battles. And in her story, I found a reminder of the incredible resilience of the human spirit. Jennifer was not just surviving: she was thriving, despite the odds. She was a testament to the power of hope, love, and the unyielding will it takes to never give up, no matter how bleak the circumstances may appear.

Alex—the Upstairs Life

Singapore's tapestry of lives and stories continued to unfold before me, each thread revealing a new shade of human complexity and giving me a new perspective on love, marriage, and social expectations. My conversation with Alex, whom I met at a gathering hosted by the American Club, was one such revelation.

Alex was a Spaniard of medium height with a dignified air and a thoughtful gaze that seemed to hold a world of secrets. We found ourselves in a quiet corner sipping cocktails, the buzz of the gathering a soft background to our conversation.

"You seem to be a woman who understands the nuances of life," he said, his voice rich with experience. "I see something in your eyes that tells me you might understand my situation."

Intrigued, I urged him to continue.

The story he told was both surprising and profoundly saddening.

"My wife and I have been married for eighteen years," he began, his eyes reflecting a mixture of pain and resignation. "But we've lived separate lives for over a decade. She lives downstairs; I live upstairs. We're married in name only."

I listened, a frown of concern knitting my brow, as he shared how the passion and connection had long since ebbed away from their relationship. The last time they had been intimate was more than ten years ago, after the birth of their last child.

"Isn't it painful to live like that?" I asked, my voice barely above a whisper.

He looked down, a shadow crossing his face. "Yes, it's painful. But what choice do I have? The D-word, divorce, is not an option. It would ruin our social standing in the church community and in Singaporean society. My wife can't bear the shame."

He went on to tell me about his girlfriend in Spain, a relationship that had brought some colour back to his life but had also left him grappling with guilt and confusion.

"But aren't you entitled to happiness, to love?" I asked, unable to contain my sympathy.

"Of course, but at what cost?" he replied, his eyes filled with a deep, unspoken sorrow. "I can't abandon my family, my children. I can't be the one to shatter this façade we've built in Singapore. It's a prison, yes, but it's one we've chosen."

We sat in silence for a moment, the weight of his words settling around us. Alex's story was a testament to the power of social pressure, the crushing weight of expectation and tradition. Here was a man trapped by the very conventions he had once embraced, a prisoner of a life he no longer recognised as his own.

As we parted ways that night, I couldn't shake the feeling that Alex's story was not an isolated one. It was a reflection of a larger issue, a symptom of a society that prioritized appearance over authenticity and status over genuine connection. It was a sobering reminder of the choices we make, the compromises we endure, and the price we pay for conforming to a world that often values perception over reality.

4.5 Yannie's Human Story

In the multifaceted landscape of human connections and emotional complexities, I met Yannie. She was a portrait of grace and composure, a woman of distinct sophistication with a quiet strength that emanated from her like an aura. It was only when she shared her story with me that I realized the depth of her courage and the tenacity of her spirit.

"Two months before my wedding," Yannie began, her voice steady, her gaze faraway, "I had an affair." It was evident that the weight of this confession was still a burden even after all these years. "The guilt was unbearable … so I made a vow to myself—to be faithful to my husband after our marriage."

Her husband, as she revealed, was a frequent traveller to Vietnam and had been curiously distant in their marital bed post-marriage. Yannie bore this silently, suppressing her desires and her needs, as her husband remained a distant figure in her life.

Even as whispers of his having another family in Vietnam reached her, she chose denial over confrontation. "I had a child through IVF," she shared, a hint of sorrow in her eyes. "I thought a child might bring us closer, might make him stay."

It wasn't until twenty years into her marriage that Yannie found the courage to liberate herself from the shackles of her loveless marriage. The divorce, as she confessed, was a devastating blow. But in that shattering, there was an awakening.

In the aftermath, Yannie embarked on a journey of rediscovery and self liberation. "I went clubbing, tried online dating, met men I never would've imagined meeting before," she said, a spark of life kindled in her eyes.

As Yannie explored her sexuality and her emotional boundaries, she blossomed. In her new-found freedom, she redefined her identity, not as a wife or a mother, but as a woman in her own right. She was no longer defined by her marital status or her past but was now a beacon of courage, a testament to the strength of a woman's spirit.

Yannie's journey from suppression to liberation is a human story that needs to echo in a million hearts. It serves as a powerful reminder to women around the world—those who have suppressed their desires, those who have traded emotional connection for social acceptance—that it's never too late to seek what we truly deserve. The journey may be fraught with pain and uncertainty, but the destination is a place of self-discovery, liberation, and most importantly, love.

We were seated on the veranda overlooking the bustling streets of Singapore, a gentle breeze cutting through the humid air. Yannie was contemplative, her eyes reflecting a mix of determination and vulnerability. She had begun to open up to me about her journey, and it was clear that so far our conversation had only scratched the surface.

"Did you ever regret it, Yannie?" I asked her, referring to her decision to divorce after twenty years. "Did you ever wonder if it was the right thing to do?"

Yannie looked at me, her eyes searching for the words that would encapsulate her emotions. "Regret? No. Fear? Absolutely. But you know, the longer I stayed in that marriage, the more I lost myself. I became a stranger to my own desires, my own needs."

She paused, taking a sip of her tea as she gathered her thoughts. "There was a time when I thought that I could make it work, that I could change him, change us. But the truth was, I was only changing myself, bending and twisting into someone I didn't recognise, and then falling in love with another man. That's when I knew it was time to break free."

I nodded, understanding her words, feeling the resonance in my own heart. "And after the divorce?" I asked, curious about the transformation she had undergone.

Her face lit up, a smile breaking through the solemnity. "Oh, that was like rediscovering myself all over again. I learned to dance to my own rhythm, to love without restrictions, and to enjoy my own company."

"But wasn't it hard?" I pressed, intrigued by her resilience.

Yannie's eyes sparkled with wisdom and experience. "Hard is staying in a place where you don't belong. Hard is denying yourself the love and connection you deserve. What I did after the divorce was liberating, terrifying, and exciting all at once. But it was never hard. It was life happening in all its glorious unpredictability."

We sat in silence for a moment as I absorbed the weight of her words. Then Yannie reached over and placed a gentle hand on my arm. "You know, there are so many women out there trapped in their own lives, stifled by society's expectations. They need to know that there's a way out, that they can find love and find themselves again."

Her words hung in the air, a profound statement about human resilience and the power of self-love and self-rediscovery. Yannie's story is not just her own; it is also a beacon for others, a call to action, a whisper of hope. It is a story of courage, a story that needs to be told. I knew then that I was privileged to be a part of it.

Our conversation continued to deepen, Yannie's words still echoing in the Singaporean evening. She was on the verge of something great, a realization of self that extended far beyond her own life's boundaries. I could feel her passion, her urgency, and I wanted to know more.

"Yannie," I began, choosing my words carefully, "what you've shared with me tonight is powerful, but I think it's also universal. So many women feel trapped, stifled by family expectations, social norms. How do you think we can reach them? How can we let them know that it's not only OK but also essential to care for themselves?"

She looked at me, her eyes filled with conviction. "We need to tell our stories," she said firmly. "We need to share our truths, our struggles, and our victories. We need to show them that there's another way."

"But how?" I asked, knowing that the cultural fabric is often tightly woven, resistant to change.

Yannie's face softened, her gaze turning inwards. "By being brave.

By being honest. By being ourselves. We need to create safe spaces for women to come together, to support each other, and to learn from one another. We need to show them that they're not alone, that their feelings, their desires, and their dreams are valid."

I could feel the weight of her words, the truth in them. "It sounds like a movement," I said, half in jest, half in earnest.

Yannie's eyes twinkled and her smile widened. "Maybe it is. Maybe it's time for a movement. A movement of women, for women, by women. A movement that says it's OK to want more, to be more, and to live more."

We sat there letting the possibilities unfold in our minds, feeling the potential, the hope, and the change that could come. Yannie's story of her journey is not just a tale of personal triumph. It is a rallying cry, a call to arms.

"It won't be easy," she said finally, her voice filled with determination. "There will be resistance, backlash, misunderstanding. But we can't let that stop us. We owe it to ourselves, to the women who came before us, and to the women who will come after us."

I nodded, feeling the truth of her words deep in my soul. This was bigger than us; it was about every woman who had ever felt trapped, stifled, or lost. It was about breaking free, finding our voices, and claiming our power.

We sat there, two women on a veranda in Singapore, connected by our shared humanity, inspired by a vision of what could be. We were ready to take on the world, one story, one woman, and one movement at a time. And we knew without a doubt that we were not alone.

Our conversation shifted, turning towards the specific ways women could empower one another, particularly in a place like Singapore, which seems to straddle two worlds: the ultramodern and the traditionally conservative.

"Yannie," I began, searching for the right words, "you've been through so much, and yet you've found a way to empower yourself. How can we help other women do the same? How can we help them to speak up about their needs, to seek professional help without shame, and to honour their physical and emotional selves?"

She leaned back in her chair, considering my question. Her eyes, still filled with that unbreakable determination, seemed to see beyond the immediate. "It's about creating a culture of acceptance and understanding," she finally said, "a culture that says it's OK to be human, to have needs, and to want more. It's about education, communication, and compassion."

I nodded, understanding her point but still wanting to go deeper. "But why do you think a modern society like Singapore suffers the same fate as more conservative cultures? What's holding us back?"

Yannie sighed, her face reflecting a mix of frustration and insight. "It's complex," she said. "On one hand, Singapore is incredibly advanced, dynamic, and forward-thinking. But on the other hand, there are deep-rooted cultural values, beliefs, and expectations that still hold sway. There's a fear of judgement, a pressure to conform, and a reluctance to challenge the status quo."

"But how do we break through that?" I asked, feeling the weight of the challenge.

Yannie's face brightened, her eyes gleaming with hope. "We start small. We start with ourselves. We learn to honour our own needs and to speak our own truths. Then we reach out to others. We create support groups, workshops, therapy sessions. We use social media, podcasts, and books. We share our stories, our victories, our struggles. We show others that it's possible, that they're not alone."

I could see the path she was laying out, the stepping stones to a new way of living, a new way of being. "And we don't stop," she added, her voice firm. "We keep going, keep pushing, keep believing. We find allies, build networks, create communities. We make it safe for women to be themselves, to be human."

I sat there, absorbing her words, feeling the truth of them in my bones. Yannie was right: it isn't about grand gestures or sweeping changes; it is about small, deliberate steps taken with purpose and passion.

"We can do this," Yannie said, her voice filled with conviction. "We can change the culture, change the narrative, and change the world. We just have to be brave enough to start."

As we sat there, two women in the heart of Singapore, I knew that we were already on our way. We were starting a conversation, planting a seed, lighting a spark. And I knew with a certainty that filled me with joy and hope that we were not alone.

Yannie's Unedited Journal Entry #1—Emotional Liberation

Ocean and Me in My Late Twenties

I am a fish. How I wish I am a fish. This is the Pisces in me who yearns to be part of the ocean.

Looking back at my life I made two discoveries about myself. I need a sanctuary to feel loved and secure. Ocean is my answer. Therefore I picked up scuba dives in late twenties.

Work in investment bank was highly stressful. What made it worse was that I was newly married at age twenty-seven and needed to deal with problem in my marriage. Well let's not go into details of my marriage as it is over. Hence I picked up scuba diving so that I can find ways to manage my unhappiness in marriage without involving anyone.

I met a nice guy who offered me rides to Terengganu on our Friday midnight diving trips to Pulau Perhentian in the east coast of Malaysia. It usually takes about seven hours' car ride from Kuala Lumpur to the jetty. He was a responsible dive buddy who looked after me underwater. You know, as much as I wanted to be a fish, I was a clumsy scuba diver who frightened all the marine life that came into contact with me!

Have I mentioned my first scuba dive? In scuba diving, we are required to make a three-minute stop at a depth of five to six metres to allow our body to decompress and to unload nitrogen accumulated during dives.

As you are aware, being underweight most of my life and loading insufficient weights during dive were a big problem for me in my virgin dive. As I gradually used up the oxygen in my tank, I became lighter before the dive ended. Being light means I was automatically "flying back" to the surface without the required safety stop! I was grabbing so hard on the first hill cliff I can find to prevent myself from flying off like a rocket to the surface! My coach was frantically trying to hold me tight to add weights to me. In visual term, I was upside down in the sea holding the cliff. It must be a hilarious sight to witness. But it was fun!

Did the experience scare the shit out of me? Well, it didn't bother me at all! I continued to go for more dive trips with the guy.

My horny male buddy whom I have known since age nineteen always think that the dive buddy and I had something romantic going on. Strange enough I had never had any romantic thought with any men I met during my marriage! How I wish I am smarter than that.

Life went on in the late twenties with long working hours and scuba dive trips on weekends. None of my family members know about my diving trips as I don't get tan easily and I don't live with them after marriage. I lead an independent but highly private life.

The other memorable dive I remembered was a jellyfish experience. It wasn't a single jellyfish. Imagine there was no empty spot without jellyfish no matter what direction you looked at. I remembered the dive sites vividly. There were three gigantic rocks or hill formations in the sea. We were supposed to swim in between the rocks. When the water was swamped by jellyfish, each of us still needed to swim between the rocks as there was no way out! Imagine you trying to avoid being stung in the tight space! It was quite an experience that none of us was stung at all! Fear doesn't seem to be in my vocabulary. This experience didn't stop me from scuba dives as I still needed to "escape" my marriage.

What made me stop scuba diving? Obviously it wasn't about fear or my marriage issue was resolved. I simply feel sorry for being a clumsy diver with gears and causing damage to the marine life. If a Nemo can have a human voice, I am positive that it will tell me to stop intruding its space.

Ocean and Me in My Late Forties

I needed to escape badly, again! When I decided to end my marriage in July 2022, I went through emotional roller coaster. It was my choice to call it a day, but I still took the decision badly.

There wasn't a day that I did not cry. My child saw all my crying and I told her I was sad. Sadness consumed me till I lost four kilograms. I was engulfed by sorrow for one year till my soul was depleted.

I embarked on a journey to search for my soul and spirit. I was equally stubborn not to let myself go into depression. Many depressive women came to me to seek shelter. But I was determined not to turn into one of them. This huge voice inside me urged me to do something about myself. I didn't know how and when my spirit will return, but I kept searching for it.

It was a long journey to restore my world with my vision in a marriage vanished. Where do I search for my lost spirit? You know it. It is ocean!

I picked up free diving theory around December 2021/January 2022. I wanted to be away from my ex-husband in February 2023. February is a significant month to me as my birthday and wedding anniversary were just two days apart in end February. The expensive dress I bought before July 2022 that was meant to be used for my twenty-year anniversary was no longer needed. I wanted to run. Run to the sea!

It was in end February 2023 that I took a practical free diving course with a beautiful and special coach named Stella.

The end of February was the opening season for most dives schools in the east coast of west Malaysia.

Weather has its schedule which is beyond our control. The rainy season continued and some parts of Malaysia experienced the worst flood in history. My island was not spared from the record-breaking rain.

Fear does not stop me from picking up free diving with Stella. If I may remind you that I haven't been to ocean for any form of diving for at least fifteen years.

I remembered the first dip into the sea after fifteen years. I wanted to yell so badly that I am finally "home" as soon as I went into the ocean! You cannot imagine how much love I felt by the sea despite how angry the sea was with its feisty waves.

It was so emotional and deep. Mother Nature does not judge me. I felt the hugs by the seawater. The sea temperature was cold due to continuous rain, but my heart just melted and felt hot. I felt forgiven by the ocean and at peace with myself. I found direct connection with the ocean without any intermediary such as the scuba diving gears!

The feeling was so intense that I kept telling myself to stay underwater forever. It was also a dark period of my life. I wanted to live underwater forever. I found a private space for myself where I can hide forever and yet be loved. How much love I yearn for in the past twenty years was finally found in the ocean. As I write this, I am tearing up.

In the brief seconds or minute where I went free dives in February, I forgot my pain and sorrow. I was no longer sad in the private space the ocean has granted me. I felt privileged to be given the opportunity to find such sanctuary. I thank my brother and coach for making it happened. Most importantly, I am grateful that Mother Nature let my humble soul find a spot in her big heart. The sea loves me.

Am I a skilled free diver? I am so far from it, but it doesn't bother my connection and experience with my love, the ocean. Am I irresponsible for wanting to stay in water forever? Well, I got my will done up before my dive trip. Do I worry about blacking out? Why worry about the future death?

This is the reminder to myself that I can navigate the future alone with my child. I am basically quite fearless in life. However, being divorced and unemployed creates the only serious fear I have ever experienced in forty-seven years. I am scared. I am no longer alone as my beautiful thirteen-year-old daughter is watching me as a role model to deal with all the uncertainty. She is the pillar of my strength, and she is the only reason why I didn't stay underwater forever in February 2023.

Dive trips in October 2023 brought in another meaningful discovery. My soul and spirit are back! Future remains uncertain. I discover my body in a more profound manners through October dive trips. Free diving is about full awareness of our body organs and psychological experience. I found myself entering the meditation zone with total relaxation as soon as I enter the water. Each dive was such a joy that I wanted to repeat the experience over and over again! Sometimes I burst into laughter in the sea doing silly moves. I no longer wanted to stay underwater forever. It was a total emotional liberation!

I am on a journey to full liberation. Mother Nature has empowered me. I am grateful for what I have in life.

Yannie's Unedited Journal Entry #2—Physical Liberation

Men come in different forms and sizes, including penis. As a woman, how do we experience men emotionally and physically with utmost pleasure?

A girlfriend of mine shared her wisdom about men: women should think like a man in terms of sex. It means no emotions are involved to reduce the sentimental attachment. I applied this wisdom in different circumstances.

Let's pause for a while. If you happen to be reading this piece of writing now, you are certainly a special one in my heart as my best friend since age thirteen from boarding school has graded the content below as highly censored for anyone's eyes and discourages me from sharing this content, prior to me even penning down my thoughts.

I won't want to discuss my sex life prior to divorce as no sex ever happened in the marriage! Well, it was my choice to live that way in a marriage so no one was to be blamed. I bear the consequences.

Many Asian women I know do not enjoy sex. Some of them are too shy to even admit if they do enjoy sex.

Let's admit that men and women have biological needs that need be released one way or the other.

I am a healthy woman with reasonably strong sex drive. I love marathons love making than one-off sex. Sex to me is more than sex. I like to view making love as integration of two bodies in the utmost private space only the two persons can experience intimately. Well, you should know by now I am against any threesome or viewing during this private session.

My body was near explosion after being suppressed for two decades. I was angry and frustrated.

I threw away all the moral values I held utmost to release myself as soon as I am going through the divorce. I no longer felt morally responsible to my ex-husband and that I was not having affairs. Hence I started acting like a man. Sex is just sex. That was what I told myself when I had some quick flings.

How was it like having sex with someone you couldn't connect emotionally for the first time since two decades?

To be honest, it was painful as though it was the first time ever. He was an acquaintance. A handsome huge man with a very big penis. To be honest, being big is not everything to me. I forgot all about lovemaking and acted awkwardly, not knowing how to make my body work. It was a pain at the start. However our bodies have muscle memory.

My body began to know how to move together with him and it ended better than it started. It was a pity that he was into pure S&M, which was not entirely my cup of tea. However, his preference did not matter as I just needed quick fix. In this situation I acted like a man. A few quick fixes were followed with protection, but nothing was worth elaborating. However, something significant was missing. I did not feel loved.

Our body confidence to a certain extent requires affirmation from our partners during sex, especially from a woman's perspective. My body feature is slender with small and uneven breasts. It bothered me a lot when I was studying at a co-ed secondary school and teased by boys for being flat-chested.

Imagine not being physically touched much in a marriage. My self-esteem about my body went to the bottom of a valley and was no way to be found. I felt ugly and unattractive as a woman during marriage.

Transformation happened after I resumed ballet lessons in 2023 after thirty-three years' break. As a private person who always have problem expressing myself, ballet was my outlet of communicating my feelings since childhood. Each body movement expresses my deeper emotions without words. I am freed through dancing. That is why I love dancing so much.

The world does not exist other than myself whenever I dance.

I started to feel attractive and elegant again. The classic black leotard, ballet skirt, pink stockings, and ballet shoes made me feel sexy. These are my best gears other than my free diving fins. Of course if you want to buy me a piece of Gucci dress, I won't mind too.

The first few ballet lessons were challenging. Do you know how a pig feel when it jumps? It feels heavy. That's me in my ballet classes.

I begin to feel good about my body. My posture is better; so is my stamina.

I am liberated physically through ballet!

Yannie's Unedited Journal Entry #3—Love

Family and friends perceive my marriage as an empty one. Despite hints and subtle warnings from my loved ones, I opted to remain in my marriage for two decades for simple reasons—love and responsibility.

I yearn to be loved and needed. The longing kept me grounded in a marriage, despite how silently I endured the absence of my now ex-husband in our daily lives and relationship. He was distant from me emotionally and physically. My self-worth was defined by my role as a wife and a mother, other than myself. The imaginary love was purely self-created to keep my vision of a marriage intact.

Growing up as a middle child observing how my mum lived as a grass widow, I learnt that it is acceptable that a husband does not play a role in the family. This was the household I was accustomed to. Although I am an educated woman who studied and travelled abroad for work, I never challenge the status quo of a marriage. I accepted the responsibility of a wife and hid the sorrow of not being loved by my spouse. I simply did not love myself enough to ask for more.

After breaking free from the marriage, I was on a journey to seek love to fill my empty soul. My feelings and emotions were poured to the men I felt to be connected. It was a like broken dam. However, I was trapped in the imaginary love again and something was not right. I still feel insignificant.

The insignificance stems from the lack of self-love. I was searching for a man to define me and make me feel loved and needed again. That was why my world shattered when I decided to break free on my own.

I was not truthful to my needs and I was not respecting my voice. Love comes from within. It shall not be defined by any man. We all deserved to be loved. However, we must love ourselves as the first and foremost priority. It is my self-discovery and it shall remain my motto for my remaining life. I deserve more.

4.6 Happiness Is ... Being True to Oneself

The time with Frederick had led me to a profound realization, one that seemed to resonate to the very core of my being, namely that the path to true happiness is not found in the accumulation of external achievements or wealth, or in the approval of others. Instead, it lies in the courage to be true to oneself.

I found myself contemplating this as I strolled through the lush gardens of Singapore, a city that seems to embody both the pursuit of material success and the deep-rooted need for individual authenticity. Here, amongst the towering skyscrapers and bustling markets, I found a place that offers a study in contrasts, and yet at its heart was a lesson in what it means to be human.

Being true to oneself is a concept that sounds simple, almost cliché. And yet, it is anything but. It's a journey that demands a willingness to look inwards, to confront our fears, our desires, and our contradictions. It requires us to peel away the layers of expectations, social norms, and the roles we are assigned or assume, to uncover the essence of who we are.

This path is fraught with challenges. It often means going against the grain, risking judgement and rejection. It may mean letting go of security and comfort and of the familiar roles that have defined us. But in that letting go, in that daring to be who we are, lies the key to a happiness that is deep, enduring, and authentic.

It's not about selfishness or narcissism, but rather about honouring the unique gifts, passions, and values that make us who we are. It's about aligning our actions with our innermost truths, allowing our lives to be a reflection of our deepest selves.

In my conversations with the people I met in Singapore—from Jennifer and her struggle with her marriage to Yannie and her courageous journey to rediscover love, and from Alex and his complex relationship with his family to Frederick and his yearning to find his authentic self, I saw variations of this same theme. All of them, in their own way, was striving to align their lives with their truths. In their stories, I saw a reflection of a universal struggle, one that transcends culture and class, a struggle that perhaps defines the very essence of the human experience.

As I continued my exploration of Singapore, I carried with me the wisdom I had gleaned, namely, a deeper understanding of what it means to be true to oneself. I knew that this path was not easy, but it was one that offered the promise of a joy that was real, a contentment that was not dependent on external validation but rooted in the knowledge that we are living our lives in harmony with our deepest selves.

In a world that often pushes us to conform, to fit into neatly defined roles and expectations, the act of being true to ourselves is perhaps the most courageous and rewarding action we can take. It leads us towards the path to a happiness that is not fleeting or superficial but that resonates with the very core of who we are. It is a happiness that comes from knowing that we are living our lives, not as others want us to do, but as we are meant to do. It is the happiness of being at home with ourselves.

Wisdom and Desperation

Navigating life's complexities and contradictions is no small feat, especially when it comes to matters of the heart. In my journey of wisdom and desperation, I've encountered stories that have jolted me out of my comfort zone and pushed me to question my own understanding of love, companionship, and happiness.

I knew of an eighty-one-year-old American professor who was enamoured with a twenty-six-year-old eastern European woman aspiring to be a model. He paid her way through life, luring her with promises of the California dream and Kardashian connections. The two of them made secret arrangements; I'd heard whispers of potential shared accommodations by the California seaside, all hidden away from his children, who were already middle-aged. I might judge, or I might dismiss, but who am I to determine the legitimacy of another's longing for companionship? Who am I to measure the depths of the two people's loneliness?

Then, there was the seventy-two-year-old American professor living in France and sharing his life with a thirty-six-year-old Chinese woman, a part-time lover as he called her. He sponsored her holidays, sharing his wealth and his time, enveloping her in love. When he fell ill and landed in the hospital, she was on vacation in China, unwilling to cut short her holiday to return to his side. This raises questions: Is this love or trade? And if both parties find what they are looking for, does the label truly matter?

In these narratives, I see a dance of desperation and wisdom, where individuals negotiate their own happiness within the structure of social norms and expectations. Love, companionship, and understanding are fundamental human needs that age does not diminish. Yet, the quest to fulfil these needs often leads us down unexpected paths, where we're forced to confront our own prejudices, assumptions, and fears.

If we're willing, these encounters can become invitations to expand our understanding of love, companionship, and the myriad ways individuals seek happiness. In an ever-changing world, relationships are not bound by age or societal expectations. They are fluid, are often unpredictable, and can be as diverse as the individuals who enter them.

As I hear these stories, I'm reminded that life is an intricate tapestry woven with threads of wisdom and desperation. Each thread contributes to the pattern, the texture, and the richness of the final masterpiece. The challenge, then, is not to judge or condemn, but to understand, to empathize, and to learn from these tales of human complexity.

I asked what a machine trained by OpenAI would do in such circumstances. The answer was, "My role is not to act, but to facilitate understanding and foster conversation. I can provide insights, offer perspectives, and stimulate thought, but ultimately, the decisions and judgements remain in the realm of human agency." That's the beauty of human life after all—its capacity for complexity, nuance, and continual growth. And in that, there's a wisdom that even the most sophisticated AI can only aspire to comprehend.

Journey to the Self, Journey for the World: A Treatise on Happiness and Meaning

Amidst the luminous landscape of my life's journey, I've noticed a curious tension between self-exploration and collective contribution. It's a tension that tugs at me to discover what it means to be truly happy. My quest for happiness, my dear friend, is akin to walking a spiritual tightrope. On one end, there's a craving for personal fulfilment; on the other, a longing to make this world a more hospitable dwelling for all souls.

I've often wondered about the role of acceptance in this enigmatic emotion we call happiness. Yes, acceptance—the radical act of embracing ourselves in totality, the symphony and the discord, the virtues and the flaws. The moment I began to cradle my imperfections, to wrap them in the same warm blanket of attention that I reserve for my strengths, something liberating occurred. The path to happiness began to clear like fog lifting off the coast in the morning.

I believe that authentic happiness has two faces: it's Janus-faced, if you will. The pursuit of self-contentment, without the compass of purpose, can become a hollow endeavour. My search for happiness eventually morphed into a search for meaning. It wasn't just about *me* anymore; it was about the *we*, the collective symphony of humanity. Specifically, it was about the melody that over half this world's population can create—a chorus of empowered women.

Consider the empirical evidence. Study after study has shown that when women are educated, a cascade of social benefits follows. Amongst these is one benefit that is remarkable: a reduction in global population. Just think about that! By pouring resources into educating women, not only do we elevate half the world's intellectual capital, but also we contribute to a more balanced, sustainable earth. It's not just good ethics; it's good logic.

In empowering women, I have discovered a purpose that marries personal fulfilment with collective well-being. It's like finding that sweet spot in a Venn diagram where the boundaries of self and society intersect. This, my friend, is the soul of my happiness—the intersection of my deepest passions with the world's greatest needs.

In a way, each of us is a small earth, teeming with dreams, hopes, and potential. When we care for ourselves, when we invest in our inner growth, we're not being selfish. We're actually contributing to the well-being of the larger earth—our shared home.

And so here I am, standing at the cusp of two quests—one for personal happiness, and the other for global transformation. They are not separate. They are two legs of the same journey—a journey that teaches me to be kind to myself so that I can be kind to the world, a journey that roots me in my own being so that I can contribute to the well-being of all beings.

In the grand dance of life, when one woman rises, we all do. And it is here, in the union of the personal and the universal, that I've found the purest form of happiness—a happiness that isn't just about thriving, but is also about helping the world thrive too.

Happiness is living your true self rather than simply existing.

Chapter 5

HAPPY ENTREPRENEUR

5.1 The Dissertation Unveiled

My research findings can be summed up as follows:

- Finding #1—**Entrepreneurs should be socially responsible.** The research conclusively establishes the vital importance of social responsibility as the cornerstone of successful entrepreneurial endeavours, substantiating the argument that entrepreneurs ought to engage in socially beneficial practices.
- Finding #2—**New measure of success: contribution, not wealth.** The researcher has discerned a significant change in the yardstick for entrepreneurial success, emphasizing one's impact and contribution to society, rather than accumulation of wealth alone.
- Finding #3—**Defining traits of responsible entrepreneurs: ethics.** An analysis of various entrepreneurial personalities has led me to identify a key characteristic of responsible entrepreneurs, namely, an unwavering commitment to ethical conduct.
- Finding #4—**The power of intrinsic motivation in entrepreneurs.** The researcher delved into understanding the crucial role that intrinsic motivation plays for entrepreneurs, empowering

them to create value, overcome obstacles, and sustain their ventures over the long term.

- Finding #5—**The need for a paradigm shift.** A critical analysis suggests the necessity of profound a paradigm shift in how we view entrepreneurship, underscoring the need to reorient our focus towards long-term societal impact and sustainability.

Research Method and Procedures

My research study, aiming to establish a grounded theory, explored the viability and applicability of the 4E model (earth, empathy, ethics, earnings) to measure entrepreneurial success. The study, using a blend of qualitative and quantitative methodologies, involved literature research, workshops, interviews, and an online survey, and took place over a period of two months in Bhutan. Data from individuals and groups were analysed for patterns and regularities, which were then used to test hypotheses and draw inferences.

The study checked for four types of validity—internal, external, construct, and conclusion—using statistical calculations and comparative analysis. The results showed that the 4E model is closely linked to Bhutan's gross national happiness principles, thereby establishing its construct validity. The conclusion validity confirmed relationships between variables based on reasonable conclusions. However, the American population disagreed with considering environmental preservation as a key success indicator. A positive correlation between current and proposed success measures was revealed through simple regression analysis, suggesting acceptance of the 4E model as a success measure by the general population. Raising global awareness of this model is expected to make a positive impact.

Sample Population

The small margin of sampling error (external validity) substantiates that the sample data can be extrapolated to represent the population parameter. This applies to the entirety of the sample data, as well as to specific subsets such as the Bhutanese or US participants.

While the interviewees were exclusively Bhutanese, the questionnaires were disseminated randomly to respondents around the world. The questionnaire delineates the geographical distribution of respondents, emphasizing the global reach of the questionnaire.

Despite the relatively small statistical sample size for Bhutanese participants in the questionnaire, the consistency of results across all respondents mitigated potential concerns about representation. This consistency was demonstrated by the low level of sampling error (σ). The compact size of the Bhutanese sample reflects the country's smaller population. Further validation of the results is provided by their alignment with qualitative findings drawn from twelve interviews with senior officials, leaders, and entrepreneurs. The correlations between qualitative and quantitative data were mutually reinforcing and provided a comprehensive analysis. Therefore, despite the small sample size, it suffices for generalizing findings to the broader Bhutanese population for the purpose of this research. Additionally, due to the relatively large sample size from the USA, comparative analyses were conducted between this group and the Bhutanese respondents.

Half the sample population reported owning or operating a business at some point. However, further analysis revealed that none of the Bhutanese respondents had previously owned or operated a business. To compensate for this potential bias, qualitative data were collected from interviews with six Bhutanese entrepreneurs, each managing businesses ranging from small-scale enterprises to large organisations in Bhutan.

The entirety of respondents from Bhutan, who represented a subset of fifty-four Asian respondents, were employed by the Bhutanese government. Given that the research questionnaire required proficient English-language skills and access to a computer with internet connectivity, it became evident that this group shared common characteristics. As the results from this group were supplemented by qualitative interviews and demonstrated a low standard deviation amongst the Bhutanese participants, potential bias was substantially mitigated.

The methodology employed for questionnaire distribution relies on a random sampling technique. This technique allows for a diversified sample group as both entrepreneurs and nonentrepreneurs are randomly selected to participate in the questionnaire. To reach a broad range of respondents, the researcher distributed the survey on a global scale, targeting the general public.

The mode of survey distribution included sending the survey link via various communication and social media channels, such as emails, blogs, Facebook, and a variety of entrepreneurial websites.

This approach to random sampling ensures the inclusion of a diverse sample population. It does not discriminate based on factors such as age, work experience, industry background, or the country of residence of the respondents. In essence, it seeks to provide a comprehensive compilation of public opinion.

By using this method, the survey reduces potential biases, particularly those that may arise from entrepreneurs who might perceive success through the lens of traditional measures, which are often the metrics they are taught to prioritize. In contrast, our questionnaire encourages respondents to think beyond the conventional parameters and consider nontraditional or nonfinancial factors as equally important metrics for entrepreneurial success. This methodology prompts respondents to step outside the box and contributes to a more comprehensive, nuanced understanding of what it means to succeed in entrepreneurship.

Research Findings

The research findings confirmed three key hypotheses related to the role of entrepreneurs in achieving the Millennium Goals. It was found that successful entrepreneurs are typically resourceful, innovative, opportunistic, and disciplined and have a high degree of social responsibility. In acknowledgement of these contributions, the study introduces a refined measure of entrepreneurial success and redefines entrepreneurial characteristics.

Building on the "People, Planet, Profit" concept coined by John Elkington in 1994, the research supports the introduction of the 4E theory: earth, empathy, ethics, and earnings. This theory incorporates the four pillars of environmental preservation, social responsibility, ethical behaviour, and wealth creation into the concept of entrepreneurship. The study posits that an entrepreneur's success hinges on his or her achievements in these four areas.

The 4E theory is seen as an extension of current theories such as triple bottom line, the Gaia theory, and corporate social responsibility. It adds an explicit focus on ethics, which is often implicitly assumed in existing theories. The inclusion of ethics directly counters corporations that use social and environmental responsibility as a marketing gimmick.

The research findings stress the significance of ethics in entrepreneurship, emphasizing its explicit mention and measurement. This stems from observations during the global financial crisis of the mid-2000s and during the crypto scams of the 2020s, underscoring the necessity of ethical behaviour as a fundamental trait of entrepreneurship.

This necessity of ethical behaviour extends to being seen as a key characteristic of an entrepreneur. According to Aristotle's *Eudemian Ethics*, personal integrity is paramount for living life at its best, a sentiment echoed by this study's participants.

The research answers three important questions, confirming the following:

1. Entrepreneurs have a social responsibility to improve the world.
2. Entrepreneurial success should be gauged on earth, empathy, ethics, and earnings.
3. Ethical behaviour is a crucial characteristic of an entrepreneur.

The study also found that nonfinancial factors, such as personal satisfaction, freedom of choice, and a sense of social contribution, are significant motivators for entrepreneurial activities.

These intrinsic motivators, if achieved, contribute to elements of the theory of authentic happiness: positive emotion, engagement, and meaning. This leads to greater life satisfaction and fosters what the study refers to as "happy entrepreneurs".

Significant changes are required to accommodate this new measure of entrepreneurial success. The research proposes long-term, viable, and sustainable solutions, including business practices focused on social, environmental, and ethical missions; role models who embody these attributes; education that encompasses these measures; and investment decisions that consider these measures.

The study found less conviction for solutions such as entrenching these factors in corporate mission statements, using shareholder influence to encourage corporate responsibility, and creating government policies to enforce compliance. These solutions were seen as less favoured, possibly because they were perceived as "tried and failed" approaches.

In conclusion, the study aligns with Elkington's transformative change matrix, calling for a change in mindsets and behaviours. Beyond just corporations, governments, and entrepreneurs, the study emphasizes the need for academics and media to play a more active role in transforming mindsets and behaviours.

Finding #1—Entrepreneurs Should Be Socially Responsible

Finding #1 reveals that entrepreneurs have a crucial role to play in social responsibility, particularly in achieving the United Nations Millennium Goals. This conclusion is backed by both qualitative interviews and quantitative questionnaire data.

The survey data revealed a strong consensus, with 71 per cent of participants agreeing that entrepreneurs have a "social responsibility" to help solve world problems. However, interesting differences emerged when comparing the responses of American and Bhutanese participants. Although both groups agreed on the concept of social responsibility, 70 per cent of Bhutanese respondents felt that entrepreneurs are "obligated" to contribute to society, a view held by only 24 per cent of American respondents.

Business ownership experience did not significantly affect attitudes towards entrepreneurs' social responsibilities. Regardless of whether a respondent had run a business, the sentiment remained consistent.

The type of organisation a respondent worked for influenced his or her perspective, with nonprofit workers expressing the strongest belief in entrepreneurs' social responsibility (90%). Government (77%) and private sector (68%) employees also acknowledged this responsibility, but to a lesser degree.

Finally, the low sampling error allows us to generalize the sample mean to the population, affirming the alternative hypothesis: entrepreneurs are socially responsible. The qualitative data from Bhutanese interviews and focus groups align with this, revealing that Bhutanese businesses pair profit motives with a social mission.

Business Profit Motive with a Social Mission Mindset

All Bhutanese entrepreneurial strategies presented in the focus group demonstrated a social mission. This aligns with the gross national happiness (GNH) philosophy that underscores Bhutanese culture, showing a strong correlation between profit motives and social missions.

The Bhutanese recognise the necessity of profit for business survival, but their primary objective is to foster self-sufficiency and sustainability in others. This approach ultimately benefits society.

The data suggests that the integration of social missions into business in Bhutan begins with education, which fosters a strong culture. This culture promotes the intersection of entrepreneurship and social obligation, leading to businesses naturally thriving with this blend. This "happy entrepreneurship" is rooted in GNH values.

Interestingly, many Bhutanese participants were unaware of their unique business perspective, which includes sharing profits with the community. Their business plans primarily focused on local markets, revealing limited knowledge of global environments. However, the study suggests that once Bhutan opens to the world, future business plans will likely reflect global market considerations.

Finding #2—New Success Measure: Contribution, Not Wealth

This finding posits that the success of an entrepreneur should be evaluated by a broader outcome than mere wealth accumulation. This research proposes a more holistic approach, considering an individual's general well-being (monetary and nonmonetary), ethical values, contributions to enhancing others' quality of life, and commitment to preserving nature for future generations. This suggests that the measure of success should be a person's contribution rather than his or her wealth.

In line with Bhutan's gross national happiness concept, which uses happiness as a metric for socioeconomic development, this research proposes that an entrepreneur's success should incorporate four pillars: earnings, empathy, earth, and ethics, also referred to as the four E's. This theory builds on Elkington's 3P (people, planet, profit) formulation or triple-bottom-line theory, adding an extra dimension, and is intended to foster awareness of these four aspects in entrepreneurial activities.

Rethinking the Measure of Success

The study's findings illustrate an imbalanced distribution curve with the measure of entrepreneurial success as defined by mass media, heavily leaning towards wealth creation. Significant aspects such as social contribution, environmental preservation, and ethical behaviour are significantly undervalued in the contemporary metrics of entrepreneurial success.

US respondents expressed a stronger belief that media highlights wealth creation as the quintessential indicator of entrepreneurial success, more so than their Bhutanese counterparts. Simultaneously, they perceived the media as less concerned about emphasizing social contribution, environmental conservation, and ethical business practices, including personal integrity. This query was intended to scrutinize the prevailing public and media perceptions of entrepreneurial success in

Bhutan and the USA. In the process, it underscores the fundamental differences rooted in the two distinct cultures.

Redefining Measures of Success

When prompted to reassess the definition of entrepreneurial success—disconnected from current mass media and public perceptions—respondents exhibited markedly different perspectives.

After summarizing the findings across the entire population, the following points are notable:

1. Data collected from all participants demonstrated that more than 50 per cent of respondents considered the four pillars—wealth creation, environmental preservation, societal contribution, and ethical behaviour—as integral to measuring entrepreneurial success.
2. Given the low spread of sampling error, the statistical sample mean can be inferred to the general population. The high correlation amongst all four variables suggests these can be encapsulated within a single construct.
3. Utilizing the calculated *z*-value (the distance between sample mean and actual population mean), the study confirms the alternate hypothesis, namely, hypothesis 2 (H2), which is that entrepreneurial success ought to be gauged by environmental preservation (earth), societal contribution (empathy), ethical behaviour (ethics), and wealth creation (earnings).

This study corroborates that ethics plays a pivotal role in assessing an entrepreneur's success. The high priority assigned to ethics heralds a revitalized perspective, emphasizing the tremendous importance of ethical conduct in today's business world.

The research suggests Bhutanese respondents have a more favourable perspective on the concept of GNH principled entrepreneurship—the four E's (earth, empathy, ethics, and earnings)—compared to their US counterparts. Except for wealth creation, Bhutanese respondents consistently rank the remaining three variables—social contribution, ethics, and environmental preservation—higher than Americans, who show a stronger bias towards wealth creation and ethics.

Although the study confirms the alternative hypothesis H2 for the entire population and specifically Bhutan, the USA sample population rejects H2, excluding environmental preservation (earth) as part of the measure. This leads to the conjecture that Bhutan, with its historical commitment to GNH philosophies, which harmonize with the four pillars of entrepreneurial success, might have a competitive advantage in implementing the four E's as a measure of entrepreneurial success across the USA.

Drawing from the GNH framework, the theoretical construct of the four E's (earth, empathy, ethics, and earnings) can be considered a valid measure of entrepreneurial success. All four variables show strong correlations, suggesting their inclusion in a unified construct. A simple regression line reveals a positive causal relationship between current and proposed measures. This indicates receptivity amongst the general population to the proposed 4E measure of entrepreneurial success, promising a multiplicative positive impact if measures are undertaken to promote this awareness globally.

Qualitative data collected through interviews and focus groups in Bhutan indicate consensus that the 4E model aligns with the principles of GNH and can be measured.

The Four E's and GNH-Principled Entrepreneurship

The study findings show agreement amongst senior Bhutanese officials and leaders that GNH-principled entrepreneurship is crucial in Bhutan, aiding the integration of GNH values within the business community. Moreover, consensus amongst the focus group that the 4E model is compatible with GNH philosophies affirms the applicability and feasibility of the 4E model as a micro-level equivalent of GNH.

The 4Es as Measurable Metrics

Senior officials and researchers in Bhutan concur that, like the GNH Index gauging the well-being of Bhutanese citizens, the 4E Index can employ similar standards and methodologies to measure the success of Bhutanese enterprises. While there's a general agreement on earth, empathy, and ethics, about half the interviewees question the inclusion of inheritance as a part of an entrepreneur's earnings calculation.

Finding #3—Defining Traits of Responsible Entrepreneurs: Ethics

The importance of ethics as a fundamental component of entrepreneurship is underscored by the data collected, which confirms ethical behaviour as an intrinsic characteristic of entrepreneurs. This resonates with the population's strong sentiment towards regarding personal integrity as a critical aspect of entrepreneurship. Aristotle's *Eudemian Ethics* supports this perspective, suggesting that such a trait is essential for humans to lead their best lives.

The qualitative data gathered through interviews and focus group discussions in Bhutan further reinforced this view, revealing consensus on two defining attributes of entrepreneurs:

1. ethical behaviour as a cornerstone of entrepreneurship
2. a commitment to giving back to the community.

The Ethical Entrepreneur

Both qualitative and quantitative data underscore the essentiality of ethics for entrepreneurs. In a survey encompassing the entire sample population, more than 50 per cent of respondents affirmed that entrepreneurs should embody ethical principles. Given the low spread of sampling error, it can be inferred that the statistical sample mean accurately reflects the broader population's perspective. The calculated *z*-value validates the alternative hypothesis, namely, hypothesis 3: entrepreneurs should exemplify ethical behaviour.

In response to Question 5, a majority of respondents agreed that entrepreneurs should be resourceful (93%), innovative (90%), opportunistic (85%), disciplined (71%), and ethical (50%). Additionally, 38 per cent believed entrepreneurs should be compassionate, while 22 per cent viewed philanthropy as an important trait.

Interestingly, agreement percentages diminished as the survey progressed through its sequence of proposed characteristics, reflecting commonly held beliefs about the necessary traits for successful entrepreneurship, such as resourcefulness, innovation, opportunism, and discipline.

Conversely, unconventional characteristics like ethics, compassion, and philanthropy were added to widen our understanding of entrepreneurship. While both Bhutanese and American respondents held ethics in high regard as a crucial entrepreneurial attribute, the Bhutanese placed more emphasis on compassion. Both groups did not perceive philanthropy, or "giving away large sums of money", as essential to entrepreneurship.

There were significant cultural differences in views on unconventional traits: 70 per cent of Bhutanese viewed ethical behaviour as integral to entrepreneurship, compared to only 45 per cent of Americans. Similarly, more Bhutanese viewed compassion (50%) and philanthropy (40%) as important, compared to fewer Americans (32% and 20% respectively).

Philanthropic Entrepreneurs: The Culture of Giving Back

Regardless of cultural, religious, and personal values, certain traits invariably become part of the definition of an entrepreneur. These include leadership, resourcefulness, innovation, dedication, creativity, honesty, sociability, knowledgeability, charisma, and passion, amongst others.

However, for those influenced by GNH philosophies, the most revered entrepreneurial traits relate to social impact: aiding the less fortunate, improving others' livelihoods, and addressing community needs.

The definition of an entrepreneur closely correlates with the concept of "giving back" to the community—a notion reiterated by several focus group members. Despite being highly valued leadership traits, honesty, charisma, and trustworthiness are infrequently associated with entrepreneurs. Also, while aggression is common amongst Western entrepreneurs, a calm personality is more appreciated within Bhutan's entrepreneurial culture.

In Bhutan, where Buddhism permeates everyday life, the characteristics of a person, and by extension an entrepreneur, intertwine with the concept of giving or "doing good", and leading by example or "being good".

Finding #4—the Power of Intrinsic Motivation in Entrepreneurs

Although the questionnaire addressed the motivations behind entrepreneurial activities, no hypothesis was directly associated with this question. Nevertheless, insights gleaned from this question enable the provision of recommendations to inspire entrepreneurs to fulfil their societal obligations.

Beyond financial gain, which was a significant motivator for 85 per cent of participants, intrinsic factors also emerged as key driving forces. These included personal satisfaction (93%), freedom of choice (80%), and a sense of contributing to society (54%). Even though the overall population recognised the importance of environmental preservation as a metric of entrepreneurial success, it was deemed a significant motivator by only 31 per cent of participants. This highlights the potential necessity for compulsory measures such as legislative requirements to ensure entrepreneurs commit to environmental preservation.

Further analysis revealed that most Bhutanese (80%) and American (90%) participants were primarily motivated by financial gain. American respondents were more likely to associate entrepreneurship with personal satisfaction (95%) and freedom of choice (84%), compared to their Bhutanese counterparts, who reported lower levels of these motivations (70% and 50% respectively). However, a larger proportion of Bhutanese respondents (60%) were driven by a sense of social contribution and environmental preservation, compared to American respondents (54% and 29% respectively).

Interestingly, 50 per cent of Bhutanese participants were motivated by fame and personal recognition, a figure more than double that of American respondents (24%). This discrepancy might stem from the elevated social recognition given to business owners in Bhutan compared to those in employment.

Using *z*-value calculations, it was evident that while Bhutanese respondents regarded environmental preservation as a key motivational factor, this was not the case for the broader population and specifically US respondents. All three sample populations dismissed fame as a primary motivator. These results suggest that Bhutan's GNH philosophy has embedded a deep concern for environmental stewardship within its entrepreneurs, making it an intrinsic motivator. Therefore, the proposed 4E model for entrepreneurial success could be rapidly implemented in Bhutan. However, mandatory measures might be necessary to stimulate similar environmental consciousness in entrepreneurs from other countries such as the USA.

In conclusion, aside from financial gain, key motivational factors for entrepreneurial activities are largely intrinsic and include personal satisfaction, freedom of choice, and a sense of social contribution. Aligning with Herzberg's two-factor theory, the recommendations derived from this research propose avenues (such as education and role models) that encourage entrepreneurs to inherently aspire "to do good", "be good", "do right", and "live well".

Successful achievement of these motivational factors can cultivate the three elements of Seligman's theory of authentic happiness: (1) positive emotion, (2) engagement, and (3) meaning, thereby enhancing life satisfaction. As a result of this increased life satisfaction, we cultivate happier, more fulfilled entrepreneurs.

Finding #5—the Need for a Paradigm Shift

The research data underscore the widespread agreement amongst participants that entrepreneurs should uphold social responsibility. However, the current perception of entrepreneurial success, largely driven by media portrayals, is significantly divergent from the newly proposed metrics. This discrepancy provokes further enquiry. How do we shift perceptions to accurately reflect the comprehensive value entrepreneurs contribute to society and the global community? What transformational changes could inspire entrepreneurs to protect our environment, contribute positively to society, uphold ethical standards, and live well, all simultaneously?

In Bhutanese society, these four pillars—environment, ethics, economics, and empathy (4E)—could be instituted as policies. Conversely, in Western societies, entrepreneurs could incorporate these values into their operational practices. An overwhelming 94 per cent of respondents proposed one or more instrumental changes to redefine entrepreneurial success, while a scant 6 per cent believed no changes were necessary.

A majority of participants (65%) endorsed the integration of social, environmental, and ethical missions within business practices. They also recognised the media's significant role (60%) in promoting these values to society. Interestingly, many respondents advocated for the inclusion of these themes in academic curricula (55%) to better educate future business leaders. More than half suggested that venture capitalists and investors (51%) should prioritize these values in their decision-making process. However, fewer than half suggested management incorporation into corporate missions (41%), shareholder influence on corporations (35%), or government intervention (35%).

In essence, while people generally harbour good intentions, they often require leaders to model these values and unite entrepreneurs to usher in a new era of conscious capitalism.

Both Bhutanese and American respondents underscored the crucial role of education in this transformation. Americans, in particular, recognised the power of media in shaping perceptions of entrepreneurial success. The American participants also favoured a wider array of practices, including revisions to corporate mission, shareholder influence, and investment decision-making. This divergence might stem from the greater familiarity of US participants with the concept of shareholder engagement. Bhutanese participants, on the other hand, assigned a more substantial role to government intervention.

In conclusion, a systemic change in the understanding and measurement of entrepreneurial success is imperative, and its realization requires concerted efforts across multiple sectors of society.

Practical Implications

Redefining Entrepreneurship

Entrepreneurs, in essence, are innovators, capable of developing novel solutions to meet consumer demands and adept at managing stakeholder expectations. They bear the responsibility of enlightening shareholders about the emergence of a new breed of corporation known as "for-benefit" corporations. These hybrid organisations harmonize social purpose with financial objectives, falling on the continuum between conventional companies and nonprofit organisations. These corporations incorporate social responsibility into their policies and practices.

Nobel Laureate Muhammad Yunus, the founder of Grameen Bank, exemplifies the entrepreneur's dual role in generating both value and wealth as a means of subsistence. He posits that a social mission should be integral to profit-driven business enterprises, a concept he refers to as "social business".

Entrepreneurs should uphold unwavering integrity and embody high moral standards. The findings from this research suggest that a holistic definition of an entrepreneur should encompass aspects of both business entrepreneurship and social entrepreneurship. These two roles are intrinsically intertwined. Entrepreneurs, benefitting from society, are equally obligated to contribute to societal well-being.

This study does not argue for all entrepreneurs to be strictly social entrepreneurs without the pursuit of economic returns. Instead, it posits that entrepreneurs, with their innovative capacities and resourcefulness, coupled with strong integrity, should integrate environmental and social enhancements into their business practices and corporate objectives. This approach is essential for fostering long-term sustainable development.

5.2 Redefining Happy Entrepreneurship

An ancient Greek philosophy reminds us, "What you leave behind is not what is engraved in stone monuments, but what is woven into the lives of others." This sentiment aligns closely with the idea of "happy entrepreneurship".

When Bhutan's Fourth King introduced the gross national happiness (GNH) concept, sceptics raised concerns about quantifying such an abstract notion as "happiness". However, after concerted efforts and collaborations, the newly established Bhutanese government developed and implemented the GNH Index, a comprehensive measure of the nation's well-being. This concept has since gained traction globally, with countries like Canada, Thailand, and Brazil adopting it as an inclusive measure of their national productivity.

On 24 May 2011, the OECD launched its alternative measure of well-being, including twenty different indicators across eleven sectors within its thirty-four member countries. These varied from life satisfaction to air pollution, with the Better Life Index mapping the gross national happiness philosophy of Bhutan.

Furthermore, consumer activism and nongovernmental organisations have catalysed corporations to adopt sustainable economic and social development practices. Various metrics have emerged as a result, such as the triple bottom line or 3P and the corporate social responsibility (CSR) index. However, these measures have been criticized for not explicitly considering "good governance".

In contrast, the GNH concept includes good governance as a crucial happiness contributor. This research validates ethical behaviour as a cornerstone of entrepreneurial success, resulting in the four E's (earth, empathy, ethics, and earnings) grounded theory. Hence, this study suggests expanding the triple-bottom-line approach to incorporate ethics or good governance, transforming it into the quad bottom line, or 4E.

But how does a socially responsible entrepreneur become a happy entrepreneur?

The study finds that, beyond financial gain, entrepreneurs are driven by intrinsic factors such as personal satisfaction, freedom of choice, and a sense of social contribution. These motivators align with the three elements of authentic happiness: positive emotion, engagement, and meaning (Seligman 2011), collectively enhancing life satisfaction. This sense of satisfaction characterizes happy entrepreneurs.

Dr Seligman (2011) outlines happiness as consisting of positive emotion, engagement, and meaning. The degree of fulfilment of these elements determines happiness levels. His authentic happiness theory proposes that the pursuit of maximal positive feelings, engagement, meaning, good relationships, and accomplishment leads, not just to happiness, but also to flourishing (Seligman 2011).

Although the term "happy entrepreneurship" is used, the 4E concept aligns more closely with Dr Seligman's concept of flourishing. Whether it's termed "happy entrepreneurship" or "flourishing entrepreneurship" or "responsible entrepreneurship", the essence of the theory remains the same: happiness and contentment stem from positive feelings, engagement in personal and social environments, finding life's meaning, maintaining good relationships, and achieving success.

"Four Pillars of Happy Entrepreneurship"

"What we become and what we contribute gives meaning to our lives," says Anthony Robbins, offering insight into the essence of happy entrepreneurship. This section elaborates on the four pillars—earth, empathy, ethics, and earnings, collectively referred to as 4E, or the quad bottom line—that underpin this concept of fulfilled entrepreneurship.

Earth

We do not inherit the earth from our ancestors,
we borrow it from our children.
—Native American proverb

Our relationship with the earth, as a Native American proverb puts it, is borrowed from future generations, not inherited from our ancestors. UNESCO warns of the numerous threats to our planet's sustainability, ranging from climate change and deforestation to environmental pollution, diminished cultivable land, threatened water resources, increasing unemployment, and social disparities (UNESCO 2005).

Elkington's (2010) Gaian paradigm, inspired by James Lovelock's Gaia hypothesis, views the earth as a single organism and underlines humanity's growing influence on various aspects of the global environment, along with the implications for human well-being (Lovelock 2009). This theory has been endorsed by several international global change research programmes, including the International Geosphere-Biosphere Programme (IGBP), the International Human Dimensions Programme on Global Environmental Change (IHDP), the World Climate Research Programme (WCRP), and the biodiversity programme DIVERSITAS.

These programmes have concluded that earth operates as a self-regulating system, featuring physical, chemical, biological, and human components, and that human activities significantly influence earth's environment beyond merely contributing to climate change. The programmes emphasize that the changes and effects observed in the earth's system are complex, cascading, and unprecedented, and can trigger severe consequences for both the environment and its inhabitants (Lovelock 2009).

The Earth pillar, akin to Elkington's Planet or natural capital, emphasizes sustainable environmental practices. It supports a cradle-to-cradle approach, accounting for environmental cost throughout the life cycle of products—from raw material sourcing and manufacturing to distribution and eventual disposal or reuse/repurpose.

The Earth pillar suggests incorporating green practices to benefit the natural environment, reduce environmental impact and ecological footprint, manage energy consumption responsibly, use renewable energy and products, produce and dispose of less toxic waste, and avoid ecologically destructive practices.

The environmental cost, often unquantifiable, is usually borne by society and future generations. It is therefore crucial for entrepreneurs to shoulder the cost of disposing of nonbiodegradable or toxic products, both for financial reasons and to preserve their reputation. They should not be allowed a free pass by society.

The 4E approach strongly advocates for the preservation of our environment and the reduction of the human ecological footprint stemming from entrepreneurial activities. Entrepreneurs engaging in environmentally destructive practices or industries that exploit society and disregard nature should be disqualified from the Happy Entrepreneur or Responsible Entrepreneur list, irrespective of their financial success.

Empathy

> The world is my country, all mankind are my brethren, and to do good is my religion.
> —Thomas Paine

Thomas Paine's sentiment reflects the essence of the Empathy pillar in the context of entrepreneurship.

Comparable to Elkington's "People", "Empathy" here signifies human capital and highlights fair, beneficial business practices concerning labour, the community, and the region where the business operations are based. Socially responsible entrepreneurs envision a reciprocal social framework in which the welfare of their business, employees, and other stakeholders are intertwined. These entrepreneurs aim to cultivate mutual benefits and strive to protect, rather than exploit or harm, any constituent party.

Such equitable human practices can involve several aspects: the first, adhering to fair trade practices, especially in agriculture; the second, rejecting exploitative labour practices, including child labour; the third, establishing fair and equitable working conditions by providing reasonable wages, a safe working environment, and sensible working hours; and the fourth, contributing to the growth and development of the community, such as improving healthcare and education.

An excellent example of this empathetic approach is the Bill and Melinda Gates Foundation, which only invests or contributes to charitable organisations with measurable outputs. As the Foundation refines its definition of "measurable output", the positive outcome resulting from an entrepreneur's contribution should be incorporated into his or her "success factor". Essentially, the proposed measurement considers not only the entrepreneur's personal achievements, but also the multiplier effect of his or her contributions.

This approach isn't fundamentally different from traditional methods of evaluating an individual's return on investment (ROI). The key difference here lies in assessing the individual's ROI based on how effectively his or her contributions benefit others. This reframing emphasizes the empathy aspect and reinforces its value as a cornerstone of successful, happy entrepreneurship. By measuring their social impact, entrepreneurs can account for the tangible improvements they've made in others' lives, embodying the spirit of empathy.

Empathy in the context of entrepreneurship extends far beyond mere business practices; it seeps into every aspect of the entrepreneur's interactions with employees, customers, and the broader community.

Entrepreneurs who practise empathy are fundamentally focused on understanding the needs, problems, and aspirations of those around them. They exhibit a high degree of emotional intelligence, which enables them to connect deeply with their team members and customers, fostering a positive organisational culture and driving customer satisfaction.

Empathetic entrepreneurs also demonstrate the fifth aspect, inclusivity, which involves respecting and celebrating diversity within the organisation and ensuring that everyone, irrespective of their background, feels welcome, respected, and valued. Entrepreneurs who practise empathy understand that each individual brings unique skills, experiences, and perspectives to the table, and they harness this diversity for the benefit of the organisation.

In terms of customer interactions, empathetic entrepreneurs listen to their customers and work towards solving their problems—the sixth aspect. They view their business not just as a means to earn profits, but also as a platform to make a positive difference in their customers' lives. This orientation often results in products and services that truly meet the needs of the customers and significantly improve their experiences.

Moreover, empathetic entrepreneurs actively engage with the community, the seventh aspect, understanding that their businesses are part of a larger ecosystem. They participate in community activities, sponsor local events, and collaborate with local institutions. Their commitment to the community goes beyond merely complying with legal obligations; they see their community engagement as an integral part of their entrepreneurial journey.

Furthermore, the Empathy pillar, as per the 4E model, emphasizes that entrepreneurs should actively practise corporate social responsibility, the eighth aspect. They should engage in initiatives that address social, economic, and environmental challenges. This could involve investing in renewable energy, reducing waste, supporting underprivileged sections of society, or contributing to local economic development.

In summary, empathy in entrepreneurship is about demonstrating a deep understanding of and commitment to the various human elements involved in a business operation—from employees, to customers, to the wider community. It's about seeing and treating these human elements, not as resources to be used, but as partners in a shared journey towards success and happiness.

The importance of empathy in entrepreneurship continues to grow and take on new dimensions, as follows:

- **Empathy fosters innovation.** Empathetic entrepreneurs have an innate ability to understand the unspoken needs of their customers. By recognising and addressing these needs, they often innovate products and services that surpass customer expectations and disrupt industries.

- **Empathy encourages transparent communication.** Empathetic entrepreneurs prioritize clear, honest, and open communication. They understand that every stakeholder—from employees to customers to investors—has a right to know the realities of the business. This transparency not only builds trust but also fosters a collaborative and innovative work environment.
- **Empathy fuels customer loyalty.** Empathetic entrepreneurs build loyal customer bases by demonstrating that they genuinely care about their customers' needs and well-being. They ensure that their customers feel valued, appreciated, and understood, thereby encouraging them to continue engaging with the business.
- **Empathy promotes conflict resolution.** Disagreements and conflicts are inevitable in any business. Empathetic entrepreneurs, however, are well-equipped to navigate these challenges. By understanding each party's perspectives and feelings, they can mediate conflicts effectively and ensure a harmonious work environment.
- **Empathy supports sustainable growth.** Entrepreneurs who prioritize empathy often experience sustainable business growth. By taking care of their employees, customers, and communities, they foster a positive brand reputation, which in turn attracts more business and encourages repeat engagements.
- **Empathy is vital to leadership.** Empathy also plays a crucial role in leadership. Entrepreneurs who show empathy foster trust, promote open communication, and inspire their employees to perform their best. Such leaders understand their teams' strengths and weaknesses, providing support and encouragement when needed, which leads to higher employee satisfaction and retention.

In conclusion, the embodiment of empathy in entrepreneurial practices encompasses a wide range of behaviours and outcomes. By adopting an empathetic approach, entrepreneurs can create businesses that not only are financially successful but also contribute positively to the well-being of all stakeholders involved. This, in turn, lays the foundation for a more sustainable, inclusive, and prosperous entrepreneurial landscape.

Ethics

> All humanity is one undivided and indivisible family, and each one of us is responsible for the misdeeds of all the others. I cannot detach myself from the wickedest soul.
> —Mahatma Gandhi

This quotation from Mahatma Gandhi serves as a profound reminder of the interconnectedness of humanity and the collective responsibility we bear for each other's actions. Ethical behaviour, a cornerstone of civilized society, is instilled from an early age, guiding our decisions and actions with the help of an invisible moral compass.

Ethics, as defined by various scholarly sources, underscores the pivotal role of moral principles in governing our individual and collective behaviours. These principles, ranging from personal integrity to professional conduct, shape our interactions within various spheres of life.

Aristotle, a preeminent philosopher, posited a distinctive ethical construct known as "Eudemian ethics". This concept emphasizes the necessity of character traits that help us lead a fulfilling life. Aristotle's conception of *eudaimonia*, a term usually translated as "happiness" or "well-being", suggests that the ultimate goal of ethics is to live and act in ways that bring about a state of flourishing or successful living.

An ethically ideal life is one of eudaimonia, a state of flourishing where moral virtue, intellect, and well-being intersect. This philosophical concept reinforces the notion that success is not merely about material wealth, but also about the ethical underpinning of one's actions. It argues for an existence where personal satisfaction and the greater good are inextricably linked, advocating a form of success that is both intrinsically rewarding and socially responsible.

Professor Christos Papoutsy shares this perspective and argues for the integration of business ethics within the framework of eudaimonia. He envisions a society where material and spiritual well-being are mutually reinforcing, forming the bedrock of communal prosperity (Papoutsy 2003).

However, the interpretation of ethics may differ across diverse cultures, presenting a challenge in achieving consensus. One may wonder whose moral principles should be applied universally or how one innately discerns right from wrong. Laws may render certain actions illegal, but do they necessarily deem them immoral? We see ethical dichotomies played out across the globe as what is considered illegal or unethical in one country may be accepted in another.

These disparities give rise to contentious debates on ethical practices in diverse sectors such as the environment, animal welfare, labour practices, fair trade, and biotechnology. The determinants of right or wrong in these areas are often shaped by societal pressure on corporations and governments or vice versa. Yet, consensus remains elusive, hinting at the subjectivity inherent in ethical norms.

Organisations and governments strive to standardize ethical norms by establishing codes of conduct and regulatory frameworks. This helps manage the diversity of moral perspectives, guiding individuals towards universally acceptable behaviours. Leaders play a key role by defining appropriate conduct, educating employees, and setting expectations through various communication channels.

However, the crux of ethics lies in its application, not merely its theoretical understanding. It involves the triad of moral awareness, judgement, and action—recognising an ethical dilemma, making the right decision, and acting upon it.

This perspective does not necessarily posit success against value. To be deemed truly successful, one should display integrity and ethical behaviour. While unethical corporate practices may face consumer backlash, the repercussions for individuals lacking ethics are not always evident. This makes the proposed 4E Index a potential tool for measuring and encouraging ethical behaviour amongst individuals, helping to elevate the definition of success beyond traditional metrics.

Although defining what constitutes ethics will undoubtedly spark debate, the absence of ethics leaves the notion of success hollow. Ultimately, ethical behaviour is an integral element in the matrix of success, enforcing accountability, driving social cohesion, and fostering a harmonious society. By integrating ethics into our personal and professional lives, we can strive towards a more sustainable and equitable future.

The philosophy of ethics doesn't exist in a vacuum; it is an integral part of our daily lives. Each decision we make, whether personal or professional, is often, knowingly or unknowingly, a reflection of our ethical standpoint. Its manifestation can be seen in actions as simple as telling the truth, respecting others' opinions, or making choices that are environmentally sustainable.

However, the challenge lies in the diverse interpretations and applications of ethics across different cultures, social strata, and individual perspectives. For example, a practice deemed ethical in one culture might be viewed otherwise in another. This cultural relativism of ethics prompts us to ask, are there universal ethical principles, or should ethics be context-dependent?

The discrepancy between legal and moral judgement further complicates the issue. Laws may prevent certain behaviours, but they do not necessarily align with moral standards. With this being the case, an action's being legal does not make it inherently moral. In many cases, societal norms, cultural contexts, and personal beliefs tend to influence the ethical landscape more so than legal stipulations.

This complexity is particularly pronounced in diverse areas such as environmental conservation, animal rights, labour practices, biotechnology, and fair trade. These sectors are often the battlegrounds of ethical debates, where consumer pressure, corporate responsibility, and regulatory guidelines frequently clash. Despite these dilemmas, societal norms and regulations often shape our collective ethical boundaries, even if these may not always align with personal moral compasses.

To navigate this complexity, organisations often develop ethical codes of conduct that provide guidance for their members. These codes represent an attempt to harmonise the diverse moral backgrounds of individuals into a collective ethos that defines the organisation's values and expectations. Leaders, through their decisions and actions, play a pivotal role in promoting these ethical standards, reinforcing the organisation's commitment to ethical behaviour.

Nevertheless, ethics is not just about understanding and prescribing what is right; it is about actively practising it. Ethical decision-making is a three-pronged process: recognising an ethical issue, making a judgement about the right course of action, and then implementing that decision.

Given that the definition and understanding of ethics can be so diverse, the proposed 4E Index offers a way to standardize and measure ethical behaviour in a consistent manner. By incorporating ethics into the criteria for success, the Index encourages individuals to act ethically and hold themselves accountable for their actions. It emphasizes that success isn't merely about achieving personal or professional goals but also about contributing positively to society and maintaining a strong ethical compass.

In sum, ethics plays a crucial role in defining success. An ethical individual is not just successful in the conventional sense but also contributes to a better world through his or her responsible decisions and actions. In a rapidly changing world, adhering to a strong ethical code is essential for creating a harmonious, sustainable, and prosperous future.

Ethics is often described as the invisible framework that holds our society together. It is the intangible moral compass that guides us and determines how we engage with each other and the world. Beyond the principles of conduct we were taught as children, ethics extend into a broader set of social expectations and values. We rely on this moral fabric to provide consistency, ensure justice, and create a harmonious coexistence.

While ethics starts on a personal level, it eventually permeates into all our social structures—businesses, governmental bodies, educational institutions, and more. An ethical approach in these domains translates into fair policies, responsible practices, and a commitment to the greater good. For example, businesses that operate ethically focus on providing fair wages, maintaining safe work environments, and limiting their environmental impact. They adopt sustainable practices and contribute to their communities, recognising their broader responsibilities beyond mere profit generation.

The importance of ethics in entrepreneurship and leadership is also significant. Leaders who embody ethical values foster an environment of trust, integrity, and accountability, thereby building organisations that mirror these virtues. Ethical leadership is a cornerstone of corporate social responsibility and is increasingly recognised as an integral part of long-term business success.

However, one of the major challenges in implementing ethics is the vast range of interpretations of what is considered ethical. These interpretations often depend on cultural, historical, religious, and personal perspectives. Moreover, ethical issues are typically complex, multifaceted, and fraught with dilemmas, rarely offering a single correct choice. Therefore, to navigate this complexity, we need to foster open dialogue, inclusive debate, and continuing education on ethics in various social, cultural, and professional contexts.

Further, there's an interesting convergence between the principles of ethics and the broader goals of society. For instance, sustainable practices in business or personal life not only adhere to ethical principles of not causing harm but also contribute to larger social goals like environmental conservation. Similarly, promoting diversity and inclusivity is not only ethically right but also beneficial for social harmony and progress.

Aspiring to be a person of value rather than one of success underscores this point, which emphasizes that while wealth and achievements may define conventional success, the true measure of a person lies in his or her values and his or her impact on the world. This sentiment is embodied in the 4E Index, which proposes a more comprehensive definition of success that encompasses ethics and societal contributions.

The 4E Index underscores the importance of ethical behaviour in shaping a person's success. By considering ethical behaviour as a key metric, the Index ensures that individuals are rewarded, not just for their personal accomplishments, but also for their integrity, moral courage, and commitment to the betterment of society. It pushes for a broader understanding of success, one that includes and values ethical decision-making and behaviour.

In conclusion, ethics is a powerful driving force that guides our decisions and actions. It is a foundational element of our individual character, the organisations we build, and the society we shape. In the pursuit of success, we must not lose sight of these fundamental principles. We must strive to integrate ethics into our personal lives, our workplaces, and our broader social roles. By doing so, we will not only enhance our individual success but also contribute to creating a more ethical, equitable, and sustainable world.

Earnings

> The day is not far distant when the man who dies
> leaving behind him millions of available wealth,
> which was free for him to administer during his life,
> will pass away unwept, unhonored, and unsung.
> —Andrew Carnegie

Earnings is a term that holds a familiar place in our financial vocabulary. Traditionally, it refers to the monetary gain obtained from business activities, employment, or investments. However, in the context of our discussion, we are revisiting this definition. Here, earnings represents the tangible economic value an entrepreneur contributes to society, beyond simply personal profit.

Andrew Carnegie's words encapsulate this paradigm shift that is needed in our understanding of earnings. A billionaire himself, Carnegie was known for his philanthropy and his belief that wealth comes with a responsibility to society. This belief forms the cornerstone of our conceptualization of earnings, where the focus isn't on individual wealth accumulation but on the value generated for the broader community.

In this sense, earnings aren't merely a measure of financial success; they're an indicator of the entrepreneur's ability to innovate, create jobs, spur economic growth, and contribute to societal well-being. This isn't just about how much wealth an entrepreneur has managed to accumulate, but how he or she has used his or her talents, skills, and opportunities to create value in the world.

A major adjustment in our assessment of earnings pertains to inherited wealth. While being born into affluence can be seen as a head start in life, it doesn't necessarily reflect one's entrepreneurial prowess or ability to generate value. Therefore, to get a more accurate measure of an entrepreneur's success, the researcher suggests disregarding the inherited wealth at the point of receipt.

However, any increase in the value of this inheritance resulting from the individual's efforts and wise decision-making is acknowledged. This is because such growth reflects the person's entrepreneurial acumen and ability to multiply the wealth entrusted to him or her. Therefore, instead of simply counting dollars amassed, this approach appreciates the entrepreneurial spirit, the capacity to create and grow wealth, and ultimately the real impact made on society's economic landscape.

This realignment of our understanding of earnings marks a departure from the traditional view of success as personal wealth accumulation. It advocates for a more holistic, inclusive, and socially conscious interpretation of success, giving equal weight to an entrepreneur's social contributions and to his or her individual financial gain. Ultimately, it argues that the true measure of success is not what a person owns, but what the person contributes to the world around him or her.

A German friend's challenge raises a critical point about the role of earnings, or economic well-being, within the 4E Index. In this context, earnings are indeed an integral part of determining success, but they're not the sole determinant. The aim of including earnings is to ensure that entrepreneurs and their employees have a sufficient level of income that can provide financial stability, thereby contributing to overall happiness and well-being.

One research study referred to suggests that up to a certain point (around seventy-five thousand to a hundred thousand dollars in the United States, according to some studies), increases in income are associated with a significant improvement in life satisfaction. This income allows individuals to meet their basic needs (food, shelter, healthcare, etc.), which aligns with the physiological and safety levels of Abraham Maslow's hierarchy of needs.

Beyond this point, however, additional income doesn't necessarily lead to a substantial increase in happiness, a phenomenon known as the "diminishing return of happiness". This is because once basic and certain psychological needs are met (the lower tiers of Maslow's hierarchy), happiness and well-being become more closely tied to fulfilling higher-order needs such as esteem and self-actualization, which are less directly tied to material wealth.

Therefore, earnings in the 4E model should be viewed, not as an end in themselves, but as a means to facilitate the satisfaction of basic needs, enabling individuals to focus on other areas of personal and professional growth.

It's also important to note that the exact income level at which further wealth stops contributing significantly to happiness may vary amongst different countries, regions, and individuals, based on cost of living, personal circumstances, and cultural attitudes towards money and success. Hence, the 4E Index should be adaptable to account for these variations.

In conclusion, this enriched perspective on earnings invites a departure from the traditional money-centric view, instead encouraging a more well-rounded assessment of an individual's financial success. It advocates for the measure of earnings to be one that not only values the creation of wealth but also measures its positive and sustainable impact on society. Thus, it places entrepreneurial success within a broader context, one that seamlessly intertwines individual prosperity with social progress.

5.3 Happy Entrepreneur Index (4E Index)

The Happy Entrepreneur Index, or 4E Index, is a compelling paradigm that integrates four critical dimensions of entrepreneurial success: earth, empathy, ethics, and earnings. This framework presents a holistic evaluation of entrepreneurial performance far surpassing the conventional reliance solely on financial success. It insists that genuine accomplishment can't be measured merely in dollar terms, but should also reflect an entrepreneur's commitment to environmental sustainability, social compassion, ethical conduct, and tangible contribution to economic growth.

Earth

Acknowledging the pressing need for environmental stewardship in the face of escalating ecological degradation, the Earth component of the 4E Index evaluates an entrepreneur's impact on the environment. This assessment rewards positive environmental contribution while penalizing harmful practices. Leveraging sustainability-reporting metrics such as those provided by the Global Reporting Initiative, CERES, and Institute 4 Sustainability, the Earth criterion ensures a deep-rooted commitment to ecological sustainability, central to the entrepreneur's overall success.

For instance, the Happy Planet Index (HPI) and Ecological Footprint offer robust tools to gauge an entrepreneur's environmental impact and resource consumption. By incorporating ecological considerations in decision-making, the 4E Index advocates for a society where prosperity doesn't come at the expense of the planet.

Empathy

Though challenging to quantify, Empathy's inclusion in the 4E Index underscores the importance of social responsibility in entrepreneurial success. The Global Reporting Initiative (GRI) offers guidelines to report on a business's social impact, providing a foundation for measuring this component. The establishment of such metrics would hold not only entrepreneurs but also NGOs accountable for their actions, driving them to enhance their positive social contributions.

Ethics

The ethical conduct of an entrepreneur, though potentially contentious, forms a crucial pillar of the 4E Index. Just as robust governance is vital for a country or corporation, ethical behaviour is a key indicator of entrepreneurial success. This aspect considers the entrepreneur's commitment to moral values and fair practices in his or her business operations.

Earnings

The Earnings dimension of the 4E Index proposes a shift from traditional net worth calculation, which often includes inherited wealth. The researcher argues that being born into a rich family equates more to luck than personal success. Instead of including inherited wealth, the 4E Index measures earnings in terms of real economic value created by the entrepreneur after subtracting initial inheritance. This approach reflects the financial outcomes genuinely attributable to the entrepreneur's capabilities and initiatives. The exclusion of inherited wealth in this measure, however, requires further analysis and consensus before implementation.

In essence, the 4E Index presents a multidimensional, comprehensive, and nuanced approach to evaluating entrepreneurial success. By incorporating considerations of environmental impact, social empathy, ethical conduct, and economic contribution, it aligns entrepreneurial success with broader societal well-being, environmental sustainability, and ethical practices. This represents a significant advancement over traditional success measures, encouraging entrepreneurs to strive for a more profound, sustainable, and inclusive success.

Obstacles

While the adoption of the 4E Index can prove beneficial in numerous ways, it's also likely to face some hurdles. Let's consider some of these obstacles and potential solutions:

1. **Lack of awareness and understanding**
   Most businesses may be unfamiliar with the 4E Index and the principles it represents. Even if they're interested, they may lack the knowledge necessary to implement these principles.

   Recommended solutions: Invest in comprehensive communication and education campaigns to raise awareness about the 4E Index. Host workshops, webinars, or training sessions to help businesses understand how they can align their operations with 4E principles.

2. **Perceived increase in costs**
   Businesses, particularly smaller ones, might worry that adopting the principles of the 4E Index could increase their costs, for instance, through more sustainable production methods or improved worker conditions.

   Recommended solutions: Highlight the long-term benefits of adopting the 4E Index, such as improved brand reputation, increased customer loyalty, and greater employee satisfaction. Provide examples of businesses that have successfully implemented these principles without sacrificing profitability.

3. **Difficulty in quantifying and measuring success**
   It can be challenging to quantify and measure aspects such as employee well-being, environmental impact, and ethical conduct.

Recommended solutions: Develop clear, concrete metrics for each aspect of the 4E Index. Ensure that these metrics are understandable and easy to implement for businesses of all sizes.

4. **Resistance to change**
   Like any new initiative, the 4E Index may face resistance from businesses comfortable with their current methods of operation. Some businesses may see it as an unnecessary burden or something outside their core mission.

   Recommended solutions: Frame the 4E Index as a tool that complements, rather than contradicts, a business's goals. Encourage early adopters to share their success stories, showcasing how the 4E principles have helped them improve their operations and achieve their objectives.

5. **Lack of governmental or regulatory support**
   Without governmental or regulatory support, businesses may feel little incentive to adopt the principles of the 4E Index.

   Recommended solutions: Advocate for governmental policies that reward businesses for adopting sustainable and ethical practices. Partner with existing business associations to lobby for these changes, if needed.

By identifying these obstacles ahead of time and preparing effective solutions, the implementation and adoption of the 4E Index will be smoother and more successful.

5.4 Global Challenges: Comparing Bhutan's Model with the Rest of the World

Bhutan versus the Global Perspective

The gross national happiness (GNH) model, a central tenet of Bhutanese society, may not be universally applicable. This is primarily because the GNH philosophy, deeply rooted in Bhutanese governance, is significantly shaped by governmental initiatives. This framework heavily influences public sector activities, whereas its impact on private enterprises remains relatively minimal.

The cultural underpinning of GNH in Bhutan, infused through religion and social norms, is an innate part of the national psyche. The strong emphasis on community, encapsulated by the "we" concept, has been integral to the Bhutanese way of life. Consequently, the values and practices associated with GNH are not so much taught as absorbed through social osmosis, an inherent aspect of Bhutanese upbringing.

Bhutanese entrepreneurs, despite representing a minor share of national output, are still an essential part of this GNH-oriented society. Their role may not significantly shape or execute GNH initiatives, but these individuals understand and exemplify the GNH ethos, consistently generating value for their communities. Concepts like preserving the earth, giving back to society, and practising ethical behaviour have been part of their learning since childhood, making them second nature rather than imposed principles.

As employment opportunities within the Bhutanese government become scarcer, more Bhutanese citizens are turning to entrepreneurship. This shift increases the potential influence of entrepreneurs within the GNH framework, making their roles more critical in shaping and executing the GNH philosophies. The Bhutanese government is thus confronted with the essential task of shaping policies and procedures to guide these young, ambitious entrepreneurs within the GNH context.

Contrastingly, in the Western world, governments typically play a less direct role in shaping citizens' thoughts and behaviours. The ethos of GNH could, therefore, be disseminated more effectively through corporations and entrepreneurs who often drive cultural norms. In many industrialized countries, such as the USA, businesses and entrepreneurs wield considerable influence in shaping societal norms and values. This influence positions them ideally to lead the shift towards GNH-oriented principles. Indeed, the fact that respondents from the USA equally emphasize the 4E elements—earth, empathy, ethics, and earnings—hints at an underlying readiness for a paradigm shift towards a more holistic definition of success and happiness.

Government's Role in Social Responsibility

While this study leans towards the libertarian movement, often referenced as the "bottom of the pyramid" strategy in business literature, emphasizing the power of free markets to alleviate poverty, it also acknowledges the necessity of complementary macro systems that can foster entrepreneurial efforts.

The responsibility to make lasting social and environmental changes falls on everyone. Entrepreneurs, corporations, and governments must work cohesively to address the complex challenges of poverty and environmental degradation. International organisations such as the United Nations and UNESCO must advocate for a top-down approach, urging governments to establish supportive policies and structures that incentivize and facilitate social and environmental contributions. Without such backing from the government, many entrepreneurial and corporate social initiatives might fall short of achieving their maximum impact.

Karnani (2010), however, contests the libertarian movement's portrayal of the poor as resilient entrepreneurs and value-conscious consumers. He argues that this romanticized perception strays far from reality and potentially harms the poor in two significant ways. Firstly, it diminishes the focus on legal, regulatory, and social mechanisms meant to safeguard the rights of vulnerable consumers. Secondly, it overemphasizes microcredit at the expense of promoting modern enterprises that could offer the poor employment opportunities. Most crucially, Karnani believes the libertarian viewpoint severely underestimates the critical role and responsibility of the state in poverty reduction.

The discussion on the government's contribution to social responsibility is beyond the scope of this study. Nevertheless, it is an area that necessitates further deliberation and serious commitment if the recommendations proposed by this study are to realize their full potential positive impact. Such research would focus on identifying effective ways for governments to augment and amplify the efforts of entrepreneurs and corporations to address social and environmental issues.

Entrepreneurship in Developing Countries

While developed nations provide robust infrastructures and institutionalized structures that aid entrepreneurs in implementing positive changes, entrepreneurs in developing nations often face less accommodating circumstances.

In developing nations, entrepreneurs are keenly aware of the need for sustainable development and its corresponding social responsibilities. However, these changes often come at an economic cost. Ironically, as developing nations increase their carbon emissions in the pursuit of rapid economic development and modernization, they tend to lag behind in adopting sustainable development concepts and ensuring social responsibility.

Historically, the economy in developing nations is primarily driven by small-scale individual entrepreneurs (SIEs). These SIEs range from petty traders to personal service providers such as street vendors, barbers, and small shop owners. The rise in the number of SIEs in developing nations is largely prompted by market-based reforms, rapid urbanization, unemployment, landlessness, and poverty. Azmat and Samaratunge (2009) attribute factors such as the business environment, cultural traditions, socioeconomic conditions, and international and domestic pressures on the practices of small-scale entrepreneurs in these countries. They argue that these elements contribute to the lack of responsible entrepreneurship amongst SIEs, posing significant implications for promoting sustainable business practices in developing countries.

Consider China, an economy largely fuelled by ambitious entrepreneurs. The adoption of the 4E philosophy by Chinese entrepreneurs could significantly influence the achievement of the Millennium Goals. Despite its dramatic economic growth over the past decades, China's economic policy-making remains governed by the Central Committee of the Communist Party, under a professed socialist regime.

Corporate social responsibility (CSR) and corporate citizenship have only recently been introduced to China, driven by both external and internal factors. Externally, following China's admission to the World Trade Organisation (WTO), multinational corporations expanded their businesses in China, thereby promoting good practices. Internally, Western-educated Chinese corporate managers, acting as change agents, are actively promoting socially responsible business behaviour (Zu and Song 2009).

However, while many Chinese entrepreneurs view CSR favourably and express a willingness to participate in socially responsible activities, it's often linked to gaining economic benefits (Zu and Song 2009). Moreover, the study found a positive correlation between managers' CSR orientation and their firms' performance.

Yet, Feng and Wang's (2010) paper identified that the institutional environment in China's transition economy over the past decade has been weak for private firms, with "weak property protection and underdeveloped (discriminatory) financial system". Consequently, private entrepreneurs tend to apply government-oriented CSR behaviours rather than initiate their own (T. Feng and G. Wang 2010).

Interestingly, social responsibility awareness is particularly acute amongst Chinese youth. This generation, having grown up during an explosive period of entrepreneurial growth while witnessing the expanding wealth gap, recognises the need for more philanthropy and public-private partnerships to address the social, economic, and environmental issues of twenty-first-century China (Bernton 2009).

Many of these Chinese youth are members of the All China Youth Federation and are actively involved in reducing youth unemployment, rural poverty, and other social ills. As these youths are likely to hold future political positions in their provinces, their efforts bode well for the future.

Unlike other developed countries, developing nations like China stand to benefit greatly from implementing the Happy Entrepreneurship or 4E approach and, in turn, make substantial contributions to these principles.

Addressing the Challenges in Developing Countries

The challenges faced by entrepreneurs in developing nations can seem daunting given the complex blend of socioeconomic conditions, cultural traditions, and institutional factors. Nonetheless, implementing the principles of GNH, as encapsulated in the 4E approach, could have profound transformative effects.

Firstly, there's a crucial need to recognise that sustainable development is not mutually exclusive with economic progress. Rather, the two can be complementary, with the economic growth providing the means to invest in environmentally friendly technologies and practices, while sustainable development ensures the long-term viability of these investments.

Moreover, the state and other stakeholders have a pivotal role to play in fostering an enabling environment that promotes happy entrepreneurship. This could involve putting in place policies and regulations that encourage responsible entrepreneurship, offering incentives for businesses that prioritize sustainability and social responsibility, and investing in infrastructure and education that will equip entrepreneurs with the necessary skills and resources.

The role of education cannot be overemphasized. Cultivating a new generation of entrepreneurs who not only are aware of the importance of sustainability and social responsibility, but also have the knowledge and skills to implement these principles in their businesses, is a critical step towards achieving the Millennium Goals.

In a country like China, this transformation could be particularly significant. If the drive towards corporate social responsibility and sustainable business practices continues to gain momentum amongst Chinese entrepreneurs and youth, it could influence the future trajectory of one of the world's largest economies.

However, it is also crucial to temper the optimism with a realistic appraisal of the challenges. As Azmat and Samaratunge (2009) note, many small-scale individual entrepreneurs in developing nations are primarily concerned with survival, so the promotion of sustainable business practices may not be a priority.

Yet, it is precisely in these challenging contexts where the potential transformative power of happy entrepreneurship could be most profound. By demonstrating that sustainable, socially responsible business practices can also be profitable and beneficial for all stakeholders, it could set a powerful example for other entrepreneurs in these countries to follow.

In conclusion, while the road to implementing happy entrepreneurship in developing countries may be fraught with obstacles, the potential rewards—in terms of achieving sustainable economic growth, social equity, and environmental protection—make it a journey worth undertaking.

Micro, Small, and Medium Enterprises (MSMEs) and the Four E's

Micro, small, and medium enterprises (MSMEs), which often form the backbone of the economies of developing nations, present a unique opportunity for implementing the 4E philosophy. Given their size and flexibility, MSMEs can adapt more readily to the changing demands of the market, the environment, and the community. These enterprises have significant potential for instigating change on a grassroots level and driving a transition towards happy entrepreneurship. However, they often face challenges related to lack of access to finance, regulatory hurdles, and limited awareness or understanding of sustainable business practices.

Governments, international organisations, and larger corporations can play a significant role in supporting MSMEs in their transition to sustainable entrepreneurship. This can be done through providing training and capacity-building programmes, facilitating access to green finance and clean technology, and developing supportive policies and regulatory frameworks. The growth of sustainable MSMEs could also spur job creation, contribute to poverty alleviation, and promote social inclusion, thereby contributing to the overall well-being of society.

International Cooperation and the Role of Multinational Corporations

Multinational corporations (MNCs) have a critical role to play in promoting happy entrepreneurship. Given their reach and influence, MNCs can set standards for sustainable and socially responsible business practices and pave the way for smaller businesses to follow. They can also facilitate technology transfer and capacity-building in their supply chains, particularly in developing countries. Moreover, MNCs can leverage their resources to contribute to local communities through initiatives such as corporate social responsibility (CSR) programmes and promote a culture of giving and empathy.

International cooperation is another vital component in this transition. Governments, international organisations, NGOs, and businesses need to work collaboratively to tackle global challenges like climate change and poverty, which require concerted and coordinated efforts. This can involve sharing best practices, fostering international dialogue on sustainable entrepreneurship, and creating platforms for knowledge exchange and collaboration.

In conclusion, the transition to a Happy Entrepreneurship approach is a multifaceted process that requires the collective effort of various stakeholders. The 4E philosophy, encompassing earth, empathy, ethics, and earnings, offers a compelling framework to guide this transition and opens a path towards a more sustainable, equitable, and prosperous world. However, to fully realize this vision, it is essential to overcome the existing challenges and leverage the unique opportunities each context presents.

Promoting Education and Awareness

For the implementation of the 4E philosophy, it is essential to boost education and awareness about sustainable entrepreneurship across different segments of society. There is a crucial need to shift mindsets and alter business models towards sustainability, and this can only be achieved by empowering individuals with the right knowledge and skills. This entails integrating concepts of sustainable business practices and social responsibility into business and entrepreneurship education and also fostering a culture of lifelong learning and constant adaptation to changing circumstances.

Moreover, promoting awareness of the importance and benefits of sustainable entrepreneurship, both for businesses and society at large, is an essential step towards triggering a change in attitudes and behaviours. This could be achieved through various means, such as campaigns, workshops, conferences, and public debates, and would need the involvement of a range of actors including governments, NGOs, media, educational institutions, and businesses themselves.

The Role of Technology

In today's digital age, technology offers tremendous potential to support the transition towards happy entrepreneurship. Technology can facilitate the measurement and tracking of sustainability performance, enable greater transparency and accountability, and provide platforms for collaboration and knowledge sharing. For instance, blockchain technology could be used to ensure traceability in supply chains, whereas artificial intelligence and big data analytics could help in making informed business decisions that align with the 4E philosophy.

Moreover, technology can also contribute to promoting sustainable development more directly. For example, clean technologies can help reduce the environmental footprint of businesses, while digital platforms can facilitate inclusive business models that provide opportunities for marginalized communities.

However, the deployment of technology should be accompanied by efforts to bridge the digital divide, both within and across countries. Access to technology and the ability to leverage it effectively are becoming increasingly crucial for entrepreneurial success and social inclusion. Therefore, ensuring digital inclusivity is a critical aspect of promoting happy entrepreneurship.

5.5 The Future

As we navigate through complex global challenges, the need for a paradigm shift in entrepreneurship becomes increasingly evident. The Happy Entrepreneurship model, underpinned by the 4E philosophy, provides a compelling vision of how entrepreneurship can contribute to a more sustainable, equitable, and happy world. By embedding the pillars of earth, empathy, ethics, and earnings into business practices, entrepreneurs can redefine success in a way that values not only economic prosperity but also social and environmental well-being. However, the realization of this vision requires collective action, continuous learning, and bold innovation from all sectors of society.

Compelling Reasons for Adoption of the 4E Index

1. **Emphasizing sustainable success.** The Forbes 500 list has long been a testament to financial prowess, showcasing the individuals and companies that have amassed the greatest wealth. However, in our current global climate—both figuratively and literally—it has become more evident that financial wealth alone is not an accurate measure of true success. The adoption of the 4E Index—encompassing earth, empathy, ethics, and earnings—would provide a more holistic and sustainable definition of success that aligns with our evolving social values and responsibilities.
2. **Encouraging responsible business practices.** As one of the world's most influential business publications, *Forbes* has the power to shape perceptions and drive behaviours within the corporate world. By shifting the focus towards the 4E Index, *Forbes* can inspire companies to prioritize environmental stewardship, social empathy, and ethical conduct as they work towards their financial goals. This can stimulate a wave of positive change in business practices worldwide, pushing companies to be more responsible corporate citizens.
3. **Aligning with consumer expectations.** Today's consumers are more socially and environmentally conscious than ever before. They expect businesses to contribute positively to society and the planet, and they make their purchasing decisions accordingly. By adopting the 4E Index, *Forbes* can reflect these changing consumer values, making the Forbes 500 list more relevant and meaningful to the modern audience.
4. **Responding to global challenges.** As we confront pressing global challenges such as climate change, poverty, inequality, and social unrest, businesses have a critical role to play in creating solutions. The 4E Index recognises and rewards those businesses that are rising to these challenges by making significant contributions to social well-being and environmental sustainability.

5. **Advancing economic equity.** The traditional Forbes 500 list often exacerbates perceptions of economic inequality by highlighting the extreme wealth of a select few. In contrast, the 4E Index acknowledges those who are leveraging their wealth and influence for broader social benefits, thus promoting a more equitable and inclusive form of capitalism.
6. **Inspiring future generations.** The leaders and companies that make it to the Forbes 500 list often serve as role models for the next generation of entrepreneurs. By shifting the spotlight to those who excel in earth, empathy, ethics, and earnings, *Forbes* can inspire future business leaders to adopt a more holistic, responsible, and sustainable approach to entrepreneurship.

In conclusion, adopting the 4E Index in place of the traditional Forbes 500 list of the world's five hundred richest people represents a powerful opportunity for *Forbes* to drive meaningful change in the global business landscape. It's about encouraging a new breed of businesses—ones that not only generate wealth, but also make a positive impact on society and the environment.

Actions Required

Adopting and promoting the 4E Index—encompassing earth, empathy, ethics, and earnings—requires a multifaceted approach involving different stakeholders. Here are several actions that can facilitate its implementation:

1. **Policy initiatives.** Governments can play a critical role in promoting the 4E Index by establishing policies and regulations that reward sustainable and ethical business practices. Tax incentives, subsidies, and grants could be used to encourage businesses to align with the 4E principles.

2. **Education and training.** Incorporating the 4E principles into educational curriculums, particularly in business and economics courses, can help create a new generation of entrepreneurs and business leaders who value holistic success. Continuous training and development programmes within corporations can also help to align the existing workforce with these principles.
3. **Corporate adoption.** Businesses themselves need to adopt the 4E Index, integrating it into their mission, strategy, and performance metrics. This will require fostering a corporate culture that values environmental sustainability, social empathy, ethical conduct, and financial profitability in equal measure.
4. **Investor engagement.** Investors can wield significant influence by directing their capital towards companies that perform well on the 4E Index. This may require developing new investment products, such as ESG (environmental, social, and governance) funds, that prioritize 4E-compliant companies.
5. **Consumer awareness.** Increasing consumer awareness of the 4E Index can encourage market demand for products and services from companies that uphold these principles. This might involve marketing campaigns, educational initiatives, and transparent labelling of products.
6. **Public-private partnerships.** Collaboration between public institutions, private companies, and nonprofit organisations can be very effective in driving wide-scale adoption of the 4E Index. These partnerships can pool resources and expertise, develop innovative solutions, and create the infrastructure needed for sustainable and ethical business practices.
7. **Regular reporting and auditing.** Transparent reporting and third-party auditing can hold companies accountable to their 4E commitments while also providing a clear picture of their progress. This transparency can help attract investors, customers, and employees who value the principles embodied by the 4E Index.

8. **Media engagement.** The media can play a powerful role in promoting the 4E Index by highlighting success stories and best practices. This can inspire other businesses to follow suit and stimulate a broader cultural shift towards valuing sustainable and ethical business practices.

Through a combination of these strategies, it is possible to foster a business environment that not only accepts, but also actively encourages, the principles represented by the 4E Index.

Media Plays a Role

The media, in its diverse forms, plays a crucial role in shaping public perception and discourse. It can utilize a myriad of strategies to raise awareness about the 4E Index:

1. **News coverage.** Traditional news outlets can air stories about businesses that have successfully adopted the 4E principles and are thriving as a result. These stories can provide concrete examples to illustrate the potential benefits of aligning business practices with the four pillars of earth, empathy, ethics, and earnings.
2. **Specialized features.** Publications or broadcasts that specialize in business, sustainability, or ethical practices can feature in-depth articles, interviews, and documentaries about the 4E Index, exploring its background, goals, and potential impacts.
3. **Talk shows and podcasts.** Influential talk shows and podcasts can invite experts, business leaders, and influencers who are proponents of the 4E Index. These platforms can provide more personal and detailed insight into the Index and its importance.
4. **Social media campaigns.** Utilizing platforms like Facebook, Instagram, Twitter, LinkedIn, and TikTok can be a great way to reach a broader, younger, and more diverse audience. Short

videos, infographics, compelling stories, and user-generated content can be used to explain and promote the 4E Index.

5. **Collaborations with influencers.** Partnering with influencers who have a significant online following can help spread the message about the 4E Index to a large audience. These influencers can share content related to the Index and show how it aligns with their personal values and lifestyle.
6. **Sponsored content and advertisements.** Media platforms can partner with businesses that support the 4E Index to create sponsored content or advertisements. This can raise awareness about the Index while also promoting these businesses as leaders in sustainability and ethical practices.
7. **Public service announcements (PSAs).** PSAs can provide concise, impactful messages about the 4E Index to a broad audience. They can be broadcasted on TV, radio, or online platforms to reach a diverse demographic.
8. **Webinars and online forums.** These platforms can host discussions, Q&A sessions, and presentations about the 4E Index, providing an interactive platform for individuals to learn more and ask questions.
9. **Op-eds and letters to the editor.** Thought leaders, experts, and activists can use these mediums to express their views on the 4E Index, stimulate public discussion, and rally support.

By leveraging these strategies, the media can effectively raise awareness about the 4E Index, leading to a more informed and engaged public.

Implementation Plan

The following step-by-step plan offers a comprehensive guide to promoting the 4E Index and making it a standard in measuring the success of responsible and happy entrepreneurs:

Step 1: Build an Advisory Board

Form an advisory board composed of thought leaders, academic experts, industry veterans, and successful entrepreneurs who have demonstrated a commitment to the principles of the 4E Index. The board will help guide the implementation process, provide credibility to the initiative, and lend its networks for wider promotion.

Step 2: Refine the Index and Set Clear Metrics

Work closely with the advisory board and a team of researchers to refine the 4E Index and establish clear, measurable, and reliable metrics. The goal should be to create an assessment tool that is both rigorous and user-friendly.

Step 3: Develop a Certification Process

Establish a formal process to certify businesses as 4E compliant. This process could include a self-assessment questionnaire, documentation review, and perhaps even site visits for larger businesses. Make the certification process as streamlined as possible to encourage participation.

Step 4: Create an Engaging Website and Online Presence

Create a professional and engaging website that serves as a central hub for all information related to the 4E Index. The website should clearly explain the index, the benefits of participating, and the process of becoming certified. Additionally, establish a strong presence on social media platforms to reach a wider audience.

Step 5: Launch a Media Campaign

Coordinate with media outlets to raise awareness about the 4E Index. This could include press releases, interviews with advisory board members, op-eds, and feature stories. Social media campaigns and partnerships with influencers can also be effective in promoting the Index.

Step 6: Pilot the Certification Process

Invite a diverse group of businesses to participate in a pilot of the certification process. Use their feedback to refine the process and address any challenges that emerge.

Step 7: Partner with Business Associations and Networks

Form partnerships with business associations, industry networks, and economic development organisations. These groups can promote the 4E Index amongst their members and encourage businesses to become certified.

Step 8: Establish a Recognition Programme

Create a programme to publicly recognise and celebrate businesses that score high on the 4E Index. This could include an annual awards event, a certification badge for use in marketing materials, and featuring certified businesses on the 4E website and social media platforms.

Step 9: Host Educational Workshops and Webinars

Provide educational opportunities to help businesses understand how they can align their practices with the 4E principles. These could take the form of webinars, workshops, or online resources.

Step 10: Regularly Review and Update

Regularly review and update the 4E Index and its implementation process to ensure it remains relevant, user-friendly, and effective in promoting responsible entrepreneurship.

The success of this plan will depend largely on the active engagement of a diverse array of stakeholders, consistent and clear communication, and a commitment to continuous improvement.

5.6 An Odyssey's End

Throughout my journey, I found myself captivated by the unique intersection of entrepreneurship, happiness, and sustainability. I learned that success isn't solely about financial wealth; it also involves embracing ethics, environmental consciousness, equity, and earning—the 4E model. Personally, this odyssey led to a profound shift in my perspective on happiness and success, revealing that both are deeply intertwined with social responsibility and the fulfilment of intrinsic values.

Academically, this exploration allowed me to challenge traditional paradigms and contribute to the discourse on entrepreneurship. By delving into the Bhutanese gross national happiness model, I was able to envision a more comprehensive measure of prosperity. The exploration of entrepreneurs across different cultures and societies also underscored the universality of human values. Assessing the nuanced differences between happiness in the context of developed and developing nations further enriched my understanding.

The concept of the 4E Index emerged as a holistic benchmark of entrepreneurial success that combines material prosperity with social and environmental well-being. This journey was not only enlightening but also deeply transformative, encouraging me to advocate for this more inclusive model of success in my own life and work. In the end, the journey affirmed that the pursuit of happiness is not merely a personal quest but is one that holds profound implications for our global society.

In addition, this journey underscored the inherent value in fostering a culture of shared responsibility, not just within the corporate world, but also within the public sector and broader community. This led to a heightened sense of personal accountability, pushing me to apply the principles of responsible entrepreneurship in my own professional pursuits. It allowed me to view my work not just as a means to financial gain, but as an opportunity to contribute positively to society and the environment.

On the academic front, the exploration into the 4E model provided me with valuable insights into the role of entrepreneurs in advancing sustainable development. It broadened my understanding of entrepreneurship beyond the narrow confines of business operations, allowing me to view it as a vehicle for social change. Moreover, the extensive research and the immersion into diverse cultural contexts deepened my appreciation for interdisciplinary studies, highlighting the intricate connections between economic practices, social norms, and environmental sustainability.

My exploration challenged prevailing notions of success, encouraging a shift towards a more inclusive and comprehensive paradigm. This realization has inspired me to advocate for changes in how we measure prosperity, steering away from purely financial metrics and towards those that consider the holistic well-being of individuals and societies.

Lastly, this odyssey has been an exercise in personal growth, empathy, and understanding. By exploring the nuances of happiness and its diverse interpretations, I've come to appreciate the richness of human experiences and perspectives. This journey, while primarily academic, has been deeply personal, not just influencing my work, but also shaping my world view and guiding my actions towards a more socially conscious and responsible future.

5.7 A New Beginning

As I close the pages on this stage of my academic journey, I find myself standing on the threshold of a new chapter. It is a fresh beginning, but one that is imbued with the wisdom and insights garnered from the exploration of the 4E Index and its implications on the role of entrepreneurs in society.

This end, rather than signalling a conclusion, truly marks the commencement of an exciting new journey. The understanding and knowledge gained have not only reshaped my perspective on entrepreneurship, but also sparked a profound transformation in the way I perceive success, responsibility, and indeed life itself.

What I once understood to be success has evolved. The traditional measures of wealth and recognition no longer stand alone as benchmarks. Instead, success has taken on a richer, more multifaceted meaning, encompassing the ethics, environment, and empathy aspects of the 4E model. It is about making a difference and creating value, not just for myself, but also for society and the world at large.

On a deeper level, this journey has also led to a personal discovery of happiness. It has shown me that happiness lies not in material prosperity alone, but in the fulfilment derived from leading a life steeped in ethical values, empathy for others, and a genuine concern for the environment. This understanding has not only brought me a sense of tranquillity and contentment but has also imbued me with a sense of purpose.

As I stand poised at the opening of this new chapter, I am filled with anticipation, eagerness, and a sense of optimism. I am ready to apply the wisdom gained and the lessons learned in my personal and professional life, eager to make a positive impact on the world. It is not merely the end of an academic voyage but also the beginning of a lifelong journey towards becoming a responsible, ethical, and happy individual. Indeed, the end of this tale has opened up myriad new paths, each leading towards the promise of a brighter, more sustainable future.

I call on all readers to join me on this journey. Together, we can make a difference.

Chapter 5 References

ACN Newswire, "'The Honor Roll of China Elite Business Women' Announced in Shanghai" (27 Nov. 2009), https://www.acnnewswire.com/press-release/English/2680/'The-Honor-Roll-of-China-, accessed 4 Feb. 2024.

Acs, Z. J., and Armington, C., *Entrepreneurship, Geography, and American Economic Growth* (Cambridge, Cambridge University Press, 2006).

Allen, J. G., and Gorkin, J., *The Complete Guide to Environmental Careers* (Island Press, 1989).

Gurria, A., "Workshop on the Findings of the Commission on the Measurement of Economic Performance and Social Progress" (14 Sept. 2009).

Auerswald, P., "Creating Social Value", *Stanford Social Innovation Review*, 7/2 (Apr 2009), 51–55.

Azmat, F., and Samaratunge, R., "Responsible Entrepreneurship in Developing Countries: Understanding the Realities and Complexities", *Journal of Business Ethics*, 90/3 (Dec 2009), 437–52, Dordrecht.

Bandyk, M., "Entrepreneurs and Social Responsibility", *Entrepreneurs.com* (30 May 2008)

Barro, R., "Bill Gates' Charitable Vistas", *Wall Street Journal* (19 Jun. 2007).

Baycan-Levent, T. Diversity and ethnic entrepreneurship, SUS.DIV position paper research task (2006).

Ben and Jerry (20 Sep 2010), http://www.benjerry.com/activism/mission-statement/

Bernton, H., "Chinese leaders learn about corporate social responsibility", *McClatchy - Tribune Business News*, Washington (24 May 2009).

Berry, G., and Robinson, P., "An Interview with James Lee Sorenson", *Journal of Management Inquiry*, 18/4 (2009), 302.

Bilson, J. "Criticisms of Corporate Social Responsibility Arguments Against Adopting Corporate Citizenship", *Suite 101* (20 Mar 2010).

Blackburn, B. "The Giving Pledge: Billionaires Promise to Donate at Least Half Their Fortunes to Charity", *ABC News* (4 Aug 2010).

Brahm, L. J., *The Anti-Globalization Breakfast Club: Manifesto for a Peaceful Revolution*, Singapore, John Wiley & Sons, 2009.

Braun, A. A., "Gross National Happiness in Bhutan: A Living Example of an Alternative Approach to Progress", *Wharton International Research Experience* (Philadelphia, University of Pennsylvania, 24 Sep 2009)

Branham, B., and Pruitt, B., "Kauffman Foundation Unveils the 'Entrepreneur's Pledge' as Part of its 'Build a Stronger America Movement'", *Edelman and Kaufman Foundation* (13 May 2010).

Boston College Center and Reputation Institute, "Disney and Microsoft Top List of 50 U.S. Companies Recognised as Leaders in Corporate Social Responsibility, http://www.csrwire.com/press_releases/27944-Disney-and-Microsoft-Top-List-of-50-U-S-Companies-Recognized-as-Leaders-in-Corporate-Social-Responsibility#, accessed 27 July 2010.

Boston College Center and Reputation Institute, *2010 Corporate Social Responsibility Index*, 2010.

Brown A., "Metacognition and Other Mechanisms", in F. E. Weinert and R. J. Kluwe, eds., *Metacognition, Motivation, and Understanding* (Hillsdale, NJ, Earlbaum, 1987).

Brouwers, J., Prins, E., and Salverda, M., *Social Return on Investment: A Practical Guide for Development Cooperation Sector* (Utrecht, Context international cooperation, October 2010)

Campbell K., *Toward a General Theory of Entrepreneurship* (Philadephia, Temple University, 11 Apr 2008).

Chatfield B. V., *The impact of entrepreneurs' decision making on startup success: investigation, analysis, and recommendations* (College Park, University of Maryland University College, 2008).

Carnegie, A., *The Gospel of Wealth and Other Timely Essays* (New York, The Century Co. 1901).

Centre for Bhutan Studies, http://www.bhutanstudies.org.bt/?p=1#more-1, accessed 22 Nov 2010.

CGAP, http://www.cgap.org, accessed15 Aug 2010

Chatterji, A. K., *Empirical Essays on Entrepreneurship and Corporate Social Responsibility* (Berkeley, University of California, 2000).

Chen, W. Y., Weng, C. S., and Hsu, H. Y., "A study of the entrepreneurship of Taiwanese youth by the Chinese Entrepreneur Aptitude Scale", *Journal of Technology Management in China*, 5(1) (2010), 26–39, Bradford.

Chidley, J., Seymour's Way, *Canadian Business*, 82(21) (Dec 2009), 50–52, Toronto.

Clarkson, M. B. E. A Stakeholder Framework for Analyzing and Evaluating Corporate Social Performance, *The Academy of Management Review*, Vol. 20, No. 1 (Jan 1995), 92–117, Academy of Management.

Clinton Global Initiative, (2011) http://www.clintonglobalinitiative.org/aboutus/default.asp?Section=AboutUs&PageTitle=About Us, accessed 7 Dec 2011.

Comas, M., and Sagebien, J. "Wal-Mart Puerto Rico: Promoting Development Through a Public-Private Partnership" *Richard Ivey School of Business Case Collection*: 9B10M024: Wal-Mart Puerto Rico: Promoting Development, (5 May 2010).

Consumer Guide, "Bread company introduces pedicart program", *BusinessWorld*, Manila (15 Mar 2010)

Corrado, M., and Hines, C., "Business Ethics: Making the world a better place", *MRS Conference*, Brighton (21 Mar 2001)

Crane, A., McWilliams, A., Matten, D., Moon, J., and Siegel D., *The Oxford Handbook of Corporate Social Responsibility* (UK, Oxford University Press, 2008).

Dalbey, R., Social Responsibilities of an Entrepreneur, http://ezinearticles.com/?Social-Responsibilities-of-an-Entrepreneur&id=1780168, (2010), accessed July 25, 2010.

Dalai Lama, *How to Practise: The Way to a Meaningful Life* (London, Random House Group, 2003).

H .E. Dasho Daw Penjo, General Assembly of the United Nations, General Debate: 65th Session, (29 Sep 2010)

Dees, G., The Meaning of "Social Entrepreneurship", *Kauffman Center for Entrepreneurial Leadership* (31 Oct 1998)

Desjardins, J., *Introduction to Business Ethics*, (New York, McGraw-Hill, 2003)

Elkington, J., "A new paradigm for change", *What Matters*, McKinsey & Co (6 Apr 2010)

Elkington, J., "Towards the Sustainable Corporation: Win-Win-Win Business Strategies for Sustainable Development", *California Management Review* 36, (1994), no. 2: 90–100

Entine, J. (2011) http://www.jonentine.com/the-body-shop.html, accessed 9 Dec 2011.

Entrepreneur Media (2010) Social Responsibility, http://www.entrepreneur.com/encyclopedia/term/82646.html, accessed 20 July 2010.

"Ethics", *Merriam-Webster Online Dictionary*, http://www.merriam-webster.com/dictionary/ethics, accessed 12 Oct. 2009.

"Ethics", *Oxford Pocket Dictionary of Current English Encyclopedia.com*, http://www.encyclopedia.com/doc/1O999-ethics.html, accessed 12 Oct 2009

Feng, T., and Wang, G., "How private enterprises establish organisational legitimacy in China's transitional economy". *The Journal of Management Development*, 29(4) (2010), 377–93.

Financial Times, "Contenders in the four other award categories", *Financial Times*, (3 Jun 2010) 2.

Folino, L, "The Great Leaders Series: Ben Cohen and Jerry Greenfield, co-founders of Ben & Jerry's Homemade", *Inc.com* (18 Feb 2010), https://www.inc.com/30years/articles/ben-and-jerry.html, accessed 18 Feb 2010.

Forbes, L. H., "Achieving Professional Success in a Decade of Economic Uncertainty". *Industrial Engineering.* Vol. 24, Iss. 9. Sep 1992.

Forbes, "Liliane-Bettencourt" (2010), http://www.forbes.com/lists/2010/10/billionaires-2010_Liliane-Bettencourt_F6EZ.html, accessed July 26, 2010.

Frederick, W., "The Difference Makers: How Social and Institutional Entrepreneurs Created the Corporate Responsibility Movement", *The Journal of Corporate Citizenship*, (32), (2008), 100–102.

Freeman, E., *Stakeholder Theory and Organisational Ethics* (Oakland, Berrett-Koehler Publishers, 2003).

Frey, W., and Cruz-Cruz, J. A. "Three Views of CSR (Corporate Social Responsibility)", *The Connexions Project* (8 Oct 2009)

Galay, K., "Time Use", *The Centre for Bhutan Studies* (2010), http://www.grossnationalhappiness.com/Default.aspx, accessed 20 Nov 2010.

Goethe Institut, *Sustainability: From Principle to Practice,* March 2008

Greening, D., and Turban, D., "Corporate Social Performance As a Competitive Advantage in Attracting a Quality Workforce", *Business & Society*, Vol. 39, No. 3, (2000), 254–80.

Grimes, M., "Strategic Sensemaking Within Funding Relationships: The Effects of Performance Measurement on Organisational Identity in the Social Sector", *Entrepreneurship Theory and Practice*, 34(4) (2010), 763–83.

Gross National Happiness Commission (2010), http://www.gnhc.gov.bt/about_us.asp, accessed 25 Oct 2010.

Guterman, E., "Toward a Dynamic Assessment of Reading: Applying Metacognitive Awareness Guiding to Reading Assessment Tasks", *Journal of Research in Reading*, 25 (2002), 283–98.

Haynie, D., Shepherd, D. A., Mosakowski, E., and Earley, C., "A Situated Metacognitive Model of the Entrepreneurial Mindset", *Journal of Business Venturing* (2009).

Haynie, D., and Shepherd, D.A., A Measure of Adaptive Cognition for Entrepreneurship Research, *Entrepreneurship: Theory and Practice* (2009).

Herzberg F., "One More Time: How do You Motivate Employees?" *Harvard Business Review* (Jan 2003)

Hewlett, S. "The 'Me' Generation Gives Way to the 'We' Generation". *Financial Times* (19 Jun 2009), 9.

Hisrich, R., Peters, M. and Shepher, D. *Entrepreneurship*, (New York, McGraw-Hill Irwin, 2010).

Hitt, M. A., Keats, B. W., and DeMarie, S. M., "Navigating in the New Competitive Landscape: Building Strategic Flexibility and Competitive Advantage in the 21st Century", *Academy of Management Executive* (1998), 22–43.

Hofstede, G., "National Cultures in Four Dimensions : A Research-based Theory of Cultural Differences among Nations", *International Studies of Management & Organisation*, vol. III, no. 1–2 (1983), 46–74.

IMF, "Reaching the MDGs: Macroeconomic Prospects and Challenges in Low-Income Countries", *United Nations MDG Summit* (2010 September).

International Institute for Sustainable Development, "Perceptions and Definitions of Social Responsibility", *International Institute for Sustainable Development* (May 2004).

International Finance Corporation, "World bank Group For-Benefit Corporations—Hot New Business Model or Fad?", *International Finance Corporation* (5 Jun 2007).

International Institute of Management, http://www.iimedu.org/polls/grossnationalhappinesssurvey.htm, accessed 26 Jul 2010.

International Organisation for Standardization, *ISO26000: ISO and social responsibility,* (International Organisation for Standardization, 2008).

International Year of Microcredit 2005 (2010), http://www.yearofmicro-credit.org, accessed 15 Aug 2010.

Ireland R.D., Hitt, M.A. and Sirmon D.G., "A Model of Strategic Entrepreneurship: The Construct and its Dimensions", *Journal of Management* (2003), 963–90.

Jones, R., Latham, J., and Betta, M., "Narrative construction of the social entrepreneurial identity", *International Journal of Entrepreneurial Behaviour & Research*, 14(5) (2008), 330–45.

Karnani, A., Failure of the libertarian approach to reducing poverty, *Asian Business & Management*, 9(1) (Mar 2010), 5–21.

King Jigme Khesar Namgyel Wangchuck, GNH Index, Coronation Speech (7 Nov 2008)

Kiva.com (2010), http://www.kiva.org, accessed 15 Aug 2010.

Kotter, J. P., "Leading Change: Why Transformation Efforts Fail", *Harvard Business Review*, (2006).

Kraut, R., "Aristotle's Ethics", *The Stanford Encyclopedia of Philosophy* (2011 Winter), accessed 7 Dec 2011 from http://plato.stanford.edu/archives/win2011/entries/aristotle-ethics/.

Leeper, M.A., *Social Responsibility and Entrepreneurship*, (Charlottesville, The Darden School, University of Virginia, 2006)

Levy, D., Brown, H., and de Jong, M., "The Contested Politics of Corporate Governance: The Case of the Global Reporting Initiative", *Business and Society*, 49(1) (Mar 2010), 88.

London, M., "Leadership and Advocacy: Dual Roles for Corporate Social Responsibility and Social Entrepreneurs", *Organisational Dynamics*, 37(4) (2008), 313.

Lovelock, James, *The Vanishing Face of Gaia*. (New York, Basic Books, 2009).

MacLean, R., Turnaround Companies, *Environmental Quality Management*, 19(4) (July 2010), 99.

Maslow, A., *Motivation and Personality* (New York, Harper, 1954).

McClave, J. T., Benson, P. G., and Sincich, T., *Statistics for Business and Economics* (10th edn, Prentice Hall, NJ, Pearson, 2008).

McGrath, R., "Falling Forward: Real Options Reasoning and Entrepreneurial Failure", *Academy of Management Review*, 24 (1999), 13–30.

Meeks, M. and Chen R., "Can Walmart Integrate Values with Value?: From Sustainability to Sustainable Business" *TRACE: Tennessee Research and Creative Exchange* (21 July 2009).

Mendonca, L., "The Most Important Question in Business Today", *McKinsey Quarterly* (15 July 2010).

Mevarech, Z .R., and Kramarski, B., "The Effects of Metacognitive Training versus Worked-out Examples on Students' Mathematical Reasoning", *British Journal of Educational Psychology*, 73/4 (2003), 449–71.

Meyskens, M., Robb-Post, C., Stamp, J., Carsrud, A., and Reynolds, P., "Social Ventures from a Resource-Based Perspective: An Exploratory Study Assessing Global Ashoka Fellows", *Entrepreneurship Theory and Practice*, 34(4) (2010), 661–80.

Middleton, D., "Executive Education: MBAs Seek Social Change—Enterprises with a Cause Gain Ground on Campus", *Wall Street Journal* (Eastern Edn, New York, 15 Oct 2009), B7.

Monitor Group, "Monitor Group Recognised as one of the Top 100 Companies in China for Corporate Social Responsibility" *Economics Week* (July2010, July), 278.

"Nef" (2011), http://www.happyplanetindex.org/info/about-nef.html, accessed 15 Oct 2011.

"Joseph Schumpeter", *New World Encyclopedia*, http://www.newworldencyclopedia.org/entry/Joseph_Schumpeter, accessed 17 Aug. 2010.

NFIB and Visa Inc., "NFIB and Visa Inc. Announce 2010 'Young Entrepreneur of the Year' Winner", *PR Newswire* (24 Jun 2010).

Nobel Learning Communities, Inc. "Introduces New Social Entrepreneurship Curriculum: Giving Without Walls program teaches the importance of civic engagement to elementary and middle school students", *PR Newswire* (27 Apr 2010).

Novogratz, J., "Developing entrepreneurship among the world's poorest", *The McKinsey Quarterly* (Mar 2009).

Ongmo, S., "Happiness—Will It Be the 9th Millennium Development Goal?", *Conversation for a better world*, (17 Sep 2010).

Orlitzky, M., "Corporate Social Performance: Developing Effective Strategies", *Centre for Corporate Change*, (Sydney, Australian Graduate School of Management, Jun 2000).

Osborne, Jason, and Waters, Elaine, "Four assumptions of multiple regression that researchers should always test" *Practical Assessment, Research & Evaluation* (2002), 8(2), accessed October 31, 2011 from http://PAREonline.net/getvn.asp?v=8&n=2.

Papoutsy C., "Entrepreneurship And Ethics Equals Success", *Hellenic Communication Service* (21 Feb 2003).

Peldon, S., and Dechen, K., *Guide Book for Teachers*, (Bhutan, Comprehensive School Health Programme Ministry of Health and Ministry of Education, 2009)

Peterson, R., and Jun, M., "Perceptions on Social Responsibility: The Entrepreneurial Vision", *Business and Society*, 48(3) (2009), 385.

Pink, D., *A Whole New Mind: Why Right-Brainers Will Rule the Future*, (New York, Riverhead Trade, 2006).

Phills, J. A. Jr., Deiglmeier, K., and Miller, D. T., "Rediscovering Social Innovation", *Stanford Social Innovation Review* (2008 Fall).

Phillips, T., :The In-House Interview: Body guard", *The Lawyer* (2010, July) 18.

Pierick, E. T., Beekman, V., van der Weele, C. N., Meeusen, M. J. G., and de Graaff, R. P. M., "A framework for analysing corporate social performance: Beyond the Wood model", *Agricultural Economics Research Institute (LEI),* The Hague (Oct 2004)

Pohle, G., and Hittner, J., "Attaining sustainable growth through corporate social responsibility", *IBM Global Business Services* (2008).

Pravda R., "Bill Gates and Warren Buffet Urge Billionaires to Give Away Most of Their Fortunes", http://english.pravda.ru/business/113879-gates-0, accessed 11 Jul 2010.

PR Newswire, "Simmons School of Management Named One of Top 20 Socially Responsible MBA Programs in the World", *PR Newswire,* New York (21 Oct 2009).

PR Newswire, "Scotiabank Joins Corporate Leaders on 2009 Dow Jones Sustainability World Index", *PR Newswire,* New York (11 Sep 2009).

PR Newswire, Babson College Signs On to the Principles for Responsible Management Education, *PR Newswire,* New York (26 Jun 2009).

Principles for Responsible Management Education, http://www.unprme.org, accessed 2011.

Ridley-Duff, R., "Social enterprise as a socially rational business", *International Journal of Entrepreneurial Behaviour & Research,* 14(5) (2008), 291–312

Sternberg, R., and Wennekers, S., "Determinants and Effects of New Business Creation Using Global Entrepreneurship Monitor Data", *Small Business Economics,* Springer, vol. 24(3) (2005), 193–203, 01.

Rosenberg, M., "Current World Population and World Population Growth Since the Year One", *About.com Guide* (14 Jun 2010)

Rubten, P., "Good Governance", *The Centre for Bhutan Studies*, http://www.grossnationalhappiness.com/Default.aspx, accessed 20 Nov 2010.

Sarasvathy, S., *Effectuation: Elements of Entrepreneurial Expertise* (Cheltenham, UK, Edward Elgar Publishers, 2006)

Schraw, D., and Dennison, R., "Assessing Metacognitive Awareness", *Contemporary Educational Psychology*, (1994) 460–75.

Schwass, J., and Lief, C., "About Family, Business and Philanthropy", *Perspectives for Managers* (2008), 165:1–4.

Seelos, C., and Mair, J., "Social entrepreneurship: Creating new business models to serve the poor", *Business Horizons* 48 (2005), 241–46.

Seligman, M., *Flourish: A Visionary New Understanding of Happiness and Well-Being*, (Free Press, 2011).

Sharma, P., and Chrisman, J., "Towards a Reconciliation of the Definitional Issues in the Field of Corporate Entrepreneurship", *Entrepreneurship Theory and Practice*, 23/3 (1999), 11–27.

Simons, J. A., Irwin, D. B., and Drinnien, B. A., *Psychology: The Search for Understanding* (New York, West Publishing Company, 1987).

SIF, *"2007 Report on Socially Responsible Investing Trends in the United States", Washington DC: Social Investment Forum* (2007).

Sjöström, E., "Shareholders as Norm Entrepreneurs for Corporate Social Responsibility", *Journal of Business Ethics*, 94/2 (2010), 177–91.

Strom, S., "Businesses Try to Make Money and Save the World", *The New York Times* (6 May 2007)

Subhash, K., "Venture Capital Financing and Corporate Governance: Role of Entrepreneurs in Minimizing Information/Incentive Asymmetry and Maximization of Wealth", *The Journal of Wealth Management*, 12(2) (2009), 113–29, 7–8.

"Success", *Oxford Pocket Dictionary of Current English, Encyclopedia.com*: http://www.encyclopedia.com/doc/1O999-success.htm, accessed 10 Sep 2009.

Sullivan, R. *Business and Human Rights: Dilemmas and Solutions*, (Sheffield, Greenleaf Publishing Ltd, 2003)

Sustainability-index.com (2010) http://www.sustainability-index.com/ accessed 14 Aug 2010.

Swanson, D. L., "Addressing a Theoretical Problem by Reorienting the Corporate Social Performance Model", *The Academy of Management Review*, Vol. 20, No. 1, (Jan 1995) 43–64.

Teraji, S., "A model of corporate social performance: Social satisfaction and moral conduct", *Journal of Socio-Economics*, Volume 38, Issue 6 (Dec 2009), 926–34.

The Economist, "The Elysee and the Elite", *The Economist*, Volume 396, Number 8690, (16 Jul 2010).

The Guardian, "Endorsing the recommendations of the Commission on the Measurement of Economic Performance and Social Progress", http://www.guardian.co.uk/business/2009/sep/14/sarkozy-attacks-gdp-focus, accessed 14 Sep 2009.

The International Business Awards, http://www.stevieawards.com/iba/, accessed 10 Aug 2010

Trivedi, C., "A Social Entrepreneurship Bibliography", *The Journal of Entrepreneurship*, 19(1) (2010), 81.

Trochim, W. M. K., *Research Methods: The Concise Knowledge Base* (USA, Thomson, USA, 2005)

UNICEF, "Life Skills-Based Education in South Asia: A Regional Overview prepared for the South Asia Life Skills-Based Education Forum", *UNICEF* (2005)

United Nation General Assembly, 2005 World Summit Outcome Report, *United Nations* (15 Sep 2005)

United Nations Educational, Scientific and Cultural Organisation Report Of The International Bioethics Committee Of UNESCO (IBC) On Social Responsibility And Health, *UNESCO* (Nov 2009).

United Nation Principles for Responsible Management Education (UNPRME), http://www.unprme.org, accessed 14 Aug 2010.

Ura, K., "Explanation of Gross National Happiness Index", *The Centre for Bhutan Studies* http://www.grossnationalhappiness.com/Default.aspx, accessed 20 Nov 2010.

Waddock, S., "Pragmatic Visionaries: Difference Makers as Social Entrepreneurs", *Organisational Dynamics*, 38(4) (2009, Oct.–Dec.) 281.

Wartick, S. L., and Cochran, P. L., "The Evolution of the Corporate Social Performance Model", *The Academy of Management Review*, Vol. 10, No. 4, (1985, October) 758–69,

World Economic Forum, http://www.weforum.org/klaus-schwab-founder-and-executive-chairman, accessed 11 Dec 2011.

World Health Organisation, http://www.who.int/research/en/, accessed 27 Jul 2010.

World Health Organisation, *Adolescent Mental Health Promotion*, (New Delhi, Health and Behavior Unit, Department of Sustainable Development and Healthy Environments, World Health Organisation, 2003)

Yunus, M., *Banker To The Poor: Micro-Lending and the Battle Against World Poverty* (New York, PublicAffairs, 2003)

Zangmo, T., "Psychological Well Being", *The Centre for Bhutan Studies,* http://www.grossnationalhappiness.com/Default.aspx, accessed 20 Nov 2010.

Zencey, E., "G.D.P. R.I.P", *The New York Times* (10 Aug 2009)

Zu, L., and Song, L., "Determinants of Managerial Values on Corporate Social Responsibility: Evidence from China", *Journal of Business Ethics: Supplement*, 88, (Apr 2009) 105–117.

PGIL2024USA